KEY CONCEPTS OF LACANIAN PSYCHOANALYSIS

Edited by

Dany Nobus

REBUS PRESS
London

First edition 1998

Printed in Great Britain

Rebus Press
76 Haverstock Hill
LONDON
NW3 2BE

ISBN 1 900877 08 2

CONTENTS

ACKNOWLEDGEMENTS

The idea for this book grew out of a discussion I had with Irish colleagues during one cold November night in Dublin, some two years ago. We were celebrating the success of the 2nd Annual Congress of the Association for Psychoanalysis and Psychotherapy in Ireland and, between mouthfuls of Guinness, expressing our dissatisfaction with the existing introductions to Lacanian thought. At one point, somebody conceded that the information provided by these introductory works is 'never enough and always too much,' a principle which somebody else had used previously to characterize the dynamics of addiction. Although it was obvious to all of us that the comparison had been triggered by the context, it struck me as quite accurate, and I started to wonder whether it would be possible to produce an introductory work on Lacan according to different criteria, which set me on the tracks leading to this book.

Apart from all those people present at my table on that memorable Irish night, I wish to express my gratitude to all the authors who have agreed to contribute to this volume for complying with the guidelines I set out for them and for patiently tolerating my repeated requests for revision. I would also like to thank Chris Lillja and Jamie Orr at Princeton University Press, and Jeffrey Czekaj at Harvard University Press for granting permission to reprint the sections in Bruce Fink's paper which appeared previously in *The Lacanian Subject* and *A Clinical Introduction to Lacanian Psychoanalysis*. Finally I thank Oliver Rathbone and Kirsty Hall at Rebus Press for supporting this project from its earliest stages and for providing invaluable editorial advice.

PREFACE

Since the 1980's, Lacanian ideas have stealthily yet steadily penetrated the social sciences, the arts and the humanities. The works of Lacan are currently a standard reference within cultural, gender and women's studies, and they also inspire many authors working within the realms of philosophy and political theory. At the same time, Lacanian ideas continue to spark off heated debates amongst psychoanalysts and 'lay-people' alike, whereby Lacan's numerous personal idiosyncrasies are often used as arguments *ad hominem* to minimize the value of his theoretical contributions.[1] Furthermore, the enormous complexity, the high level of abstraction, and the partial publication and translation of Lacan's works continue to trigger scholarly disputes about how to interpret terms and formulae.[2]

Confronted with this broad dissemination of Lacanian thought and the multifarious controversies surrounding it, professional researchers, health care workers and students often try to find solace in psycho-analytic works of reference. Over the past decade, many works have been published in which psychoanalytic concepts, schemas, and symbols are defined in a brief, accessible format, although mainly in French and dealing with psychoanalysis in general rather than Lacanian theory as such.[3] For the Anglo-American reader, and strictly oriented towards Lacanian terminology, there is currently Dylan Evans's *An Introductory Dictionary of Lacanian Psychoanalysis*, which is likely to remain an invaluable source of information for students and profes-sionals in years to come.[4] Besides this unique compendium, numerous general introductions to Lacan in English exist, and there is even a *Reader's Guide* to the English *Ecrits*.[5]

Considering the scope and the quality of these materials, the primary Lacan-needs of the Anglo-American reader are already well catered for, which reduces the desirability of yet another 'introduction to

Lacan.' In conceiving *Key Concepts of Lacanian Psychoanalysis* I have tried to ensure that the book is neither an alternative, nor a complement to the existing works of reference. In the essays that follow, the newcomer to Lacanian psychoanalysis will not find any short definitions of terms, nor any concise expositions of what concepts and symbols mean within the various contexts in which they have appeared. Rather than a ready reference, each author provides an in-depth discussion of one particular notion, paying attention to the theoretical and/or practical context in which Lacan introduced it, the way in which the notion developed throughout his works, the questions it was designed to answer, and its relevance for clinical and/or sociocultural issues. Contrary to a 'reader's companion,' *Key Concepts of Lacanian Psychoanalysis* probes into the sources, dimensions and purposes of as few as eight Lacanian concepts, exploring how they relate to other Lacanian and non-Lacanian notions, and questioning their value for present-day clinical and non-clinical issues. In this sense, the book is not an alternative to the available compendia and introductions. Yet *Key Concepts of Lacanian Psychoanalysis* is neither a complement to these books, since it does not focus on Lacan's general sociocultural legacy, nor strictly speaking on his 'life and works.'[6]

One might therefore assume that these essays are addressed to professional psychoanalysts, advanced Lacan-scholars and highbrow academics. Nothing could be less true. *Key Concepts of Lacanian Psychoanalysis* does not presuppose any familiarity with Lacanian theory on the part of the reader, nor a prior acquaintance with Lacan's *Ecrits* or seminars. Although all the essays proceed from a close reading of Lacan's writings and lectures, they invite the reader to start his or her own reading rather than consolidating and building on an already accomplished groundwork. To facilitate the reader's personal 'return to Lacan,' each essay contains detailed and extensive references to primary and secondary source materials, as well as suggestions for further reading.

As the reader will notice, some of the primary sources are still unpublished and many of those which have already been published are not yet available in English. For the purposes of this book, the inclusion of these materials was necessary, since it is for example impossible to discuss the development of a concept throughout Lacan's works without taking into account his unpublished seminars (some eighteen volumes) and those already published yet hitherto not officially translated into English (four volumes).[7] I hope the reader who has no access to these original and/or unpublished sources, rather than being deterred by this book, will find it a valuable tool for adding some epistemological continuity to his or her (inescapably fragmented) reading of Lacan. For if one thing will become clear after a reading of these essays, it is that Lacan's works are not governed by a succession of epistemological rifts, as some Lacan-scholars have tried to prove. Rather than being characterized by ruptures and radical shifts of attention, Lacan's work bears witness to a lasting continuity, in keeping with the Wundtian principle of 'hierarchy without loss' that was also dear to Freud.[8]

In this sense, Lacan's ideas from the 1970's display a higher degree of complexity than those from the 1950's, without the latter completely disappearing under the influence of the former. The 'early' Lacan is often recognizable behind the faces of the 'middle' and 'late' Lacan. This does not mean that Lacan's entire theory is 'always already there,' contained *in utero* in his earliest contributions, since such an interpretation does not acknowledge the fact that when 'early concepts' surface in a 'later context,' they always acquire new meaning. But it neither implies that his is a theory of ongoing progress. A cursory reading of his texts and seminars from the 1970's suffices to recognize that his later developments are not a synthesis of the early ones. Lacan does not work towards the realization of absolute psychoanalytic knowledge, but rather towards a destabilization of knowledge — whether somebody else's or his own — that gives the impression of being firmly established. Lacan's incessant challenge of 'ready-made' psychoanalytic knowledge might also explain why there is currently no solid, unitary Lacanian Theory, and why such a Theory is unlikely to emerge from a close reading of his works.

In selecting the concepts for this book, I have used the criteria of prevalence, penetrance and transferability. Initially, I started with terms that are so intricately linked to Lacanian theory that their emergence within any given context almost immediately conjures up Lacan's name. Having produced a list of these 'prevalent' Lacanian concepts, I then highlighted those spanning a substantial period of Lacan's teachings, excluding those which only appear in a limited number of seminars, or in a couple of lessons of one single seminar. I thus rejected for instance 'quilting point' (*point de capiton*), extimacy (*extimité*), holophrase and passage-à-l'acte. Finally, I reduced the list even further by only retaining those concepts that are applicable to a broad range of issues: clinical as well as sociocultural, psychoanalytic as well as psychological, philosophical and ideological. In this way, I excluded concepts that are quite important, yet fairly technical, such as 'logical time' (*temps logique*) and 'lack of being' (*manque à être*). On this final list of 'key concepts,' limitations of space imposed an additional restriction, a more or less random selection process yielding the eight concepts discussed in the essays that follow. The concepts presented in this book are thus by no means *the* key concepts of Lacanian psychoanalysis. Many Lacanian concepts, such as the object *a*, the pass, the optical schema, the Name-of-the-Father and the subject-supposed-to-know, are at least as key as those discussed here. A second volume of *Key Concepts of Lacanian Psychoanalysis* could therefore be envisaged.

Finally, I must say something about the translation of Lacan's works into English. Since Anthony Wilden's landmark translation and annotation of Lacan's 'Rome discourse' in 1968, translations have been undertaken by various scholars, and Lacanian concepts have often been rendered in different ways. The most notorious example of these differing translations concerns Lacan's notions of *parole*, *sens* and *signification*, which Wilden has rendered as word, meaning and signification, Schneiderman as speech, sense and meaning, and both Forrester and Sheridan as speech, meaning and signification.[9] Despite the obvious advantages of a standard translation, I have not imposed some kind of shared Lacanian English on the authors of this volume, allowing them to use their own translations of Lacanese, yet including the original French term when necessary and adding a note whenever an existing English translation has been modified. I hope this will enable the reader to regard these texts as interpretations rather than definitive statements reflecting the view of a particular Lacanian 'school,' and that this will also contribute to a further discussion of Lacanian concepts.

DANY NOBUS
London, November 1997

Notes

1. To mention but two striking, recent examples of *ad hominem* argumentation, see: T. Eagleton, Sickness unto Death, *The Times Literary Supplement*, October 17 1997, pp. 15-16; R. Tallis, The Shrink from Hell, *The Times Higher Education Supplement*, October 31 1997, p. 20.

2. For a fine discussion of some persistent Lacanian misreadings, see: J. Gallop, Reading the Phallus, *Reading Lacan*, Ithaca NY-London, Cornell University Press, 1985, pp. 133-156.

3. For the most recent ones, see: E. Wright (Ed.), *Feminism and Psychoanalysis: A Critical Dictionary*, Oxford, Blackwell, 1992; P. Kaufmann (Ed.), *L'apport freudien. Eléments pour une encyclopédie de la psychanalyse*, Paris, Bordas, 1993; R. Chemama, *Dictionnaire de la psychanalyse*, Paris, Larousse, 1993; B.E. Moore & B.D. Fine (Eds.), *Psychoanalysis: The Major Concepts*, New Haven CT-London, Yale University Press, 1995; E. Roudinesco & M. Plon, *Dictionnaire de la psychanalyse*, Paris, Fayard, 1997; Encyclopaedia Universalis (Ed.), *Dictionnaire de la psychanalyse*, Paris, Encyclopaedia Universalis, 1997.

4. D. Evans, *An Introductory Dictionary of Lacanian Psychoanalysis*, London-New York NY, Routledge, 1996.

5. For introductions to Lacan in English, see for example: A. Lemaire, *Jacques Lacan* (1970) (trans. D. Macey), London, Routledge & Kegan, Paul, 1979; C. Clément, *The Lives and Legends of Jacques Lacan* (1981) (trans. A. Goldhammer), New York NY, Columbia University Press, 1983; S. Schneiderman, *Jacques Lacan: The Death of An Intellectual Hero*, Cambridge MA-London, Harvard University Press, 1983; B. Benvenuto & R. Kennedy, *The Works of Jacques Lacan: An Introduction*, London, Free Association Books, 1986; E. Ragland-Sullivan, *Jacques Lacan and the Philosophy of Psychoanalysis*, Chicago IL-London, The University of Illinois Press, 1986; D. Macey, *Lacan in Contexts*, London-New York NY, Verso, 1988; E. Grosz, *Jacques Lacan: A Feminist Introduction*, London-New York NY, Routledge, 1990; J.S. Lee, *Jacques Lacan*, Ann Arbor MI, The University of Michigan Press, 1991; M. Bowie, *Lacan*, London, Fontana, 1991; M. Borch-Jacobsen, *Lacan: The Absolute Master* (1990) (trans. D. Brick), Stanford CA, Stanford University Press, 1991; S. Žižek, *Looking Awry: An Introduction to Jacques Lacan through Popular Culture*, Cambridge MA-London, The MIT Press, 1991; S. Weber, *Return to Freud: Jacques Lacan's Dislocation of Psychoanalysis* (trans. M. Levine), Cambridge, Cambridge University Press, 1991; M. Sarup, *Jacques Lacan*, New York NY-London, Harvester Wheatsheaf, 1992; R. Samuels, *Between Philosophy and Psychoanalysis: Lacan's Reconstruction of Freud*, London-New York NY, Routledge, 1993; Ph. Julien, *Jacques Lacan's Return to Freud: The Real, the Symbolic and the Imaginary* (1981) (trans. D. Beck Simiu), New York NY-London, New York University Press, 1994; D. Leader, *Lacan for Beginners*, Cambridge, Icon, 1995; B. Fink, *The Lacanian Subject: Between Language and Jouissance*, Princeton NJ, Princeton University Press, 1995; Ph. Hill, *Lacan for Beginners*, London, Writers & Readers, 1997; J. Dor, *Introduction to the Reading of Lacan: The Unconscious Structured Like a Language* (1985) (trans. S.

Fairfield), Edited by J. Feher Gurewich in collaboration with S. Fairfield, Northvale NJ-London, Jason Aronson Inc., 1997; B. Fink, *A Clinical Introduction to Lacanian Psychoanalysis: Theory and Technique*, Cambridge MA-London, Harvard University Press, 1997; J. Dor, *The Clinical Lacan* (1986) (trans. S. Fairfield), Edited by J. Feher Gurewich in collaboration with S. Fairfield, Northvale NJ-London, Jason Aronson Inc., 1997. For the reader's guide to *Ecrits*, see: J. Muller & W. Richardson, *Lacan and Language: A Reader's Guide to Ecrits*, Madison CT, International Universities Press, 1982.

6. For detailed, yet controversial accounts of Lacan's life and works, see: E. Roudinesco, *Jacques Lacan & Co.: A History of Psychoanalysis in France 1925-1985* (1986) (trans. J. Mehlman), London, Free Association Books, 1990; S. Turkle, *Psychoanalytic Politics: Jacques Lacan and Freud's French Revolution* (2nd Edition, Revised and Updated), London, Free Association Books, 1992; E. Roudinesco, *Jacques Lacan* (1993) (trans. B. Bray), New York NY, Columbia University Press, 1997. For a brief chronology, see: D. Evans, *An Introductory Dictionary of Lacanian Psychoanalysis, o.c.*, pp. xix-xxii. The most complete Lacan-bibliography is: J. Dor, *Nouvelle bibliographie des travaux de Jacques Lacan*, Paris, E.P.E.L., 1993. For summaries of Lacan's works and listings of secondary sources, see: M. Clark, *Jacques Lacan: An Annotated Bibliography*, 2 vols., New York NY-London, Garland, 1988; M. Marini, *Jacques Lacan: The French Context* (1986) (trans. A. Tomiche), New Brunswick NJ, Rutgers University Press, 1992.

7. Translations of *Seminar IV* (*La relation d'objet*), *Seminar VIII* (*Le transfert*), *Seminar XVII* (*L'envers de la psychanalyse*) and *Seminar XX* (*Encore*) are currently underway, as is a new complete translation of *Ecrits*.

8. For the Wundtian principle, see: S. Freud, Totem and Taboo (1912-13*a*), *Standard Edition*, XIII, pp. 1-161.

9. See: J. Lacan, *Speech and Language in Psychoanalysis* (1968) (trans. with notes and commentary A. Wilden), Baltimore MD-London, The Johns Hopkins University Press, 1991; J. Lacan, *Ecrits: A Selection* (1966) (trans. A. Sheridan), London, Tavistock, 1977; S. Schneiderman, Translator's Preface, in *How Lacan's Ideas are Used in Clinical Practice* (1980) (Selections edited and translated by S. Schneiderman), Northvale NJ-London, Jason Aronson Inc., 1993, pp. vii-viii; J. Forrester & S. Tomaselli, Translators' note, in J. Lacan, *The Seminar. Book I: Freud's Papers on Technique* (1953-54) (trans. with notes J. Forrester), Edited by J.-A. Miller, New York NY, W.W. Norton & Company, 1988, pp. vii-viii.

CHAPTER 1

From Kantian Ethics to Mystical Experience: An Exploration of Jouissance

Dylan Evans

I. Introduction

No survey of Lacanian terms would be complete without a discussion of jouissance.[1] And yet, as more than one commentator has pointed out, jouissance is certainly among the most complex and ambiguous terms in the Lacanian oeuvre.[2] The problem begins with translation. The closest literal translation is 'enjoyment,' both in the sense of deriving pleasure from something, and in the legal sense of exercising certain property rights. But while jouissance is often rendered simply 'enjoyment' in many English works on Lacan, this obscures the directly sexual connotations of the French term, which can also mean 'orgasm.'[3] In order to escape these difficulties of translation, most have opted simply to retain the French term, thus consolidating the tendency of many anglophone Lacanians to intersperse their discourse with the ocassional French word.[4]

The difficulties of finding an appropriate way of rendering the term in English are matched by the complexities of its conceptual references. During the course of Lacan's teaching, jouissance is used in a series of different contexts, in each of which it acquires a different nuance. The first step, then, in examining this term, must be to examine these different contexts in order to unravel these various nuances. Only then will it be possible to examine and assess the clinical and cultural applications of the term.

II. The Various Nuances of Jouissance in Lacan's Work

It is perhaps surprising, given the importance that jouissance comes to acquire in Lacan's later work, that the term does not appear at all in his early writings. There is no mention of it in the pre-war writings, and in fact it does not make its first appearance until Lacan's first public seminar, which he gave in the year 1953-54.[5] Even then, it figures only occasionally, and it is not until 1958 that it begins to play a major part in Lacan's theoretical vocabulary. From then onwards it takes on an ever greater significance until, in the 1970's, it is so crucial to Lacan's thinking that, were one to single out the most important Lacanian concept, the only contenders would be jouissance and the object *a*.

In the course of this rise to prominence, the term jouissance does not retain a stable meaning. On the contrary, like most Lacanian terms, its resonances and articulations shift dramatically over the course of his teaching. One way to examine these shifts would be to read them as the progressive unfolding of a single concept; this is how Nestor Braunstein presents jouissance in his informative work on the topic.[6] However, such an approach is peculiarly at odds with Lacan's own style of exposition, which never aims at producing a single consistent meaning for each term, but rather at developing different meanings which are often at odds with one another. In what follows, therefore, I have simply sketched some of the different nuances of jouissance as they emerge at different sites in Lacan's texts, without trying to reconcile them in some masterful synthesis. It is not that such syntheses are necessarily wrong, since one attraction of Lacan's teaching is that it invites the reader to construct such syntheses for himself or herself. It is simply that when the commentator on Lacan constructs a synthesis, care must be taken to foreground its interpretative nature, for otherwise one runs the risk, as Braunstein does, of presenting a particular reading as immanent in the text itself. In opting to discuss jouissance in a fragmentary way, I hope to leave the task of synthesis up to the reader, as well as providing the grounds for criticising the syntheses that are produced.

1. Jouissance as pleasure

Before Lacan, the term jouissance did not figure in the terminological apparatus of psychoanalysis; the closest German equivalent (*Genuß*) does not form part of Freud's theoretical vocabulary, nor had any French psychoanalyst assigned any special value to the term. Lacan seems to have imported the term into psychoanalysis from a certain tradition in philosophy, namely the Hegelian tradition as it was developed by Alexandre Kojève, whose lectures on Hegel Lacan attended in the 1930's. Lacan himself attributes the notion of jouissance to Hegel, but such a remark must be qualified by the fact that, whenever Lacan refers to Hegel, it is always Kojève's Hegel he has in mind.[7] Thus it is Kojève, rather than Hegel himself, who first stresses the dimension of enjoyment in the dialectic of the master and the slave:

> [The Master] can also force the Slave to *work* for him, to yield the result of his *Action* to him. Thus, the Master no longer needs to make any effort to satisfy his (natural) desires . . . Now, to preserve oneself in Nature without fighting against it is to live in *Genuß*, in Enjoyment. And the enjoyment that one obtains without making any effort is *Lust*, Pleasure.[8]

It is not hard to detect the influence of Kojève when the term jouissance first appears in Lacan's work, in the seminar of 1953-54. Here, the term is used exclusively in the context of discussions of the dialectic of the master and the slave, and seems to denote no more than a form of pleasure. Thus, when the master puts the slave to work, the slave produces objects which only the master can possess and enjoy:

> Indeed, beginning with the mythical situation [of the master and the slave], an action is undertaken, and establishes the relation between pleasure [*jouissance*] and labour. A law is imposed upon the slave, that he should satisfy the desire and the pleasure [*jouissance*] of the other.[9]

Thus the slave becomes the paradigm of the obsessional neurotic, who is dead, not to himself, but for his master, because he has effaced his own enjoyment.[10] Giving up his own enjoyment, the obsessional neurotic transfers it onto an imaginary other whom he can then watch with the envious eyes of a caged animal.[11]

2. Jouissance as orgasm

If the sexual connotations of jouissance are absent from Lacan's initial use of the term in the seminars of 1953-54 and 1954-55, they become explicit a few years later, when Lacan uses the term to refer to the pleasures of masturbation.[12] This marks a turning point in Lacan's use of the term, after which it is always marked explicitly by the dimension of sexuality, even though at first the sexuality in question has a distinctly biological flavour. In other words, jouissance is equated simply with the pleasurable sensation of orgasm, and thus still located in the register of need and biological satisfaction. In 1958 for example, in a paper on feminine sexuality, Lacan speaks of frigidity as a lack of 'clitoral jouissance.'[13] This must be read alongside another paper dating from the same year, in which frigidity is defined as 'a lack in the *satisfaction* proper to sexual *need*.'[14] Even much later in Lacan's work, when jouissance has taken on multiple significations far removed from the simple equation with the orgasm, this register is never completely abandoned. Thus Lacan can gloss jouissance simply as 'orgasm' in 1963 and play on this meaning overtly in his remarks on Bernini's Saint Theresa in 1973.[15]

If Lacan's first uses of the term jouissance in 1953-55 are inspired by Kojève, the shift towards the sexual connotations of the term after 1956 may be inspired by the work of Georges Bataille. Lacan himself does not acknowledge this debt; there is, in fact, only one direct reference to Bataille in the whole of the *Ecrits*, and Bataille's name is mentioned only once in the seminar *The Ethics of Psychoanalysis*, where the discussion of Sade might well have merited more.[16] However, as both François Perrier and David Macey have argued, there are many indications of the influence of Bataille in Lacan's later conceptualisation of jouissance.[17] Not only is the deadly character of jouissance strongly reminiscent of Bataille's view of the erotic as a realm of violence which borders on death itself, but Bataille also characterises erotic joy (*joie*) as necessarily excessive in character, and compares it to an incommunicable mystical experience (as does Lacan).[18] Again, anticipating Lacan's remarks on the paradoxical character of jouissance, Bataille writes that 'we should, enduring it without too much anxiety, enjoy [*jouir*] the feeling of being lost or being in danger.'[19] For Bataille, this paradox arises from the very nature of the orgasm itself, which is always finalised by a death-like shudder.

3. Jouissance versus desire

Prior to 1958, Lacan's occasional uses of the term jouissance seem to be in keeping with common usage; it is a synonym for pleasure, particularly pleasure of a brute physical kind, the paradigm of which is the pleasure of orgasm. However, beginning in 1958, the term gradually acquires a completely new, specifically Lacanian meaning. This new meaning emerges from distinctions which Lacan develops, first between jouissance and desire, and then between jouissance and pleasure.

The distinction between jouissance and desire is first developed in the seminar on the formations of the unconscious, in the sessions of March 1958.[20] Here, Lacan states that it is important to distinguish carefully between these two terms, but provides only a few hints on how he understands this distinction. His most explicit statement on the matter comes in the lecture of 26 March 1958, when he claims that 'the subject does not simply satisfy a desire, he enjoys [*jouit*] desiring, and this is an essential dimension of his jouissance.'[21] In other words, desire is not a movement towards an object, since if it were then it would be simple to satisfy it. Rather, desire lacks an object that could satisfy it, and is therefore to be conceived of as a movement which is pursued endlessly, simply for the enjoyment (jouissance) of pursuing it. Jouissance is thus lifted out of the register of the satisfaction of a biological need, and becomes instead the paradoxical satisfaction which is found in pursuing an eternally unsatisfied desire. It is no surprise, then, that Lacan immediately links it with the phenomenon of masochism.

These first remarks on the relationship of jouissance and desire suggest that jouissance is what sustains desire, since it is the enjoyment of desiring for desire's sake that keeps one desiring in the absence of satisfaction. Later, however, the relationship between desire and jouissance is presented differently. In the seminar on anxiety, for example, when Lacan states that 'desire presents itself as a will to jouissance,' this seems to posit jouissance as the terminus of desire, as that which desire aims at.[22] It is now a question of explaining why desire never attains that jouissance which it seeks out, of explaining why the will to jouissance is always 'a will which fails, which encounters its own limit, its own restraint.'[23]

It is important to note the difference between these two accounts of the relationship between jouissance and desire. In the first account, the two coexist: if the subject enjoys desiring, then jouissance sustains desire. In the second account, in which desire aims at jouissance, desire is predicated on a lack of jouissance, since one can only desire what one does not have. In the later works of Lacan, it is the latter account which is predominant.

4. Jouissance as a radical ethical stance

If the distinction between jouissance and desire, which Lacan begins to develop in 1958, constitutes the first specifically Lacanian axis of the term, then the opposition between jouissance and pleasure constitutes the second. Lacan develops this opposition in 1960, in the context of his seminar *The Ethics of Psychoanalysis*.[24] Here, jouissance is no longer simply equated with the sensation of pleasure, but also comes to designate the opposite sensation, one of physical or mental suffering. This is not to equate jouissance with masochism, for there is an important difference. In masochism, pain is a means to pleasure; pleasure is taken in the very fact of suffering itself, so that it becomes difficult to distinguish pleasure from pain. With jouissance, on the other hand, pleasure and pain remain distinct; no pleasure is taken in the pain itself, but the pleasure cannot be obtained without paying the price of suffering. It is thus a kind of *deal* in which 'pleasure *and* pain are presented as a single packet.'[25] Lacan illustrates this with an example from Kant's *Critique of Practical Reason*: a man is given the opportunity to have sex with the woman he most desires, but told that if he does so he will be executed afterwards.[26]

The opposition between jouissance, understood in this newer sense, and pleasure also involves a revised understanding of the latter term. Pleasure now signifies on the one hand the *sensation* of pleasure and on the other hand the pleasure *principle*. The pleasure principle is one of the 'two principles of mental functioning' which Freud discusses in his metapsychological writings (the other being the reality principle).[27] It is the innate tendency of the subject to govern his actions on the basis of avoiding pain and obtaining pleasure. Now, it should be clear that whereas pleasure in the former sense is synonymous with the earlier meaning of jouissance, pleasure in the latter sense is actually opposed to the later meaning of jouissance. If the man in Kant's example is governed by the pleasure principle, he will not pay the price of death simply in order to have a brief sexual encounter with the lady of his dreams. The pleasure principle involves a kind of cost-benefit analysis which makes the man reject the deal of jouissance. Or, in Lacan's words: 'it is pleasure that sets the limits on jouissance.'[28]

However, it is precisely the merit of psychoanalysis to point out that there is something 'beyond the pleasure principle.'[29] In other words, not all human decisions are governed by a 'rational' calculation in which potential pleasure is weighed against potential pain. There are those who would indeed pay the price of death in order to spend one night with the woman of their dreams. The deal of jouissance is not always rejected.

Kant uses this example of the man faced with the choice of paying the price of death for sex to illustrate the hypothetical imperative, which precedes his discussion of the true ethical decision. If the man chooses to renounce the deal because of selfish 'pathological' considerations — that is, if the man decides not on the basis of the moral law but on the basis of a calculation which weighs up the gain in pleasure against the price to be paid for it — this is not a radical ethical stance. Only an act which disregards the normal calculations of weighing up potential pleasure against potential pain can be called ethical. If this is now transposed to Lacan's opposition between the pleasure principle and jouissance, the pleasure principle would correspond to Kant's pathological calculation of pleasure and pain, whereas jouissance would be located on the side of the ethical, 'given that jouissance implies precisely the acceptance of death.'[30]

By distinguishing pleasure and jouissance in terms of Kantian ethics, Lacan also clarifies the nature of the death drive. What is it that allows someone to disregard the normal, 'rational' calculations of pleasure and pain, and thus become capable of a truly ethical act? Is it not precisely the fact that the pleasure principle does not hold universal sway? In other words, Lacan's point is that it is precisely the existence of the death drive, the 'beyond' of the pleasure principle, which makes possible the ethical zone.

5. The jouissance of the Other

In the previous section it was seen how the meaning of jouissance shifts, in 1960, from a simple equation with pleasure, to a deal in which pleasure and pain are presented 'in a single packet.' However, as with most of Lacan's terminological innovations and conceptual shifts, the earlier meaning of jouissance is not simply replaced by the newer one; rather, they coexist. After 1960, then, it is possible to detect an oscillation between the older meaning of jouissance (as a synonym for pleasure) and the newer meaning of jouissance (as pleasure and pain 'in a single packet'), and it is always important to discern which meaning is operating at any particular point where the term is used. At the risk of oversimplifying things, it could be argued that, after 1960, when Lacan speaks of the jouissance of the subject it is the newer meaning which is relevant, whereas his discussion of the jouissance of the Other invokes the older equation of jouissance with pleasure. In other words, the jouissance of the Other is not marked by that element of pain and suffering that characterises the jouissance of the subject.

This reading is borne out by some remarks that Lacan makes on a common clinical phenomenon: the widespread illusion that there are other people who are 'not fucked up like me,' other families which are not beset by the dark forces that mar one's own, asymptomatic subjects who are completely happy, who do not ask questions, and who sleep soundly in their beds. Lacan refers to this mirage as a jouissance which is only accessible to the Other, which would seem to confirm the idea that, when associated with the Other, jouissance harks back to the earlier equation with pleasure and lacks the connotation of suffering.[31]

The origin of this illusion of a superabundant jouissance accessible only to the Other is to be found in the very first experiences of the child, when the primordial Other, the mother, may seem to be complete, self-sufficient, and happy with herself independently of the child. Since this leaves no space for the child, the child attempts to inscribe a lack in the Other, by seeking to introduce, for example, a note of anxiety in the mother, perhaps by screaming or refusing to eat. If unsuccessful (that is, if the child's screams do not perturb the mother's enjoyment at all), the child will not be able to elaborate its own desire; desire and jouissance are here clearly opposed. If successful, however, this proves to the child that the Other is not complete, that the mother's jouissance is not superabundant. Even then, the memory of the first impression of the mother's complete jouissance will persist in the illusion of a superabundant jouissance accessible only to the Other.

6. Feminine jouissance

The remarks in the previous section implied that the belief that the jouissance of the Other is somehow more complete than our own is simply an illusion. However, there are moments in Lacan's teachings which suggest that this is not always the case, that there really *is* an Other whose jouissance is greater. These suggestions emerge when the Other is identified with *the Other sex*, which for Lacan is always woman. This idea first emerges in the seminar on anxiety, when Lacan states (with Tiresias) that: 'it is women who enjoy [*jouissent*]. Their jouissance is greater.'[32]

While the idea that feminine jouissance is somehow greater than male jouissance is new in 1963, the articulation of jouissance with femininity is certainly not. Lacan had already used the term jouissance in his discussions of feminine sexuality in 1958, marking what would become a constant conjunction.[33] Indeed, in no context does Lacan use the term jouissance more frequently than that of feminine sexuality. It is this which has led some commentators to observe that Lacan's discussions of femininity are usually the site of a significant displacement, in which the question of female sexuality becomes a question of female jouissance.[34]

In this context, jouissance is to be understood as the achievement of some form of sexual satisfaction, often (but not always) equated with orgasm. The distinction between male and female jouissance thus depends on the assumption that there are distinct forms of sexual satisfaction for men and women. At first this distinction is presented by

Lacan as merely a matter of degree, as in the remark above on female jouissance being greater than that of men. The distinction does not therefore affect the nature of jouissance as such, which is held by Lacan to be phallic: 'Jouissance, insofar as it is sexual, is phallic, which means that it does not relate to thc Other as such.'[35] However, later on, Lacan posits the idea of a different *form* of jouissance, a specifically feminine jouissance which is 'beyond the phallus.'[36] Lacan had already spoken of feminine jouissance in his 1958 paper on feminine sexuality, but this was simply a clitoral jouissance opposed not to male jouissance but to vaginal satisfaction.[37] Given the Freudian equation between the clitoris and the penis, this early reference to feminine jouissance cannot be read as denoting a qualitatively different form of jouissance, but simply as referring to the female experience of a phallic form of jouissance common to both sexes. In the seminar of 1972-73, however, Lacan does speak of feminine jouissance as a qualitatively different form. Phallic jouissance continues to be something universal, experienced by both sexes, but women have, in addition to this phallic jouissance, access to another form.[38] Unlike phallic jouissance, this 'supplementary jouissance' does relate to the Other as such. But beyond this, very little can be said about it. Lacan himself is not very forthcoming on the nature of this form of enjoyment; indeed, he suggests that it is impossible to articulate it, since the experience of this kind of jouissance does not lead to any knowledge about it.[39] The ineffable nature of feminine jouissance leads Lacan to characterise it in terms of mystical experience, of which ineffability has always been one of the hallmarks. The image which he points to in his discussion is that of Bernini's Saint Theresa, about to be pierced by the golden spear of the angel. As is clear from Saint Theresa's own description of the event, this moment of mystical ecstasy is strongly suggestive of orgasmic enjoyment, and Lacan remarks in *Seminar XX* that one has only to look at the statue to realise that Saint Theresa is coming.[40]

7. The jouissance of the body

Since in Lacan's discourse the Other designates not only the Other *sex*, but also the body, it is hardly surprising that Lacan links the jouissance of the Other not only with femininity but also with the body. In fact, the two are intimately linked. When Lacan first introduces the idea of a jouissance beyond the phallus, he immediately specifies it as a 'jouissance of the body.'[41] This bodily jouissance is furthermore described as a 'substance,' a word that Lacan uses in awareness of all its philosophical resonances. Jouissance, he suggests, is the only substance that psychoanalysis recognises.[42] Like the Freudian concept of the libido, to which Lacan relates the concept of bodily jouissance, this substance is usually described in hydraulic metaphors.[43] Thus it can be described as a kind of fluid with which the body is loaded at birth, some of which must be drained away in order to accomplish the 'work of civilization' (Freud) and allow entry into the symbolic (Lacan). This operation of drainage is what psychoanalysis designates by the term castration. In other words, castration may be theorised as the renunciation of a certain portion of the bodily jouissance with which one is born: 'Castration means that *jouissance* must be refused, so that it can be reached on the inverted ladder (*l'échelle renversée*) of the Law of desire.'[44]

This Lacanian account of the castration complex takes up an important theme running through Freud's writings. Throughout Freud's work we find the idea that in order to enter into society, the subject must give something up. This 'something' which the subject must renounce is described variously as 'the sense of omnipotence' or a 'piece of instinctual satisfaction.'[45] The condition for taking up a position in the social order is that part of the initial quota of instinctual life with which the person is born must be lost forever. This part is 'unserviceable'; it does not fulfil any useful purpose in society and must therefore be eliminated:

> Generally speaking, our civilization is built up on the suppression of instincts. Each individual has surrendered some part of his assets . . . [T]he piece of instinctual satisfaction which each person had renounced was offered to the Deity as a sacrifice . . .[46]

Like the Freudian 'piece of instinctual satisfaction,' the Lacanian jouissance is an unserviceable surplus which must be sacrificed. In Lacan's discussion of sacrifice, however, he provides a critique of the utilitarian model of society implicit in Freud's account. The sacrifice of a piece of instinctual satisfaction, Lacan argues, does not simply lead to its extinction. On the contrary, the sacrificed jouissance collects in the superego whence it can return in the form of evil. The 'Deity' of which Freud speaks is thus to be conceived not as a beneficient God, nor even as the serene but detached God of Spinoza, but primarily as 'the dark God.'[47]

There is, then, no hygienic way to eliminate this excess bodily jouissance which is surplus to the requirements of utility; though 'jouissance is useless,' as Lacan claims, it cannot simply be disposed of.[48] The term 'surplus' is used advisedly, for Lacan himself goes on, towards the end of the 1960's, to link jouissance to Marx's concept of surplus value, and coins the term 'surplus jouissance' (*plus-de-jouir*).[49] The concept of surplus jouissance indicates that after castration has drained jouissance from the body, there is always a certain amount left over.[50] This remainder of jouissance then gets trapped in bits of the body, in borders which constitute the erotogenic zones, or in the nuclei of hysterical symptoms.

8. Jouissance and language

To speak of the jouissance trapped in the symptom is to signal another important shift in Lacan's discourse, from the symptom as a linguistic phenomenon to something that can no longer be reduced entirely to language. Lacan had begun to move towards this view in the early 1960's, as is evident from his remark in 1963 that the symptom, unlike acting out, does not call for interpretation, since it is, in itself, not a call to the Other but a pure jouissance addressed to no one.[51] But it is not until the 1970's that this move becomes fully articulated in the concept of the *sinthome*.[52] Whereas Lacan had seen the symptom in the 1950's as a message to be deciphered and dissolved, the *sinthome* designates a signifying formulation beyond analysis, a kernel of enjoyment immune to the efficacy of the symbolic. It is no longer simply a case of *ça parle* (it speaks); it is now also necessary to state that *ça jouit* (it enjoys).[53] The later view reflects Freud's discovery of resistance; in other words, after interpretation, there remains an element of jouissance which is beyond symbolization and thus resists the linguistic interventions of the analyst.

This development in Lacan's thought answers one problem, only to raise another. The problem it answers relates to one of the main criticisms levelled at Lacan's work, namely, that Lacan reduces everything to language. In developing the concept of jouissance, Lacan rebuts such a criticism, by pointing to a powerful force beyond language. But this creates another theoretical difficulty, namely, the problem of the relationship between language and jouissance. For if jouissance is simply beyond language, how can the analyst gain any purchase on the symptom, given that his only tools are linguistic ones?

This question can be answered in a number of ways. On the one hand, it can be pointed out that castration, the operation by which jouissance is drained away from the body, is primarily a symbolic operation of language. It is the imposition of rules and prohibitions that drains the initial quota of jouissance from the child's body in the castration complex, and the analyst extends this castrating process in the course of a psychoanalysis by imposing other rules. However, this still leaves the question of what to do with that element of the symptom that *cannot* be interpreted, that kernel of jouissance that cannot be drained away. In other words, what can one do with the *sinthome*? Lacan's answer was that analysis can lead the subject to *identify* with the *sinthome*, that is, to realise that, far from requiring some sort of analytic dissolution that would render the subject asymptomatic, the pathological mark of the *sinthome* is precisely what can 'allow the subject to live' by providing him or her with a unique organisation of his or her jouissance.

On the other hand, Lacan also goes on to question the simple opposition between language and jouissance which is present in his earlier works, proposing that the signifier itself is the cause of jouissance.[54] Language (*langage*) as the network of signifiers may well operate by excluding jouissance, but this disguises the fact that *langage* is underpinned by *lalangue*, in which unconnected, free-floating, meaningless signifiers are in fact completely permeated by jouissance.[55] This is another radical twist in Lacan's work which complicates many of the previous oppositions developed in the 1950's. There is now a realm in which meaning (*sens*) is contaminated by an upsurge of enjoyment, a realm for which Lacan coins the neologism *jouis-sens* ('enjoyment in meaning' or, perhaps, 'enjoy-meant'). Jouissance is no longer simply a force *beyond* language; it is now also a force *within* language.

III. The Clinical Applications of the Concept of Jouissance

Having sketched the various meanings of the concept of jouissance in Lacan's work, I shall now examine some of its clinical applications. However, before doing so, it is worth commenting on the division between theory and clinical practice that this approach implies.

As should be clear from the preceding discussion of the development of the concept of jouissance, theoretical and practical concerns are constantly interwoven in Lacan's work in such a way as to make them impossible to separate. One example is the way that, as noted above, the concept answers a theoretical question ('Why does the symptom persist after interpretation?') but raises a technical one ('How can the analyst gain purchase on such resistant symptoms?'). The distinction between theory and practice is so much part and parcel of the Anglo-American tradition that an author such as Lacan, who refuses this division, is simply assigned to the category of 'theory.' Lacan's work is, therefore, often criticised by English and American psychoanalysts for being 'too theoretical' and for not engaging with the nitty-gritty of the clinic.

To deal first with the concept of jouissance and then with its clinical applications might be seen as lending support to the erroneous division between theory and practice on which this criticism is based. On the other hand, precisely because this misconception does exist, the clinical relevance of Lacanian concepts must be spelled out here in black and white, under a separate heading ('The clinic'), lest the Anglo-American reader miss the practical import of Lacan's work.

1. Frigidity

Given the sexual connotations of the term, it is hardly surprising that when Lacan first speaks of jouissance in the context of the clinic it is in relation to the phenomenon of frigidity.[56] Unlike Freud, who attributed frigidity to the inhibiting effect of female hostility towards men (itself a product of penis envy), Lacan puts the emphasis on the *symbolic* conditions which are necessary for a woman to be able to enjoy coitus.[57] Foremost among these conditions is the acceptance of the man's castration. In other words, whereas for Freud castration affects the woman and provokes frigidity via envy of the un-castrated man, in Lacan's account castration bears primarily on the man, and, rather than provoking frigidity, it is precisely (the woman's acceptance of) his castration that allows her to *enjoy* sexual intercourse.[58] This is the case because, according to Lacan, the woman's enjoyment of coitus with her sexual partner (or, in Lacan's own words, 'the sensitivity of holding the penis') depends on the presence of an invisible third term, which Lacan identifies as 'a castrated lover or a dead man (or even both at the same time).'[59] This unconscious element (which Lacan also calls the 'ideal incubus') is what bears the trace of the Name-of-the-Father, the instance of castration.[60] Now, Lacan argues that if the woman, in her game of seduction, becomes overly identified with the phallic masquerade she assumes, a veil is drawn between her and the ideal incubus, thus blocking off the precondition for her jouissance of her lover's penis. In other words, the woman's real partner is the demonic incubus; without *him*, she cannot enjoy sexual intercourse with the man who is called (not entirely accurately) her sexual partner.

This 1958 account of what Geneviève Morel aptly calls the 'feminine conditions of jouissance' clearly antedates the opposition between jouissance and pleasure which Lacan introduces not long after.[61] At this point, jouissance is identified with orgasmic ecstasy and is not yet tinged with the paradoxical note of pain. Jouissance is thus still linked to the real, and conceived primarily in biological terms, and thus frigidity (or lack of jouissance) can be defined by Lacan in another paper from the same year as 'a lack in the *satisfaction* proper to the sexual *need*.'[62] But by the time Lacan returns to the subject of frigidity, in 1973, his concept of jouissance has undergone so many modifications that he can happily call the existence of frigidity into question. Now that Lacan has specified that in addition to the universal phallic form of jouissance there is another specifically feminine form, the absence of the former in a woman cannot be taken to imply the absence of the latter. And furthermore, given that the latter, 'supplementary' form of jouissance is marked by ineffability, it follows that if a woman complains of a lack of enjoyment this must not always be taken at face value; it may be that she experiences that other form of jouissance, of which she knows nothing: 'If it was simply that she experiences it and knows nothing of it, then we would be able to cast considerable doubt on this notorious frigidity.'[63] In this passage, Lacan is very far removed from the position he adopted in 1958, in which frigidity was equated with an absence of clitoral orgasm and was seen as necessarily symptomatic, even though it might be 'relatively well tolerated.'[64] Now frigidity is equated with the absence of any kind of jouissance, and thus its very existence is called into question, on the grounds that the subject is always enjoying, even though she may know nothing about it.

2. Anxiety and psychosis

Besides frigidity, the concept of jouissance also sheds light on another clinical phenomenon: anxiety. In one of his later seminars, Lacan remarks that anxiety is that which exists in the interior of the body when the body is overcome by jouissance.[65] This is a departure from Lacan's earlier remarks on anxiety as a signal, and is reminiscent of Freud's first theory of anxiety, in which anxiety is seen as the direct transformation of excessive quantities of libido that cannot otherwise be discharged. This may be seen especially clearly in certain cases of psychosis. The psychotic has not accepted symbolic castration, and thus the normal process by which jouissance is drained away by the imposition of rules and regulations has not occurred. As a result, excessive quantities of jouissance constantly threaten to overwhelm the psychotic subject in the form of anxiety, although the way that this occurs differs according to the form of psychosis in question. That is, jouissance manifests itself in different ways in the schizophrenic and the paranoiac.

For the schizophrenic, jouissance is primarily a bodily phenomenon. One schizophrenic patient of mine described a terrifying incident in which this is clearly illustrated. For one whole day she was pinned to the floor of her apartment by an invisible force which crushed down on top of her. This somatic hallucination was accompanied by the most intense form of anxiety, which she desperately wanted to release 'by piercing something.' She knew that the thing to be pierced had to be a surface of some kind, but whether this surface was her own skin or the window of her apartment did not seem to matter to her; the important thing was simply to 'let it out.' The 'it' in this phrase was her way of talking about a jouissance that could not be discharged.

For the paranoiac, on the other hand, jouissance is located not in the subject's own body but in the Other. The Other's jouissance then takes the form of a persecution directed at the subject. For example, the Other may be represented as the CIA, which the subject imagines to be sending out agents to watch his or her every move, note down his or her words, etc. The paranoiac is thus the object of the Other's enjoyment, his or her 'complement.' A classic example of this is provided by Schreber, the most famous paranoiac in the psychoanalytic pantheon, who saw himself as God's sexual partner.[66]

3. Sadism and the superego

The concept of the jouissance of the Other is not only relevant for the clinic of psychosis; it is also very important in understanding the clinic (or perhaps the non-clinic) of perversion. In his essay entitled *Kant with Sade*, Lacan proposes that the sadist sees himself as acting, not for his own jouissance, but for the jouissance of the Other.[67] Thus, while it is true that on one level there is an object which the pervert seeks in his victim, on another level this is not done for himself but for the Other.[68] For example, the sadist inflicts pain on his victims because he is convinced that by this means he will procure the enjoyment of a shadowy, obscene Other who stands behind him as he carries out his acts of violence. Unlike the psychotic, who is the *object* of the Other's jouissance, the pervert is thus the *instrument* of the Other's jouissance. The pervert sees himself as a neutral tool carrying out the 'will-to-enjoy' (*volonté-de-jouissance*) of the Other, who, in the case of sadism, assumes the form of the Sadean 'Supreme-Being-in-Evil' (*Etre-suprême-en-méchanceté*).[69]

This brief discussion of sadism also throws light on another important clinical issue, namely, the nature of the superego. Freud pointed out that the superego acts in a sadistic manner towards the ego, subjecting it to ever greater cruelty in proportion to the ego's subservience to its commands.[70] This is why Lacan characterises the superego as an 'obscene, ferocious figure' whose command to the subject is not to feel guilty but to enjoy.[71] Given the paradoxical nature of jouissance, the command 'Enjoy!' is the cruellest of all. This can be seen clearly by relating it to the first topic discussed in this section: the phenomenon of frigidity. For there is nothing that inhibits orgasm more easily than the suspicion that one's partner *demands* that one come.

4. Jouissance and the neurotic symptom

Lacan's discussions of frigidity, anxiety, sadism and the superego give some idea of the clinical applications of the concept of jouissance. But the clinical relevance of the concept is certainly not limited to such areas; indeed, the problematic of jouissance extends into almost every sphere of clinical experience. In many ways, it could be argued that jouissance is the most fundamental problem faced by the analyst in clinical practice, since it encapsulates the paradox of painful pleasure and pleasurable pain which constitutes the heart of the neurotic symptom. Why do people usually come to see an analyst? Because, at some level, they are suffering. There is a demand for the analyst to alleviate their pain. But the moment the analyst begins to intervene, s/he is faced with the same discovery that Freud made a century ago; namely, that the subject resists cure because of the libidinal satisfaction that the symptom affords him or her. It now becomes necessary to expose the enjoyment hidden in the symptom before the subject will let go of it. For this reason, a psychoanalysis may be described as a struggle between the analyst and the jouissance of the analysand; the task of the analyst is to enable the analysand to channel his or her enjoyment through other, less painful forms of release. These other forms of release are provided by the signifying material that is generated in the course of free association.

One need only think of the Rat Man for an example of this enjoyment which lurks at the heart of the symptom.[72] The Rat Man tells Freud that he is tormented by the idea that a certain punishment may be inflicted upon the woman he loves. The punishment involves the woman being tied up while a pot of rats is placed upside down on her buttocks, with the result that the rats bore their way into her anus. The idea torments the Rat Man to such an extent that he is forced to perform all kinds of obsessional rituals to ward off the thought. But Freud notes something peculiar about the Rat Man's expression as he tells the story:

> At all the more important moments while he was telling his story his face took on a very strange, composite expression. I could only interpret it as one of *horror at pleasure of his own of which he himself was unaware.*[73]

The expression on the Rat Man's face gives away the jouissance in the obsessional symptom. Like jouissance, it is 'composite,' a paradoxical mixture of horror and pleasure. But only the horror is conscious, while the element of pleasure is hidden from the Rat Man's awareness.

The preceding survey of the clinical applications of the concept of jouissance is certainly not exhaustive; reasons of space have meant that other, equally interesting clinical phenomena on which the concept of jouissance throws light (such as sexual jealousy) have had to be left aside.[74] However, it is hoped that the foregoing discussion provides at least some indication of the important clinical dimensions of the concept, and goes some way towards showing that jouissance is not merely a theoretical term devoid of practical import.

IV. The Cultural Applications of the Concept of Jouissance

To speak of the cultural 'applications' of any psychoanalytic concept raises questions as complex as, though different from, those discussed above in relation to the separation of theoretical and clinical matters. Lacan himself distrusted the notion of 'applied psychoanalysis,' writing that: '[P]sychoanalysis is only applied, in the proper sense of the term, as a treatment, and thus to a subject who speaks and listens.'[75] Nevertheless, there is a long tradition, going back to Freud himself, of using psychoanalytic concepts to analyse cultural artifacts and social issues. Perhaps it is better to speak, in such cases, of the cultural *implications* of psychoanalysis rather than of its *applications*, as the former term avoids the idea of psychoanalytic theory as a metadiscourse which is implicit in the latter.

Given this important caveat, how might we proceed to define the cultural implications of jouissance? Lacan himself opened up one possible avenue for answering this question in a question and answer session televised in 1973.[76] At one point, the interviewer asks Lacan about a remark he had made predicting the rise of racism. Lacan replies by remarking that there is something peculiarly disordered about the contemporary organisation of jouissance.[77] A whole set of intriguing assumptions are implicit in this statement; namely, that jouissance is not merely a private affair but is structured in accordance with a social logic, and moreover that this logic changes over time, presumably by virtue of some economic or other determinant. Lacan does not elaborate much on these assumptions, however, except to hint that the causes of the present disorder have something to do with a galloping excess, related to the intrinsic need of capitalism to multiply our demand for more products to satisfy ever more 'false needs.' Such a reading is supported by the fact that Lacan uses the term *plus-de-jouir*, which is related, as has already been noted, to the Marxist concept of surplus value.

According to Lacan, this capitalist logic has the effect of 'derailing' the organisation of jouissance in modern Western society, by which he means that it becomes impossible for us to conceive of enjoyment except in relation to a cultural Other. The phenomenon is thus intimately linked with another contemporary social phenomenon, namely multiculturalism (the term Lacan uses is 'the melting pot').[78] But as soon as we are forced to have recourse to the Other in order to mark the position of our own jouissance (a feature which is a fairly recent development, according to Lacan, suggesting that in previous historical epochs jouissance was enclosed in some kind of interiority, defined only in relationship to itself), a curious paradox results. On the one hand, we need to preserve the jouissance of the Other in order to be able to define our own; but on the other hand, we seek to destroy that Other enjoyment because we suspect it may be more superabundant than our own. This recalls Lacan's earlier remarks about the common illusion that the jouissance of the Other is untainted by the note of pain which marks the jouissance of the subject. Then, he had commented on the strangeness of this phenomenon whereby we become 'jealous of something in the other to the point of hatred and the need to destroy.'[79] Now, Lacan goes on to remark how the same logic of envy impels us to define the Other as 'underdeveloped,' to distrust his mode of jouissance and 'imposing our own on him.'[80]

Reading between the lines, Lacan seems to be saying something like this: jouissance is as much a problem for society as it is for the individual. In Freudian terms, civilization is built up on the renunciation of instincts, and must therefore find a way of dealing with the pieces of instinctual satisfaction it demands that each person renounce. Different civilizations find different ways of doing this. In Lacanian terms, different cultural groups have different ways of collectively organising their jouissance. Given Freud's remark about the renunciation of instinctual satisfaction as a sacrificial offering, it could be argued that religion is one major way in which jouissance is collectively structured. It might then be possible to speak of a Catholic mode of jouissance, or a Hindu mode, and so on. Lacan argues that in the present social situation, in which our jouissance is 'going off the track,' a multicultural society leads inevitably to a rise in racism.[81] The very proximity of groups with different modes of jouissance, especially when combined with the tendency of each group to define its own mode of jouissance in opposition to that of another group, exacerbates the tendency to impose 'our' mode of jouissance on 'them.'

The theme of racism is taken up by Jacques-Alain Miller in his 1985-86 seminar entitled *Extimité*.[82] Developing Lacan's thoughts in *Television*, Miller argues that it is the jouissance of the Other that makes the Other truly Other. Racism, as a hatred of difference, is thus founded on the kernel of this difference; the fact that the Other takes his jouissance in a way different from ours. All the arguments employed by racists to justify their hatred ultimately focus on the way in which the Other obtains some *plus-de-jouir* that he does not deserve; either he does not work, or he works too hard, or he eats smelly food or has too much sex, etc. Thus true intolerance, concludes Miller, is nothing other than intolerance of the Other's jouissance.

The same theme is further developed by Slavoj Žižek in relation to the concept of the nation. Žižek reads the ethnic moment of the 'nation' as the object *a*, the leftover, of the universalising concept of democracy. In other words, democracy inevitably produces a surplus, without which it cannot exist, and which is identified by Žižek with the fact of the nation-state. Nationalism thus becomes 'the privileged domain of the eruption of enjoyment into the social field.'[83] The 'national Cause' is then cleverly related to Lacan's concept of 'the Thing' (in French: *la Chose*; in German: *das Ding*), which is closely linked with the concept of jouissance; it is itself a materialization of jouissance. This allows Žižek to state that:

> What is at stake in ethnic tensions is always the possession of the national Thing: the 'other' wants to steal our enjoyment (by ruining our 'way of life') and/or it has access to some secret, perverse enjoyment. In short, what gets on our nerves, what really bothers us about the 'other,' is the peculiar way he organizes his enjoyment. . .[84]

In a similar vein, Juliet Flower MacCannell builds on Žižek's arguments to analyse the logic of fascism; she also uses Lacan's concept of the 'will-to-enjoy' (*volonté-de-jouissance*) to demonstrate the perverse nature of fascist ethics.[85]

These speculations on racism and fascism provide one way of developing the cultural implications of the concept of jouissance by linking it to the field of the social. But the importance of psychoanalysis for cultural theory is certainly not limited to its incidence in social and political thought; there is also a long tradition of using psychoanalytic concepts to analyse works of art and literature. To conclude this section, then, I shall look at two examples of how the concept of jouissance has been used in discussions of popular culture.

An instructive example of the use of Lacanian theory to examine film is provided by Parveen Adams in her essay on Michael Powell's *Peeping Tom*, which tells the story of a young man, Mark Lewis, who films women as he kills them.[86] The film raises questions about the pleasure of the spectator, since the spectator is placed in a position similar to that of Mark Lewis, who Adams argues is a pervert. Such a comparison between the pleasure of the spectator and the enjoyment of the pervert is certainly not new to film theory; it has even become somewhat of a cliché. However, it is precisely this comparison that Adams objects to, on the grounds that it 'fails to distinguish between a pleasure and the question of jouissance.'[87] Adams argues that while Mark Lewis is (almost) entirely caught up within the perverse circuit of jouissance, the spectator is gradually separated from this scenario by a number of crucial shots in the film which disrupt his/her identification with the protagonist. The jouissance of the perverse Mark Lewis leads him eventually to his death; the framing of certain key images in the film puts the spectator in quite a different position, a position from which a safe *pleasure* may be derived.

Whereas Adams shows how the concept of jouissance can be used to critique a commonplace of contemporary film theory, Joan Copjec uses the concept to draw a structural distinction between two types of film that are often confused: the crime film and film noir. In the crime film, Copjec argues, the criminals are still ruled by the Other even when they try to cheat it, whereas in film noir, the Other is suspended altogether. Since the reign of the Other is that which protects the subject from jouissance, the film noir hero can be conceived of as 'a man who enjoys too much.' Copjec thus concludes: 'The difference between the crime film and film noir amounts to this question of enjoyment.'[88]

V. Conclusion

From Kantian ethics to mystical experience, from frigidity to racism: judging by the range of the contexts in which it appears, the concept of jouissance is certainly versatile. Indeed, it could be argued that no other Lacanian concept is quite so versatile, with the exception of the object *a*. This versatility may be partially accounted for by the various nuances which the term acquires during the course of Lacan's teaching. However, with such semantic inflation there is the risk of devaluation. Thus the critic might object that, if the term jouissance can be used in so many ways, it becomes so general and vague as to lose all value.

This objection can be countered by pointing to the various qualifiers that can be attached to the term jouissance (phallic or feminine, of the Other, of the body, etc.). These qualifiers reintroduce a certain specificity which enables the term to function as a rigorous conceptual tool. A useful stricture that those working with Lacanian theory might impose on themselves, then, would be to clarify the type(s) of jouissance to which they are referring. This would not aim at erasing ambiguity (which is, in any case, an impossibility), but simply at encouraging a minimal level of rigour.

Notes

1. My thanks go to Joan Copjec and Dany Nobus, who both provided me with helpful comments and constructive criticism as I was writing this essay.

2. See, for example: D. Macey, *Lacan in Contexts*, London-New York NY, Verso, 1988, p. 201.

3. Žižek, for example, almost always uses the term 'enjoyment' in preference to the term 'jouissance.' See: S. Žižek, *Looking Awry: An Introduction to Jacques Lacan through Popular Culture*, Cambridge MA-London, MIT, 1991.

4. Even this, however, turns out to have a curious twist, for it has since been pointed out, for example by Macey, that the word 'jouissance' does in fact figure in the Shorter Oxford English Dictionary. One might therefore argue that the use of the term jouissance by anglophone Lacanians is not an obscure gallicism and need not therefore be italicised. However, this observation has passed most English-speaking Lacanians by, and thus they continue to write jouissance in italics, preserving its mystery by marking it with the sign of untranslatability. See: D. Macey, *Lacan in Contexts*, *o.c.*, p. 288, note 129.

5. J. Lacan, *The Seminar. Book I: Freud's Papers on Technique* (1953-54) (trans. with notes J. Forrester), Edited by J.-A. Miller, Cambridge, Cambridge University Press, 1988.

6. N. Braunstein, *La jouissance: un concept lacanien* (1990), Paris, Point Hors Ligne, 1992.

7. See: J. Lacan, *Le Séminaire XIV, La logique du fantasme* (1966-67), unpublished, seminar of 31 May 1967.

8. A. Kojève, *Introduction to the Reading of Hegel* (1947[1933-39]) (trans. J.H. Nichols, Jr.), New York NY-London, Basic Books, 1969, p. 46. This piece by Kojève may also have inspired Lacan's later opposition between enjoyment and pleasure; even though Kojève sees pleasure (*Lust*) as a type of enjoyment (*Genuß*) rather than opposing the two terms, it may well be that this conjunction sowed a seed in Lacan's mind that was only to come to fruition many years later, in the antithesis between pleasure and jouissance.

9. J. Lacan, *The Seminar. Book I: Freud's Papers on Technique*, *o.c.*, p. 223. Forrester's decision to translate jouissance as pleasure in this passage, rather than enjoyment reinforces the fact that, at this point in Lacan's work, jouissance is not yet opposed to pleasure (*plaisir*), but practically synonymous.

10. See: J. Lacan, *The Seminar. Book II: The Ego in Freud's Theory and in the Technique of Psychoanalysis* (1954-55) (trans. S. Tomaselli, notes J. Forrester), Edited by J.-A. Miller, Cambridge, Cambridge University Press, 1988, p. 269.

11. See: J. Lacan, La psychanalyse et son enseignement (1957), *Ecrits*, Paris, du Seuil, 1966, p. 453.

12. See: J. Lacan, *Le Séminaire, Livre IV, La relation d'objet* (1956-57), texte établi par J.-A. Miller, Paris, du Seuil, 1994, p. 241.

13. J. Lacan, Propos directifs pour un congrès sur la sexualité féminine (1958), *Ecrits*, *o.c.*, p. 727. In her English translation of this text, Jacqueline Rose has rendered *jouissance clitoridienne* simply as 'clitoral orgasm.' See: J. Lacan, Guiding Remarks for a Congress on Feminine Sexuality (1958) (trans. J. Rose), in J. Mitchell & J. Rose (Eds.), *Feminine Sexuality: Jacques Lacan and the école freudienne*, New York NY-London, W.W. Norton & Company, 1985, p. 89.

14. J. Lacan, The Signification of the Phallus (1958) (trans. A. Sheridan), *Ecrits: A Selection*, London, Tavistock, 1977, p. 290, emphasis added.

15. See: J. Lacan, *Le Séminaire X, L'angoisse* (1962-63), unpublished, seminar of 6 March 1963; J. Lacan, *Le Séminaire, Livre XX, Encore* (1972-73), texte établi par J.-A. Miller, Paris, du Seuil, 1975, p. 70; J. Lacan, God and the Jouissance of The Woman (1973) (trans. J. Rose), in J. Mitchell & J. Rose (Eds.), *Feminine Sexuality: Jacques Lacan and the école freudienne*, *o.c.*, p. 147.

16. See: J. Lacan, On a Question Preliminary to any Possible Treatment of Psychosis (1957-58), *Ecrits: A Selection*, *o.c.*, p. 225, note 40; J. Lacan, *The Seminar. Book VII: The Ethics of Psychoanalysis* (1959-60) (trans. with notes D. Porter), Edited by J.-A. Miller, New York NY-London, W.W. Norton & Company, 1992, p. 201.

17. See: F. Perrier, Démoïsation (1978), *La Chaussée d'Antin*, Vol. 2, Paris, Christian Bourgeois, coll. «10/18», 1979, pp. 163-178; D. Macey, *Lacan in Contexts*, *o.c.*, pp. 204-205.

18. G. Bataille, Histoire de l'érotisme (1957), *Œuvres complètes*, VIII, Paris, Gallimard, 1976, p. 89.

19. *Ibid.*, p. 91. My translation.

20. See: J. Lacan, *Le Séminaire V, Les formations de l'inconscient* (1957-58), unpublished.

21. *Ibid.*, seminar of 26 March 1958. My translation.

22. J. Lacan, *Le Séminaire X, L'angoisse*, *o.c.*, seminar of 27 February 1963. My translation.

23. *Ibid.*, seminar of 27 February 1963. My translation.

24. J. Lacan, *The Seminar. Book VII: The Ethics of Psychoanalysis*, *o.c.*, pp. 166-240.

25. *Ibid.*, p. 189.

26. Kant's example runs as follows: 'Suppose that someone says his lust is irresistible when the desired object and opportunity are present. Ask him whether he would not control his passion if, in front of the house where he has this opportunity, a gallows were erected on which he would be hanged immediately after gratifying his lust.' I. Kant, Critique of Practical Reason (1788), *Critique of Practical Reason and Other Writings in Moral Philosophy* (trans. with an introduction L.W. Beck), Chicago IL, The University of Chicago Press, 1949, p. 141.

27. See: S. Freud, Formulations on the Two Principles of Mental Functioning (1911*b*), *Standard Edition*, XII, pp. 213-226.

28. J. Lacan, The Subversion of the Subject and the Dialectic of Desire in the Freudian Unconscious (1960), *Ecrits: A Selection*, *o.c.*, p. 319.

29. See: S. Freud, Beyond the Pleasure Principle (1920*g*), *Standard Edition*, XVIII, pp. 1-64.

30. J. Lacan, *The Seminar. Book VII: The Ethics of Psychoanalysis*, *o.c.*, p. 189.

31. See: J. Lacan, *The Seminar. Book VII: The Ethics of Psychoanalysis*, *o.c.*, p. 237.

32. J. Lacan, *Le Séminaire X, L'angoisse*, *o.c.*, seminar of 20 March 1963.

33. See: J. Lacan, Guiding Remarks for a Congress on Feminine Sexuality, *o.c.*, p. 89; J. Lacan, *Le Séminaire V, Les formations de l'inconscient*, *o.c.*, seminar of 19 March 1958.

34. See: D. Silvestre, Chercher la femme, *Ornicar ?*, 1982, no. 25, pp. 57-62 and p. 61 in particular; D. Macey, *Lacan in Contexts*, *o.c.*, p. 200.

35. J. Lacan, *Le Séminaire, Livre XX, Encore*, *o.c.*, p. 14.

36. J. Lacan, God and the Jouissance of The Woman, *o.c.*, p. 145.

37. See: J. Lacan, Guiding Remarks for a Congress on Feminine Sexuality, *o.c.*, p. 89.

38. The two 'sexes' are here understood by Lacan in logical rather than biological terms. Thus feminine jouissance is not limited to biological women; it may be experienced by any human being who follows the logic of female sexuation. Cases of biological men who follow this logic and thereby have access to feminine jouissance may be rare, but Lacan does cite one example: Saint John of the Cross. See: J. Lacan, God and the Jouissance of The Woman, *o.c.*, pp. 146-147.

39. *Ibid.*, p. 147.

40. *Ibid.*, p. 147. For Saint Theresa's comments on her mystical experiences, see: Saint Theresa, *The Complete Works*, Edited by S. de Santa Teresa, London, Sheed & Ward, 1946.

41. J. Lacan, God and the Jouissance of The Woman, *o.c.*, p. 145.

42. J. Lacan, *Le Séminaire, Livre XX, Encore*, *o.c.*, p. 26.

43. Lacan also uses a biological metaphor to describe that which is lost to the subject *ab initio*. He conceives of a mythical organ called the 'lamella' which is 'subtracted from the living being by virtue of the fact that it is subject to the cycle of sexed reproduction.' J. Lacan, *The Four Fundamental Concepts of Psychoanalysis* (1964) (trans. A. Sheridan), Edited by J.-A. Miller, London, The Hogarth Press and the Institute of Psycho-Analysis, 1977, p. 198.

44. J. Lacan, The Subversion of the Subject and the Dialectic of Desire in the Freudian Unconscious, *o.c.*, p. 324.

45. S. Freud, 'Civilized' Sexual Morality and Modern Nervous Illness (1908*d*), *Standard Edition*, IX, pp. 188-189.

46. *Ibid.*, pp. 186-187.

47. J. Lacan, *The Four Fundamental Concepts of Psychoanalysis*, *o.c.*, p. 275.

48. J. Lacan, *Le Séminaire, Livre XX, Encore*, *o.c.*, p. 10.

49. J. Lacan, *Le Séminaire, Livre XVII, L'envers de la psychanalyse* (1969-70), texte établi par J.-A. Miller, Paris, du Seuil, 1991, p. 18. Here, Lacan refers to his previous seminar, *D'un Autre à l'autre*, in which he had introduced *plus-de-jouir* in the context of a theoretical development on the dialectic of frustration.

50. The concept of 'surplus jouissance' is closely related to the object *a*. Indeed, in the diagrams of the four discourses which Lacan presents in 1972, he glosses the symbol *a* simply as 'surplus jouissance.' The object *a* is both that which is lost *ab initio* and the trace of this loss, that which remains as a left-over to remind the subject of the lost jouissance. See: J. Lacan, *Le Séminaire, Livre XX, Encore*, *o.c.*, p. 21.

51. J. Lacan, *Le Séminaire X, L'angoisse*, *o.c.*, seminar of 23 January 1963.

52. See: J. Lacan, Le Séminaire, Livre XXIII, Le sinthome (1975-76), texte établi par J.-A. Miller, *Ornicar ?*, 1976, no. 6, pp. 3-20; 1976, no. 7, pp. 3-18; 1976, no. 8, pp. 6-20; 1977, no. 9, pp. 32-40; 1977, no. 10, pp. 5-12; 1977, no. 11, pp. 2-9.

53. J. Lacan, *Le Séminaire, Livre XX, Encore*, *o.c.*, p. 104.

54. *Ibid.*, p. 27.

55. See: J. Lacan, A Love Letter (1973) (trans. J. Rose), in J. Mitchell & J. Rose (Eds.), *Feminine Sexuality: Jacques Lacan and the école freudienne*, *o.c.*, p. 155.

56. See: J. Lacan, Guiding Remarks for a Congress on Feminine Sexuality, *o.c.*, pp. 93-96.

57. See: S. Freud, Contributions to the Psychology of Love: The Taboo of Virginity (1918*a*[1917]), *Standard Edition*, XI, pp. 191-208.

58. See: G. Morel, Conditions féminines de jouissance, *La Cause freudienne*, 1993, no. 24, pp. 96-106 and p. 97 in particular.

59. J. Lacan, Guiding Remarks for a Congress on Feminine Sexuality, *o.c.*, p. 95.

60. *Ibid.*, p. 95.

61. See: G. Morel, Conditions féminines de jouissance, *o.c.*, pp. 96-106.

62. J. Lacan, The Signification of the Phallus, *o.c.*, p. 290, emphasis added.

63. J. Lacan, God and the Jouissance of The Woman, *o.c.*, p. 146.

64. J. Lacan, The Signification of the Phallus, *o.c.*, p. 290.

65. See: J. Lacan, Le Séminaire XXII, R.S.I. (1974-75), texte établi par J.-A. Miller, *Ornicar ?*, 1975, no. 2, p. 104.

66. See: D.P. Schreber, *Memoirs of My Nervous Illness* (1903) (trans. I. Macalpine & R. A. Hunter), with a new introduction by S.M. Weber, Cambridge MA-London, Harvard University Press, 1988; S. Freud, Psycho-Analytic Notes Upon an Autobiographical Account of a Case of Paranoia (Dementia Paranoides) (1911*c*[1910]), *Standard Edition*, XII, pp. 3-82.

67. J. Lacan, Kant with Sade (1962) (trans. J.B. Swenson, Jr.), *October*, 1989, no. 51, pp. 55-75.

68. For the voyeur, this object is the gaze; for the sadist, the object is the voice. What the sadist longs for is to hear the sound of his victim's screams, and thus his jouissance is summed up in the phrase 'I hear.' The homophony between 'I hear' (*j'ouis*) and 'enjoy' (*jouis*) illustrates the privelege of the sadomasochistic drive in Lacan's account; the sadomasochistic (or invocatory) drive is the one in which the problematics of jouissance are most clearly exemplified.

69. J. Lacan, *The Seminar. Book VII: The Ethics of Psychoanalysis*, *o.c.*, p. 215; J. Lacan, Kant with Sade, *o.c.*, p. 63 & p. 61. Swenson has rendered *Etre-suprême-en-méchanceté* as 'Being-Supreme-in-Wickedness.' For Sade's term, see: D.A.F. de Sade, *Juliette* (1797) (trans. A. Wainhouse), New York NY, Grove Press, 1968, p. 399.

70. See: S. Freud, Civilization and its Discontents (1930*a*), *Standard Edition*, XXI, pp. 123-133.

71. J. Lacan, The Direction of the Treatment and the Principles of its Power (1958), *Ecrits: A Selection*, *o.c.*, pp. 226-280 and p. 256 in particular; J. Lacan, The Subversion of the Subject and the Dialectic of Desire in the Freudian Unconscious, *o.c.*, p. 319.

72. See: S. Freud, Notes upon a Case of Obsessional Neurosis (1909*d*), *Standard Edition*, X, pp. 151-249.

73. *Ibid.*, pp. 167-168.

74. Lacan argues that the object of jealousy is not an unconsciously loved rival but the jouissance of the partner. Male jealousy bears on the woman's access to the Other jouissance which is not available to the man; female jealousy bears on the man's phallic jouissance which he extracts selfishly from intercourse with her. See: J. Lacan, L'étourdit, *Scilicet*, 1973, no. 4, pp. 5-52.

75. J. Lacan, Jeunesse de Gide ou la lettre et le désir (1958), *Ecrits*, *o.c.*, p. 747.

76. J. Lacan, *Television/A Challenge to the Psychoanalytic Establishment* (1973) (trans. D. Hollier, R. Krauss & A. Michelson), Edited by J. Copjec, New York NY-London, W.W. Norton & Company, 1990.

77. *Ibid.*, p. 32.

78. *Ibid.*, p. 32.

79. J. Lacan, *The Seminar. Book VII: The Ethics of Psychoanalysis*, *o.c.*, p. 237.

80. J. Lacan, *Television/A Challenge to the Psychoanalytic Establishment*, *o.c.*, p. 32.

81. *Ibid.*, p. 32.

82. J.-A. Miller, *Extimité* (1985-86), unpublished seminar; J.-A. Miller, Extimité (trans. F. Massardier-Kenney), in M. Bracher, M. Alcorn Jr., R. Corthell & F. Massardier-Kenney (Eds.), *Lacanian Theory of Discourse: Subject, Structure and Society*, New York NY, New York University Press, 1994, pp. 74-87.

83. S. Žižek, *Looking Awry: An Introduction to Jacques Lacan through Popular Culture*, *o.c.*, p. 165.

84. *Ibid.*, p. 165. Those interested in pursuing Žižek's ideas on the social and political dimensions of jouissance may find further comments at various other points in his work. Curiously, however, there is almost no discussion of jouissance in the one book by Žižek which incorporates the term in its title. See: S. Žižek, *For They Know Not What They Do: Enjoyment as a Political Factor*, London-New York NY, Verso, 1991.

85. J. Flower MacCannell, Facing Fascism: A Feminine Politics of Jouissance, in W. Apollon & R. Feldstein (Eds.), *Lacan, Politics, Aesthetics*, Albany NY, State University of New York Press, 1996, pp. 65-100.

86. P. Adams, Father, can't you see I'm filming?, *The Emptiness of the Image*, London-New York NY, Routledge, 1996, pp. 91-107.

87. *Ibid.*, p. 91.

88. J. Copjec, *Read My Desire: Lacan against the Historicists*, Cambridge MA-London, MIT Press, 1994, p. 191.

CHAPTER 2

The Master Signifier and the Four Discourses

Bruce Fink

I. Introduction

Lacanian psychoanalysis constitutes a very powerful theory and a socially significant practice. Yet it is not a *Weltanschauung*, a totalized or totalizing world view, though many would like to make it such.[1] It is a discourse and, as such, has effects in the world. It is but one discourse among many, not *the* final, ultimate discourse.

The dominant discourse in the world today is no doubt the discourse of power: power as a means to achieve x, y, and z, but ultimately power for power's sake. Lacanian psychoanalysis is not, in and of itself, a discourse of power. It deploys a certain kind of power in the analytic situation, a power that is unjustifiable according to many American schools of psychology wherein the 'client's' autonomy (read: ego) is sacrosanct and must remain untrammeled and unchallenged. Psychoanalysis deploys the power of the cause of desire, in order to bring about a reconfiguration of the analysand's desire. As such, analytic discourse is structured differently from the discourse of power. Lacan's 'four discourses' (the master's discourse, the university discourse, the hysteric's discourse and the analyst's discourse) seek to account for the structural differences among discourses, and I will turn to this accounting in a moment.

First let me raise the question of relativism. If psychoanalysis is not somehow the ultimate discourse, being but one discourse among others, what claim can it make to our attention? Why should we bother to concern ourselves with analytic discourse at all, if it is just one of several or one of many? I will provide but one simple answer here: because *it allows us to understand the functioning of different discourses in a unique way.*[2]

Before taking up the particulars of Lacan's four discourses, let me point out that, while Lacan terms one of his discourses the 'hysteric's discourse,' he does not mean thereby that a given hysteric always and inescapably adopts or functions within the hysteric's discourse. As an analyst, the hysteric may function within the analyst's discourse; as an academic, the hysteric may function within the discourse of the university. The hysteric's psychical structure does not change as he or she changes discourses, but his or her efficacy changes. Situating him or herself within the analyst's discourse, his or her effect on others corresponds to the effect allowed by that discourse, and suffers from the obstacles and shortcomings endemic to that discourse. A particular discourse facilitates certain things and hinders others, allows one to see certain things while blinding one to others.

Discourses, on the other hand, are not like hats that can be donned and doffed at will. The changing of discourses generally requires that certain conditions be met. An analyst does not always function within analytic discourse; insofar, for example, as he or she teaches, the analyst could very well adopt the university discourse or the master's discourse, or for that matter the hysteric's discourse (and Lacan's own teaching often seems to come under this latter head).

One thing that is immediately striking is that, while Lacan forges a discourse of the hysteric, there is no such discourse of the obsessive neurotic, phobic, pervert, or psychotic. Their discourses can no doubt be formalized to some extent, and Lacan went a long way towards formalizing the structure of fantasy in phobia, perversion, and so on.[3] Yet they are not primary focuses of the four major discourses he outlines. I will not go into the four discourses in all their complexity, especially as concerns their development over time from *Seminar XVII*, where they are introduced, to *Seminar XX* and beyond, where they are somewhat reworked.[4] Instead I will present the basic features of each of the four discourses.[5]

II. The Master's Discourse

Lacan's discourses begin in a sense with the discourse of the master, both for historical reasons and because it embodies the alienating functioning of the signifier to which we are all subject. As such, it holds a privileged place in the four discourses, as a sort of primary discourse (both phylogenetically and ontogenetically). It is the fundamental matrix of the coming to be of the subject through alienation, but Lacan ascribes it a somewhat different function in the context of his four discourses.

$$\frac{S_1}{\$} \rightarrow \frac{S_2}{a}$$

The master's discourse[6]

In the master's discourse, the dominant or commanding position (in the upper left-hand corner) is filled by S_1, the nonsensical signifier, the signifier with no rhyme or reason, in a word, the master signifier. The master must be obeyed — not because we will all be better off that way or for some other such rationale — but because he or she says so.[7] No justification is given for his or her power: it just is.

The master (represented here by S_1) addresses (that addressing is represented by the arrow) the slave (S_2), who is situated in the position of the worker (in the upper right-hand corner, also referred to by Lacan as the position of the other). The slave, in slaving away for the master, learns something: he or she comes to embody knowledge (knowledge as productive), represented here by S_2. The master is unconcerned with knowledge: as long as everything works, as long as his or her power is maintained or grows, all is well.[8] He or she has no interest in knowing how or why things work. Taking the capitalist as master here and the worker as slave, object (a), appearing in the lower right-hand corner, represents the surplus produced: surplus value. That surplus, deriving from the activity of the worker, is appropriated by the capitalist, and we might suppose that it directly or indirectly procures the latter enjoyment of some kind: surplus jouissance.[9]

The master must show no weakness, and in this sense carefully hides the fact that he or she, like everyone else, is a being of language and has succumbed to symbolic castration. The split between conscious and unconscious ($\$$) brought on by the signifier is veiled in the master's discourse and shows up in the position of truth: dissimulated truth.

The various positions in each of the four discourses can now be designated as follows:

$$\frac{\text{agent}}{\text{truth}} \rightarrow \frac{\text{other}}{\text{product/loss}}$$

Positions in the four discourses[10]

Whichever matheme (S_1, S_2, $\$$, or a) Lacan places in one of these four positions, it takes on the role ascribed to that position.

The other three discourses are generated from the first by rotating each element counter-clockwise one quarter of a turn or 'revolution.' One might suppose that these further or 'derivative' discourses either came into being, or at least were grasped later in time. This seems true of at least the last two of the four, for the analyst's discourse only came into being at the end of the nineteenth century, which eventually allowed the hysteric's discourse to be grasped.[11]

Note that other discourses than the four discussed here could be generated by changing the *order* of the four mathemes used here. If, instead of keeping them in the order in which they are found in the master's discourse ($\$ \rightarrow S_1 \rightarrow S_2 \rightarrow a$), we changed the order to $S_2 \rightarrow S_1 \rightarrow \$ \rightarrow a$, four different discourses could be generated. In effect, a total of twenty-four different discourses are possible using these four mathemes in the four different positions, and the fact that Lacan only mentions four discourses suggests that he finds something particularly important about the *order* of the elements. As is true of many of his quadripartite structures, it is this particular configuration, and not just any old combination of its constitutive elements, that Lacan considers of value and interest to psychoanalysis.

III. The University Discourse

For centuries, knowledge has been pursued as a defense against truth.

Jacques Lacan[12]

In the discourse of the university, 'knowledge' replaces the nonsensical master signifier in the dominant, commanding position.

$$\frac{S_2}{S_1} \rightarrow \frac{a}{\$}$$

The university discourse[13]

Systematic knowledge is the ultimate authority, reigning in the stead of blind will, everything having its reason. Lacan almost goes so far as suggesting a sort of historical movement from the master's discourse to the university discourse, the university discourse providing a sort of legitimation or rationalization of the master's will. In that sense he seems to agree with the argument put forward in the 1960's and 1970's that the university is an arm of capitalist production (or of the 'military-industrial complex,' as it was known at the time), suggesting that the truth hidden behind the university discourse is, after all, the master signifier.[14]

Knowledge here interrogates surplus value (the product of capitalist economies, which takes the form of a loss or subtraction of value from the worker), and rationalizes or justifies it. The product or loss here is the divided, alienated subject. Since the agent in the university discourse is the knowing subject, the unknowing subject or subject of the unconscious is produced, but at the same time excluded. Philosophy, Lacan says, has always *served* the master, has always placed itself in the service of rationalizing and propping up the master's discourse, as has the worst kind of science.[15]

Note that whereas Lacan at first associates the university discourse with scientific formalization, with the increasing mathematization of science, he later dissociates true scientific work from the university discourse, associating it instead with the hysteric's discourse.[16] Surprising as that may seem at first, Lacan's view of genuine scientific activity (explained in *Science and Truth*, for example) does correspond to the structure of the hysteric's discourse, as I shall try to explain it below.[17]

That shift is reflected in *Television* by an association of the scientific and hysteric's discourses.[18] It implies that the kind of knowledge involved in the university discourse amounts to mere rationalization, in the most pejorative Freudian sense of the term. We can imagine it, not as the kind of thought that tries to come to grips with the real, to maintain the difficulties posed by apparent logical and/or physical contradictions, but rather as a kind of encyclopaedic endeavour to exhaust a field.[19]

Working in the service of the master signifier, more or less any kind of argument will do, as long as it takes on the guise of reason and rationality.

IV. The Hysteric's Discourse

In the hysteric's discourse (which is actually the fourth generated by the succession of quarter turns, not the third as I am presenting it here), the split subject occupies the dominant position and addresses S_1, calling it into question. Whereas the university discourse takes its cue from the master signifier, glossing over it with some sort of trumped-up system, the hysteric goes at the master and demands that he or she show his or her stuff, prove his or her mettle by producing something serious by way of knowledge.[20]

$$\frac{\$}{a} \rightarrow \frac{S_1}{S_2}$$

The hysteric's discourse[21]

The hysteric's discourse is the exact opposite of the university discourse, all the positions being reversed. The hysteric maintains the primacy of subjective division, the contradiction between conscious and unconscious, and thus the conflictual, or self-contradictory nature of desire itself.

In the lower right-hand corner, we find knowledge (S_2). This position is also the one where Lacan situates jouissance, the enjoyment produced by a discourse, and he thus suggests here that an hysteric gets off on knowledge.[22] Knowledge is perhaps eroticized to a greater extent in the hysteric's discourse than elsewhere. In the master's discourse, knowledge is prized only insofar as it can produce something else, only so long as it can be put to work for the master; yet knowledge itself remains inaccessible to the master. In the university discourse, knowledge is not so much an end in itself as that which justifies the academic's very existence and activity.[23] Hysteria thus provides a unique configuration with respect to knowledge, and I believe this is why Lacan finally identifies the discourse of science with that of hysteria.

In November 1969, at the beginning of *Seminar XVII*, Lacan views science as having the same structure as the master's discourse.[24] He makes the same point six months later, in the closing speech of a congress of the *Ecole freudienne de Paris*.[25] Here, Lacan seems to see science as serving the master, as did classical philosophy. By 1971-72, in *Seminar XIX*, ...*ou pire*, and in *Television* (1973), Lacan claims that the discourse of science and the discourse of the hysteric are *almost* identical.[26] What leads him to do so?

Consider Heisenberg's uncertainty principle. In simple terms, it states that we cannot precisely know both a particle's position and its momentum at the same time. If we have been able to ascertain one parameter, the other must necessarily remain unknown. In and of itself, that is a startling proposition for a scientist to put forward. Naively, we often think of scientists as people who relentlessly refine their instruments until they can measure everything, regardless of its infinitesimal proportions or blinding speed. Heisenberg, however, posited a limit to our ability to measure, and thus a true limit to scientific knowledge.

If, for a moment, we view scientific knowledge as a whole or a set, albeit expanding (we could imagine it as an ideal set of all scientific knowledge, present and future) then Heisenberg can be understood as saying that the set is incomplete, the whole is not whole, for there is an 'unfillable' hole in the set.[27]

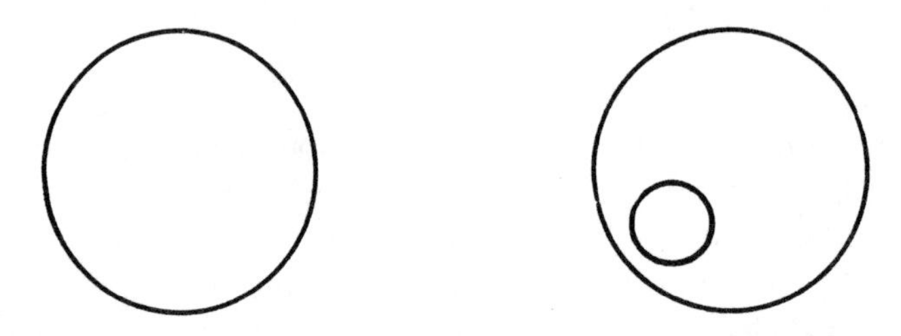

Now that is similar to what Lacan says of the hysteric: the hysteric pushes the master — incarnated in a partner, teacher, or whomever — to the point where he or she can find the master's knowledge lacking. Either the master does not have an explanation for everything, or his or her reasoning does not hold water. In addressing the master, the hysteric demands that he or she produce knowledge and then goes on to disprove his or her theories. Historically speaking, hysterics have been a true motor force behind the medical, psychiatric, and psychoanalytic elaboration of theories concerning hysteria. Hysterics led Freud to develop psychoanalytic theory and practice, all the while proving to him in his consulting room the inadequacy of his knowledge and know-how.

Hysterics, like good scientists, do not set out to desperately explain everything with the knowledge they already have — that is the job of the systematizer or even the encyclopaedist — nor do they take for granted that all the solutions will be someday forthcoming. Heisenberg shocked the physics community when he asserted that there was something that structurally speaking could not be known: something that is impossible for us to know, a kind of conceptual anomaly.

Similar problems and paradoxes have arisen in logic and mathematics. In Lacan's terminology, these impossibilities are related to the real that goes by the name of object (*a*).

In the hysteric's discourse, object (*a*) appears in the position of truth. That means that the truth of the hysteric's discourse, its hidden motor force, is the real. Physics too, when carried out in a truly scientific spirit, is ordained and commanded by the real, that is to say by that which does not work, by that which does not fit. It does not set out to carefully cover over paradoxes and contradictions, in an attempt to prove that the theory is nowhere lacking — that it works in every instance — but rather to take such paradoxes and contradictions as far as they can go.

V. The Analyst's Discourse

Let us now turn to analytic discourse:

$$\frac{a}{S_2} \rightarrow \frac{\$}{S_1}$$

The analyst's discourse[28]

Object (*a*), as cause of desire, is the agent here, occupying the dominant or commanding position. The analyst plays the part of pure desirousness (pure desiring subject), and interrogates the subject in his or her division, precisely at those points where the split between conscious and unconscious shows through: slips of the tongue, bungled and unintended acts, slurred speech, dreams, etc. In this way, the analyst sets the patient to work, to associate, and the product of that laborious association is a new master signifier. The patient in a sense 'coughs up' a master signifier that has not yet been brought into relation with any other signifier.

In discussing the discourse of the master, I referred to S_1 as the signifier with no rhyme or reason. As it appears concretely in the analytic situation, a master signifier presents itself as a dead end, a stopping point, a term, word, or phrase that puts an end to association, that grinds the patient's discourse to a halt. It could be a proper name (the patient's or the analyst's), a reference to the death of a loved one, the name of a disease (AIDS, cancer, psoriasis, blindness), or a variety of other things. The task of analysis is to bring such master signifiers into relation with other signifiers, that is, to dialectize the master signifiers it produces.

That involves reliance upon the master's discourse, or as we might see it here, recourse to the fundamental structure of signification: a link must be established between each master signifier and a binary signifier such that subjectification takes place. The symptom itself may present itself as a master signifier; in fact, as analysis proceeds and as more and more aspects of a person's life are taken as symptoms, each symptomatic activity or pain may present itself in the analytic work as a word or phrase that simply is, that seems to signify nothing to the subject. In *Seminar XX*, Lacan refers to S_1 in the analyst's discourse as *la bêtise* (stupidity or 'funny business'), a reference back to the case of Little Hans who refers to his whole horse phobia as *la bêtise* (*Dummheit*), as Lacan translates it.[29] It is a piece of nonsense produced by the analytic process itself.[30]

S_2 appears in analytic discourse in the place of truth (lower left-hand position). S_2 represents knowledge here, but obviously not the kind of knowledge that occupies the dominant position in the university discourse. The knowledge in question here is unconscious knowledge, that knowledge that is caught up in the signifying chain and has yet to be subjectified. Where that knowledge was, the subject must come to be.

Now, according to Lacan, while the analyst adopts the analytic discourse, the analysand is inevitably, in the course of analysis, hystericized.[31] The analysand, regardless of his or her clinical structure — whether phobic, perverse, or obsessive compulsive — is backed into the hysteric's discourse. Why is that? Because the analyst puts the subject as divided, as self-contradictory, on the firing line, so to speak. The analyst does not question the obsessive neurotic's theories about Dostoevsky's poetics, for example, attempting to show the neurotic where his or her intellectual views are inconsistent. Such an obsessive may attempt to speak during his or her analytic sessions from the position of S_2 in the university (academic) discourse, but to engage the analysand at that level allows the analysand to maintain that particular stance. Instead, the analyst, ignoring, we can imagine, the whole of a half-hour-long critique of Bakhtin's views on Dostoevsky's dialogic style, may focus on the slightest slip of the tongue or ambiguity in the analysand's speech — the analysand's use, for example, of the graphic metaphor 'near misses' to describe her bad timing in the publishing of her article on Bakhtin, when the analyst knows that this analysand had fled her country of origin shortly after rejecting an unexpected and unwanted marriage proposal ('near Mrs.').

Thus the analyst, by pointing to the fact that the analysand is not the master of his or her own discourse, instates the analysand as divided between conscious speaking subject and some other (subject) speaking at the same time through the same mouthpiece, as agent of a discourse wherein the S_1s produced in the course of analysis are interrogated and made to yield their links with S_2 (as in the hysteric's discourse). Clearly the motor force of the process is object (*a*) — the analyst operating as pure desirousness.[32]

What does it mean concretely for the analyst to occupy the position of object (*a*) for an analysand, the position of cause of the analysand's desire? Many analysands tend, at an early stage of analysis, to thrust responsibility for slips and slurs onto the analyst. As one patient said to her therapist, 'You're the one who always sees dark and dirty things in everything I say!' At the outset, analysands often see no more in a slip than a simple problem regarding the control of the tongue muscles or a slight inattention.[33] The analyst is the one who attributes some Other meaning to it.

As time goes on, however, analysands themselves begin to attribute meaning to such slips, and the analyst, rather than standing in for the unconscious, for that strange Other discourse, is viewed by the analysand as its cause: 'I had a dream last night because I knew I was coming to see you this morning.' In such a statement, very often heard in analysis, the analyst is cast in the role of the cause of the analysand's dream: 'I wouldn't have had such a dream were it not for you,' 'The dream was for you,' 'You were in my dream last night.' Unconscious formations, such as dreams, fantasies, and slips, are produced for the analyst, to be recounted to the analyst, to tell the analyst something. The analyst, in that sense, is behind them, is the reason for their production, is, in a word, their cause.

When the analyst is viewed as an other like the analysand, the analyst can be considered an imaginary object or other for the analysand.[34] When the analyst is viewed as a judge or parent, the analyst can be considered a sort of symbolic object or Other for the analysand.[35] When the analyst is viewed as the cause of the analysand's unconscious formations, the analyst can be considered a 'real' object for the analysand (which is denoted by the expression 'object (*a*)').

Once the analyst has manoeuvred in such a way that he or she is placed in the position of cause by the analysand (cause of the analysand's dreams and of the wishes they fulfil — in short, cause of the analysand's desire), certain manifestations of the analysand's transference love or 'positive transference,' typically associated with the early stages of analysis, may well subside, giving way to something far less 'positive' in coloration.[36] The analysand may begin to express his or her sense that the analyst is 'under my skin,' like an irritant. Analysands who seemed to be comfortable or at ease during their sessions at the outset (by no means the majority, however) may well display or express discomfort, tension, and even signs that they are rebelling against the new configuration, the new role the analyst is taking on in their lives and fantasies. The analyst is becoming *too* important, is showing up in their daydreams, in their masturbation fantasies, in their relationships with their significant other, and so on.

Such a predicament is generally not what people expect when they go into analysis, and indeed non-Lacanian analyses often never go this far. Certain analysands are inclined to break off their treatment when they sense that the analyst is taking on an 'intrusive' role in their lives, and many analysts are loath to invite, shoulder, and deal with such feelings (sometimes referred to as the 'negative therapeutic reaction').[37] Indeed, the very theory of therapy such analysts embrace considers such an intrusive role to be unproductive. Lacan, on the contrary, considers it *the Archimedean point of analysis* — that is, the very point at which the analyst can apply the lever that can move the symptom. The analyst in the position of *cause* of desire for the analysand is, according to Lacan, *the motor force of analysis*; in other words, it is the position the analyst must occupy in order for transference to lead to something other than identification with the analyst as the endpoint of an analysis (identification with the analyst being considered the goal of analysis by certain psychoanalysts).

'Negative transference' is by no means the essential sign indicating that the analysand has come to situate the analyst as cause of desire; it is but one possible manifestation of the latter. Nevertheless, the attempt by therapists of many ilks to avoid or immediately neutralize any emergence of negative transference — which, after all, is but the flipside of transference love (love and hate being intimately related through the essential ambivalence of all affect) — means that aggression and anger are turned into feelings which are inappropriate for the analysand to project onto the therapist.[38] Patients thereby learn not to express them in therapy; or, if they do express them, the therapist quickly seizes the opportunity to point out that the analysand is projecting — that the anger and aggression are *not really directed at the therapist* — thereby defusing the intensity of the feeling and the possible therapeutic uses of the projection. Anger and aggression are thus never worked out with the therapist, but rather examined 'rationally.'

Consider, by way of contrast, Freud's characterization of analysis as a struggle or battle between the analyst and analysand:

> The patient regards the products of the awakening of his unconscious impulses as contemporaneous and real; he seeks to put his passions into action without taking any account of the real situation. [The ensuing] struggle between the doctor and the patient . . . is played out almost exclusively in the phenomena of transference. It is on that field that the victory must be won — the victory whose expression is the permanent cure of the neurosis. It cannot be disputed that controlling the phenomena of transference presents the psychoanalyst with the greatest difficulties. But it should not be forgotten that it is precisely they that do us the inestimable service of making the patient's hidden and forgotten erotic impulses immediate and manifest. For when all is said and done, it is impossible to destroy anyone *in absentia* or *in effigie*.[39]

In other words, it is only by making psychical conflicts — such as aggression against one's parents or hatred of a family member — *present* in the relationship with the analyst that the patient can work them through. To work them through means not that they are intellectually viewed and 'processed,' but rather that the internal libidinal conflict which is holding a symptomatic relationship to someone in place must be allowed to repeat itself in the relationship with the analyst and play itself out. If verbalization (putting things into words) is the only technique allowed the analysand, a true separation from the analyst and from analysis never occurs.[40] Projection must be allowed to go so far as to bring out all the essential aspects of a conflict-ridden relationship, all the relevant recollections and dynamics, and the full strength of the positive/negative affect. It should be recalled that one of the earliest lessons of Freud and Breuer's *Studies on Hysteria* was that verbalizing traumatic events without reliving the accompanying affect left symptoms intact.[41]

Transference, viewed as *the transfer of affect* (evoked in the past by people and events) *into the here and now of the analytic setting*, means that the analysand must be able to project onto the analyst a whole series of emotions felt in relation to significant figures from his or her past and present. If the analyst is concerned with 'being himself' or 'being herself,' or with being the 'good father' or 'good mother,' he or she is likely to try to immediately distance him- or herself from the role in which the analysand is casting him or her, by saying something like, 'I am *not* your father' or 'You are projecting.' The message conveyed by such a statement is, 'Don't confuse me with him,' or 'It is not appropriate to project.' But the analyst would do better to neither encourage nor discourage the case of mistaken identity that arises through the transfer of feelings, and to let the projection of different personas occur as it will — unless, of course, it goes so far as to jeopardize the very continuation of the therapy.

Rather than interpreting the *fact* of transference, rather than pointing out to the analysand that he or she is projecting or transferring something onto the analyst, the analyst should direct attention to the *content* (the ideational and affective content) of the projection, attempting to get the analysand to put *it* into words. Not to dissipate it or prohibit it, not to make the analysand feel guilty about it, but to speak it. Here the analyst works — often more by asking questions than by interpreting — to re-establish the connections between the content (thought and feeling) and the persons, situations, and relationships that initially gave rise to it.

Just as one should interpret not the fact of transference but rather its content, one should avoid interpreting 'resistance,' transference being but one manifestation of resistance. Resistance, rather than being nothing more than an ego defense, is — in Lacan's view — structural, arising because the real resists symbolization; when the analysand's experience resists being put into words, he or she grabs onto, digs into, or takes it out on the only other person present: the analyst. Transference is thus a direct product of resistance, of the resistance the real (e.g., trauma) erects against its symbolization, against being spoken. What sense could it possibly make, then, to *accuse* the analysand of resisting? Of course the analysand resists — that is a given, a structural necessity. Interpretation must aim at the traumatic event or experience that is resisting verbalization, not the mere fact of resistance.[42]

VI. The Social Situation of Psychoanalysis

I mentioned earlier that psychoanalysis is not, in and of itself, a discourse of power: it does not collapse into the master's discourse. Yet an American's view of the Lacanian psychoanalytic scene — both in France and elsewhere — often encompasses little more than the power struggles engaged in by individual analysts and schools against other analysts and schools.[43] Insofar as psychoanalysis is a social practice, it obviously operates in social and political environments that contain competing and oftentimes antagonistic discourses: medical discourse promoting the physiological basis and treatment of mental 'disorders,' 'scientific' and philosophical discourses aiming at undermining the theoretical and clinical foundations of psychoanalysis, political and economic discourses seeking to reduce the length and cost of psychoanalytic therapy, psychological discourse hoping to attract patients to its own adherents, etc. In such circumstances, psychoanalysis becomes one political lobbyist among many and can do no more than attempt to defend its right to exist in ever-changing political contexts.

In Paris and other cities where Lacanian psychoanalysis has become a major movement, individuals and schools compete for theoretical and/or clinical dominance, vying for political influence, university support, hospital positions, patients, and simple popularity. Is that a necessary outgrowth of psychoanalytic discourse as we see it operating in the analytic setting? I think not. It may certainly have a negative impact upon an analyst's ability to completely adhere to analytic discourse in the analytic setting, but it does not seem to be inherent to analytic discourse as such. This claim will no doubt be disputed by many, given psychoanalysis' long history of schisms and infighting, but I would sustain that the latter results from the adoption of other discourses by analysts as soon as institutionalization begins (the formation of schools, the consolidation of doctrine, the training of new analysts, the stipulation of licensing requirements, etc.), not from analytic discourse itself. There are limits to the extent to which analytic discourse can and should be adhered to in contexts other than the analytic setting!

VII. There's No Such Thing as a Metalanguage

There is no such thing as a metalanguage or metadiscourse that would somehow escape the limitations of the discourses thus far discussed, for one is always operating within a particular discourse, even as one talks about discourse in general terms. Psychoanalysis' claim to fame does not reside in providing an Archimedean point *outside of discourse*, but simply in elucidating the structure of discourse itself. Every discourse requires a loss of jouissance and has its own mainspring or truth (often carefully dissimulated).[44] Each discourse defines that loss differently, starting from a different mainspring. Marx elucidated certain features of capitalist discourse and Lacan elucidates features of other discourses as well. It is not until we have identified the features peculiar to a discourse that we can know how it operates.

When Lacan first presents the four discourses, he seems to suggest that there are no others. Does that mean that every conceivable form of discourse activity comes under one of those four? As I have argued elsewhere, Lacan introduces a new way of thinking about discourses in *Seminar XXI*, whereby he defines each discourse according to the order in which the three registers — imaginary, symbolic, and real — are taken up in it.[45]

Notes

1. See Lacan's remarks on this point in *Seminar XI*: J. Lacan, *The Four Fundamental Concepts of Psychoanalysis* (1964) (trans. A. Sheridan), Edited by J.-A. Miller, London, The Hogarth Press and the Institute of Psycho-Analysis, 1977, p. 77.

2. Without itself constituting a 'metalanguage.'

3. See, in particular: J. Lacan, *Le Séminaire VI, Le désir et son interprétation* (1958-59), unpublished.

4. See: J. Lacan, *Le Séminaire, Livre XVII, L'envers de la psychanalyse* (1969-70), texte établi par J.-A. Miller, Paris, du Seuil, 1991; J. Lacan, *Le Séminaire, Livre XX, Encore* (1972-73), texte établi par J.-A. Miller, Paris, du Seuil, 1975.

5. In Chapter 10 of my *The Lacanian Subject: Between Language and Jouissance*, I discuss a second way of talking about different kinds of discourses that Lacan presents in *Seminar XXI*. See: B. Fink, *The Lacanian Subject: Between Language and Jouissance*, Princeton NJ, Princeton University Press, 1995, pp. 138-146; J. Lacan, *Le Séminaire XXI, Les non-dupes errent* (1973-74), unpublished.

6. See: J. Lacan, *Le Séminaire, Livre XVII, L'envers de la psychanalyse, o.c.*, p. 12.

7. Indeed, Lacan says in *Seminar XX* that the first function of language is the 'imperative.' See: J. Lacan, *Le Séminaire, Livre XX, Encore, o.c.*, p. 33.

8. See: J. Lacan, *Le Séminaire, Livre XVII, L'envers de la psychanalyse, o.c.*, pp. 23-24.

9. *Ibid.*, p. 19.

10. See: J. Lacan, *Le Séminaire, Livre XX, Encore, o.c.*, p. 21.

11. The master's discourse had long since been recognized by Hegel. See: J. Lacan, *Le Séminaire, Livre XVII, L'envers de la psychanalyse, o.c.*, p. 20.

12. J. Lacan, *Le Séminaire XIII, L'objet de la psychanalyse* (1965-66), unpublished, seminar of 19 January 1966. My translation.

13. See: J. Lacan, *Le Séminaire, Livre XVII, L'envers de la psychanalyse, o.c.*, p. 31.

14. *Ibid.*, p. 119.

15. *Ibid.*, pp. 22-23.

16. *Ibid.*, pp. 119-122 (university discourse and scientific formalization).

17. See: J. Lacan, Science and Truth (1965) (trans. B. Fink), *Newsletter of the Freudian Field*, 1989, no. 3, pp. 4-29.

18. See: J. Lacan, *Television/A Challenge to the Psychoanalytic Establishment* (1973) (trans. D. Hollier, R. Krauss & A. Michelson), Edited by J. Copjec, New York NY-London, W.W. Norton & Company, 1990, p. 19.

19. Consider Charles Fourier's 810 personality types and Auguste Comte's goal of a total sociology. See: Ch. Fourier, *The Passions of the Human Soul*, New York NY, Augustus M. Kelley, 1968, p. 312.

20. See: J. Lacan, Radiophonie, *Scilicet*, 1970, nos. 2/3, p. 89.

21. See: J. Lacan, *Le Séminaire, Livre XVII, L'envers de la psychanalyse, o.c.*, p. 13.

22. *Ibid.*, pp. 105-107.

23. Indeed, the academic, rather than getting off on knowledge, would seem to get off on alienation.

24. See: J. Lacan, *Le Séminaire, Livre XVII, L'envers de la psychanalyse, o.c.*, pp. 21-23.

25. See: J. Lacan, Allocution prononcée pour la clôture du congrès de l'Ecole freudienne de Paris le 19 avril 1970, par son directeur, *Scilicet*, 1970, nos. 2/3, pp. 391-399 and pp. 395-396 in particular.

26. See: J. Lacan, ...ou pire. Compte rendu pour l'Annuaire de l'Ecole Pratique des Hautes Etudes du Séminaire de l'année 71-72, *Scilicet*, 1975, no. 5, pp. 5-10 and pp. 6-7 in particular; J. Lacan, *Television/A Challenge to the Psychoanalytic Establishment, o.c.*, p. 19.

27. This could be associated with S(Ⱥ), which Lacan, in *Seminar XX*, qualifies as the 'one-less' (*l'un-en-moins*). See: J. Lacan, *Le Séminaire, Livre XX, Encore, o.c.*, p. 118.

28. See: J. Lacan, *Le Séminaire, Livre XVII, L'envers de la psychanalyse, o.c.*, p. 31.

29. See: J. Lacan, *Le Séminaire, Livre XX, Encore, o.c.*, pp. 16-18; S. Freud, Analysis of a Phobia in a Five-Year-Old Boy (1909*b*), *Standard Edition*, X, pp. 27-28.

30. Recall that in the case of Little Hans, the boy suffers from a kind of generalized anxiety state before latching onto the horse phobia; the latter appears after he has already begun a kind of analytic treatment with his father, under Freud's tutelage. Some detailed comments on the Hans case can be found in Chapter 8 (Neurosis) and Chapter 9 (Perversion) of my *A Clinical Introduction to Lacanian Psychoanalysis: Theory and Technique*. See: B. Fink, *A Clinical Introduction to Lacanian Psychoanalysis: Theory and Technique*, Cambridge MA-London, Harvard University Press, 1997, pp. 112-202.

31. See: J. Lacan, *Le Séminaire, Livre XVII, L'envers de la psychanalyse, o.c.*, pp. 35-36.

32. Object (*a*) as cause occupies four different positions in the four discourses. At the end of *Science and Truth* Lacan associates four other discourses with the four Aristotelian causes: science and formal cause, religion and final cause, magic and efficient cause, psychoanalysis and material cause. It seems to me a fruitful venture to compare the four disciplines thus analyzed in the text from 1965 and their causes with the four discourses outlined in 1969 and the position of the object *a* in each of them. The four components of the Freudian drive (pressure, aim, object and source) might help situate the different objects at stake at the different levels. See: J. Lacan, Science and Truth, *o.c.*, pp. 19-25.

33. Consider, in this regard, the expression, 'My tongue got in the way of my eye teeth and I couldn't see what I was saying.'

34. Lacan writes this other as *a'*, '*a*' being the first letter of *autre*, the French word for 'other.' Lacan puts it in italics to indicate that it is imaginary. In contrast to *a'*, the subject's own ego is denoted by *a*. See, for example: J. Lacan, *The Seminar. Book II: The Ego in Freud's Theory and in the Technique of Psychoanalysis* (1954-55) (trans. S. Tomaselli, notes J. Forrester), Edited by J.-A. Miller, Cambridge, Cambridge University Press, 1988, pp. 243-244.

35. *Ibid.*, p. 243. Lacan writes this as A, for *Autre*, 'Other.'

36. As Freud tells us, positive transference — also known as 'transference love' — can serve as a form of resistance just as much as negative transference can. See, in particular: S. Freud, Observations on Transference Love (1915*a*[1914]), *Standard Edition*, XII, pp. 159-171.

37. For negative therapeutic reaction, see for example: S. Freud, The Ego and the Id (1923*b*), *Standard Edition*, XIX, pp. 49-50.

38. As Freud says, the 'simultaneous presence [of affectionate and hostile feelings] gives a good picture of the emotional ambivalence which is dominant in the majority of our intimate relations with other people.' S. Freud, Introductory Lectures on Psycho-Analysis (1916-17*a*[1915-17]), Lecture 27: Transference, *Standard Edition*, XVI, p. 443.

39. S. Freud, The Dynamics of Transference (1912*b*), *Standard Edition*, XII, p. 108.

40. Another way of saying this might be that there is always a quantitative factor involved: affect or libido.

41. See: S. Freud & J. Breuer, Studies on Hysteria (1895*d*), *Standard Edition*, II, Chapter 1.

42. On resistance and its 'interpretation,' see J. Lacan, Variantes de la cure-type (1955), *Ecrits*, Paris, du Seuil, 1966, pp. 332-336. On the symbolization of the real, see Chapter 3 of my *The Lacanian Subject*. On transference and resistance, see my more detailed theoretical and clinical discussions in *A Clinical Introduction to Lacanian Psychoanalysis*, above all the case of hysteria discussed in Chapter 8. See: B. Fink, *The Lacanian Subject: Between Language and Jouissance, o.c.*, pp. 24-31; B. Fink, *A Clinical Introduction to Lacanian Psychoanalysis: Theory and Technique, o.c.*, pp. 145-160.

43. Provided by numerous books, including: S. Turkle, *Psychoanalytic Politics: Jacques Lacan and Freud's French Revolution*, New York NY, Basic Books, 1978; E. Roudinesco, *Jacques Lacan & Co.: A History of Psychoanalysis in France 1925-1985* (1986) (trans. J. Mehlman), Chicago IL, University of Chicago Press, 1990. Roudinesco's recently translated 'biography' of Lacan is tantamount to pure slander. See: E. Roudinesco, *Jacques Lacan* (1993) (trans. B. Bray), New York NY, Columbia University Press, 1997.

44. Analytic discourse, for example, requires the analysand to give up the jouissance associated with his or her symptoms or master signifiers.

45. See: B. Fink, *The Lacanian Subject: Between Language and Jouissance, o.c.*, pp. 138-146.

CHAPTER 3

From the Mechanism of Psychosis to the Universal Condition of the Symptom: On Foreclosure

Russell Grigg

I. Introduction

Lacan introduces the term 'foreclosure' to explain the massive and global differences between psychosis and neurosis; neurosis operates by way of *repression*, while psychosis operates by way of *foreclosure*. This distinction is complemented by a third category, though arguably less secure and more problematic than the first two, of *disavowal*, as a mechanism specific to perversion. These three terms which correspond respectively to Freud's *Verdrängung*, *Verwerfung* and *Verleugnung*, along with the three-part division of neurosis, psychosis and perversion, form the basis of what is effectively a differential diagnosis in Lacan's work, one that aspires to being truly psychoanalytic, deriving nothing from psychiatric categories. Thus, underlying the elaboration of the notion of foreclosure is a clear and sharp distinction between three separate subjective structures.

Two features of this psychoanalytic nosology worthy of note are firstly that it assumes a structural unity behind often quite different symptoms that are expressions of the one clinical type and secondly that there is no continuum between the various clinical types uncovered. A corollary is that in the case of psychosis this structure, a quite different structure from that of neurosis, is present even before the psychosis declares itself clinically.

II. Origin of the Term

While 'foreclosure' is a common French legal term, with a meaning very close to its English equivalent, for Lacan's purposes it clearly derives more directly from the work of the French linguists Jacques Damourette and Edouard Pichon. In their *Des mots à la pensée: Essai de grammaire de la langue française*, these authors speak of 'foreclosure' in certain circumstances when an utterance repudiates facts that are treated as either true or merely possible.[1] In their words, a proposition is 'foreclosed' when 'expelled from the field of possibilities as seen by the speaker,' who thereby 'scotomises' the possibility of something's being the case.[2] They take the presence of certain linguistic elements as an indication of foreclosure, so that when it is said that 'Mr Brooke is not the sort of person who would *ever* complain' (*M. Brooke n'est pas de ceux qui se plaignent* jamais), on Damourette and Pichon's analysis, the word 'ever' would flag the foreclosure of the very possibility of Mr Brooke's complaining. That Mr Brooke should complain is 'expelled from the field of possibilities.'[3]

Whether this analysis is correct or not is largely irrelevant as far as Lacan is concerned since, although he derives foreclosure from Damourette and Pichon, he puts it to quite a different use. For Lacan, what is foreclosed is not the possibility of an event's coming to pass, but the very signifier, or signifiers, that makes the expression of impossibility possible in the first place. Thus, 'foreclosure' refers not to the fact that a speaker makes a statement which declares something impossible — a process closer to disavowal — but to the fact that the speaker lacks the very linguistic means for making the statement at all.

This is where the difference between repression and foreclosure lies. In Lacan's analysis of Freud's classic studies on the unconscious — *The Interpretation of Dreams*, *The Psychopathology of Everyday Life*, *Jokes and their Relation to the Unconscious* — the mechanisms of repression and the return of the repressed are linguistic in nature.[4] Lacan's thesis that the unconscious is structured like a language implies that for something to be repressed it has first of all to be registered in the symbolic.[5] Thus, repression implies the prior recognition of the repressed in the symbolic system or register. In psychosis, on the other hand, the necessary signifiers are lacking and so the recognition required for repression is impossible. However, what is foreclosed does not simply disappear altogether but may return, albeit in a different guise, from outside the subject.

Lacan chooses 'foreclosure' to translate Freud's *Verwerfung*, a term which is difficult to chart through the *Standard Edition* because it is not indexed, but is there usually given the more literal translation of 'rejection.'[6] For a number of years Lacan also employed more literal French translations, like *rejet* or on occasion *retranchement*.[7] It was not until the very last session of his *Seminar III* on psychosis in 1955-56 that he finally opted for the term that has since become so familiar:

> I shan't go back over the notion of *Verwerfung* I began with, and for which, having thought it through, I propose to you definitively to adopt this translation which I believe is the best — *foreclosure*.[8]

It is reasonable to regard this choice as an acknowledgement that Lacan raised to the level of a concept what in Freud had remained less clear in its meaning and more ambiguous in its employment. Freud does not use only the term *Verwerfung* in connection with psychosis, since at times, and specially late in his work, he prefers to speak in terms of the *disavowal* (*Verleugnung*) of reality in psychosis.[9] On a number of different occasions Freud appeared to be grasping for a way of characterising different mechanisms underlying neurosis and psychosis, without ever coming to a satisfactory conclusion. It is fair to say that with the work of Lacan the mechanism of foreclosure and the structure of psychosis are understood in a new way, one that has given the psychoanalytic treatment of psychosis a more secure basis.

Indeed, on more than one occasion Lacan declared that psychoanalysts must not back away from psychosis, and the treatment of psychotics is a significant feature of analytic work within the Lacanian orientation.[10] It should be noted, though, that Lacan's remark is not to be taken as an admonition to shoulder fearlessly the clinical burden imposed by the psychotic patient. It rather reflects his belief that the problems the psychotic raises are central to psychoanalysis and not a mere supplement to a supposed primary concern with neurosis.

Lacan observed that Freud's breakthrough in his examination of President Schreber's *Memoirs* was discovering that the discourse of the psychotic, as well as other bizarre and apparently meaningless phenomena of psychosis, could be deciphered and understood, just as dreams can.[11] Lacan compares the scale of this breakthrough with that obtained in the interpretation of dreams. Indeed, he is inclined to regard it as even more original than dream interpretation, arguing that while Freudian interpretation of dreams has nothing in common with previous interest in the meaning of dreams, the claim that dreams have meaning was itself not new.[12] However, Lacan also indicates that the fact that the psychotic's discourse is just as interpretable as neurotic phenomena such as dreams leaves the two disorders at the same level and fails to account for the major, qualitative differences between them. Therefore, if psychoanalysis is to account for the distinction between the two, it cannot do so on the basis of meaning alone.

It is on this issue of what makes psychosis different from neurosis that Lacan focuses. How are we to explain the massive, qualitative differences between the two disorders? It is because Lacan is convinced that the delusional system and the hallucinations are so invasive for the subject, have such a devastating effect upon his or her relations with the world and with fellow beings, that he regards prior psychoanalytic attempts to explain psychosis, ultimately including Freud's own, as inadequate.

Freud explains psychosis in terms of a repressed homosexual relationship to the father. According to Freud, it was the emergence in Schreber of an erotic homosexual relationship towards his treating doctor, Professor Flechsig, and the conflict this desire produced in him that led in the first instance to the delusion of persecution and ultimately to the fully developed delusional system centred on Schreber's special relationship to God.[13]

Freud also compares the mechanisms of neurosis and psychosis in the following terms: in both there is a withdrawal of investment, or object-cathexis, from objects in the world. In the case of neurosis this object-cathexis is retained but invested in fantasized objects within the neurotic's internal world. In the case of psychosis the withdrawn cathexis is invested in the ego. This takes place at the expense of all object-cathexes, even in fantasy, and the turning of libido upon the ego accounts for symptoms such as hypochondria and megalomania. The delusional system, the most striking feature of psychosis, arises in a second stage. Freud characterises the construction of a delusional system as an attempt at recovery, in which the subject re-establishes a new, often very intense relation with the people and things in the world by way of his or her delusions.[14]

One can see that despite the differences in detail between the mechanisms of neurosis and psychosis in Freud's account, both still operate essentially by way of repression: withdrawal of libido onto fantasized objects in neurosis, withdrawal of object libido onto the ego in psychosis. It is basically for this reason that Lacan finds it inadequate:

> It is difficult to see how it could be purely and simply the suppression of a given [homosexual] tendency, the rejection or repression of some more or less transferential drive he would have felt toward Flechsig, that led President Schreber to construct his enormous delusion. There really must be something more proportionate to the result involved.[15]

III. The Foreclosure of Castration in the Wolf Man

It is apparent in Lacan's work prior to *Seminar III* that he was already thinking about a mechanism in psychosis that is different from repression. In his *Réponse au commentaire de Jean Hyppolite sur la 'Verneinung' de Freud*, published in 1956 but dating back to a discussion in his seminar in early 1954, Lacan refers to Freud's use of the term *Verwerfung* to characterise the Wolf Man's attitude towards castration.[16] The discussion focuses on a series of comments in this case study where Freud first contrasts repression and foreclosure categorically, stating: 'A repression is something very different from a foreclosure.'[17] Freud then observes:

> [The Wolf Man] rejected [*verwarf*] castration. . . When I speak of his having rejected it, the first meaning of the phrase is that he would have nothing to do with it in the sense of having repressed it. This really involved no judgement upon the question of its existence, but it was the same as if it did not exist.[18]

Lacan considers that the Wolf Man's attitude towards castration shows that, at least in his childhood, castration is foreclosed. It lies outside the limits of what can be judged to exist, because it is withdrawn from the possibilities of speech. While no judgement can be made about the existence of castration, it may nevertheless appear in the real in an erratic and unpredictable manner which Lacan describes as being 'in relations of resistance without transference,' or again, 'as a punctuation without text.'[19] While clearly indicating that a difference of register is at stake here, these formulations remain somewhat metaphorical. They will subsequently be developed into a more complex position concerning the vicissitudes of the foreclosed.

The implication in Freud is, then, that foreclosure is a mechanism that simply treats the foreclosed as if it did not exist, and as such is distinct from repression where the repressed manifests itself in symptomatic formations. Pursuing this line of thought further, Lacan turns to Freud's paper *Negation*, the topic of his discussion with Hyppolite during the seminar. In this paper Freud distinguishes between *Einbeziehung ins Ich* and *Ausstossung aus dem Ich*.[20] Regarding these respectively as 'introduction into the subject' and 'expulsion from the subject,' Lacan argues that the latter constitutes the domain of what subsists outside symbolisation.[21] This initial, primary expulsion constitutes a domain that is external to — in the sense of radically alien or foreign to — the subject and the subject's world. Lacan calls this domain the real. He regards it as distinct from reality, since reality is to be discriminated within the field of representation (Freud's notion of *Vorstellung*), which Lacan, in taking Freud's *Project* as his point of departure, considers to be constituted by the imaginary reproduction of initial perception.[22] Reality is thus understood as the domain in which the question of the possible existence of the object of this initial perception can be raised, and in which this object can also be refound (*wiedergefunden*) and located.[23] Although the real is excluded from the symbolic field within which the question of the existence of objects in reality can be raised, it may nevertheless appear in reality, but it will do so in the form of a hallucination. Thus Lacan's remark: 'That which has not seen the light of day in the symbolic appears in the real.'[24]

Though there is no explicit statement to this effect, it is clearly implied in *Réponse au commentaire de Jean Hyppolite* that it is castration that is foreclosed. This issue is taken up again in *Seminar III*:

> What is at issue when I speak of *Verwerfung*? At issue is the rejection [foreclosure] of a primordial signifier

> into the outer shadows, a signifier that will henceforth be missing at this level. Here you have the fundamental mechanism that I posit as being at the basis of paranoia. It's a matter of a primordial process of exclusion of an original within, which is not a bodily within but that of an initial body of signifiers.[25]

However, Lacan shifts ground in this seminar, concluding that the foreclosure of castration is secondary to the original foreclosure of the primordial signifier of the Name-of-the-Father.

IV. Schreber's Way

Lacan devoted his seminar in the year 1955-56 to a re-examination of Schreber's *Memoirs* and Freud's discussion of the case. Already armed with the distinction between *Verdrängung* and *Verwerfung*, Lacan intended to explore the clinical, nosographical and technical difficulties the psychoses raise.

In further examining the nature of foreclosure in *Seminar III*, the earlier views outlined above undergo a number of modifications. While it is a common assumption that foreclosure entails psychosis, there in fact appears to be nothing to rule out the possibility that foreclosure is a normal psychic process. Indeed, although he does not do this systematically, Lacan does not hesitate to speak of the foreclosure of femininity, or, later and in a different context, of the foreclosure of the subject of science.[26] Foreclosure in psychosis is the foreclosure of the Name-of-the-Father, a key signifier that 'anchors' or 'quilts' signifier and signified.[27] Thus it is only when what is foreclosed is specifically concerned with the question of the father, as in Schreber's case, that psychosis is produced. The term 'Name-of-the-Father' indicates that what is at issue is not a person but a signifier, one that is replete with cultural and religious significance.[28] It is a key signifier for the subject's symbolic universe, regulating this order and giving it its structure. Its function in the Oedipus complex is to be the vehicle of the law that regulates desire — both the subject's desire and the omnipotent desire of the maternal figure. It should also be noted that since foreclosure of the Name-of-the-Father is one possible outcome of the Oedipus complex, neurosis and perversion being the others, these structures are laid down at the time of negotiating the Oedipus complex.

In contrast to Freud and also, in part, to his own earlier views, Lacan sees the foreclosure of castration and the homosexual identification as effects and not causes of psychosis. In fact, he claims that Schreber's symptoms are not really homosexual at all and that it would be more accurate to call them *transsexual*. These transsexual and other phenomena, for which Lacan will later coin the phrase 'push towards woman' (*pousse à la femme*), are the result of the initial foreclosure of the Name-of-the-Father and the corresponding lack in the imaginary of phallic meaning.[29] The paternal metaphor is an operation in which the Name-of-the-Father is substituted for the mother's desire, thereby producing, as a new species of meaning, phallic meaning, which heralds the introduction of the subject to the phallic economy of the neurotic and, therefore, to castration. This phallic meaning, as both the product of the paternal metaphor and the key to all questions of sexual identity, is absent in psychosis. The operation of the paternal metaphor is expressed in the following formula:[30]

$$\frac{\text{Name-of-the-Father}}{\text{Desire of the Mother}} \cdot \frac{\text{Desire of the Mother}}{\text{Signified for the subject}} \rightarrow \text{Name-of-the-Father}\left(\frac{\text{O}}{\text{Phallus}}\right)$$

The paternal metaphor

In psychosis, then, the foreclosure of the Name-of-the-Father is accompanied by the corresponding absence (foreclosure) of the phallic meaning that is necessary for libidinal relations. Without this phallic meaning the subject is left prey to — 'left in the lurch' (*liegen lassen*) as Schreber puts it — the mother's unregulated desire, confronted by an obscure enigma at the level of the jouissance of the Other which the subject lacks the means to comprehend.

It is not that the absence of this signifier, the Name-of-the-Father, prevents the symbolic from functioning altogether. Schreber is after all within the symbolic; indeed, he is a very prolix author, as his *Memoirs* so clearly demonstrate. Yet his entire literary output revolves around two connected, fundamental issues which he is unable to resolve: the question of the father and the question of his own sexual identity.

The difference between Schreber and the neurotic here is striking: the neurotic finds a response, in the form of a neurotic compromise, a more or less satisfactory solution to the questions of the law and of sexual identity. Schreber on the other hand finds himself completely incapable of resolving them because the material he needs to do so, the requisite signifiers, are missing.

Yet what is foreclosed from the symbolic is not purely and simply abolished. It returns, but, unlike the return of the repressed, it returns from outside the subject, as emanating from the real. As Lacan henceforth puts it: what has been foreclosed from the symbolic reappears in the real. It is important to recognise not only that what returns in the real is actual bits of language, signifiers, but also that the effects of this return are located at both the symbolic and imaginary levels.

With the emphasis upon the function of speech in *Seminar III*, where the Other is understood as the Other of speech and of subjective recognition, Lacan pays very close attention to the imaginary means by which the subject makes good the lack in the symbolic. For instance, Lacan considers that in psychosis there is a form of regression involved; there is regression, which is topographical rather than chronological, from the symbolic register to the imaginary.[31] Thus, when he declares that what has been foreclosed from the symbolic reappears in the real, it is marked by the properties of the imaginary.

Whereas the symbolic is linguistic in nature, the imaginary groups together a series of phenomena the cornerstone of which is the mirror stage.[32] The mirror stage, which refers to the infant's early experience of fascination with its own image in a mirror, relates how the child responds with jubilation and pleasure to seeing a reflection of its own image. Lacan claims that the child is fascinated with its image because it is here that the child experiences itself as a whole, as a unity, for the first time. Furthermore, the experience of a self-unity lays the basis for the ego, which is formed through the subject's identification with this image. The reference to the mirror is not essential, but is intended to capture the fact that the ego and the other both come into existence together. Moreover, the ego and the other (or more strictly speaking, the image of the other, i(*a*)) are dependent upon one another, and indeed are not clearly differentiated. The reference to the mirror captures this ambiguity by emphasizing that the ego is built upon an image of one's own body as it would be perceived from another's point of view. The ego and its other are locked together in the sense that they come into existence together and depend upon one another for their sense of identity. For Lacan, this dual relationship epitomizes the imaginary relationship, which is characterized by identification and alienation, and marked by an ambivalent relationship of aggressive rivalry with and erotic attachment to the other. In psychosis this means that relations with the other are marked by the erotic attachment and aggressive rivalry characteristic of the imaginary. Thus, Professor Flechsig becomes an erotic object for Schreber, but also the agent of Schreber's persecution.

In *On a Question Preliminary to Any Possible Treatment of Psychosis* there is a shift away from the function of speech to the laws of language, which is accompanied by a simultaneous shift away from intersubjectivity towards the relationship with the Other as the Other of language. As a consequence, there is a somewhat more detailed analysis of language phenomena and language disorders in psychosis. This appears very clearly in Lacan's analysis of the psychiatric term 'elementary phenomena.' Throughout his work Lacan makes repeated references to these elementary phenomena, a term which embraces thought-echoes, verbal enunciations of actions, and various forms of hallucination. In *Seminar III* he uses it as a general term for the phenomena produced in psychosis by the appearance of signifiers in the real.[33] These are classically referred to as primitive phenomena, are considered to be instrumental in the onset of the psychosis, while they themselves lack any apparent external cause. Lacan's use of the term dates back to his 1932 thesis in medicine where he observes:

> By this name [of primitive or elementary phenomena], in effect, according to a schema frequently accepted in psychopathology . . . , authors designate symptoms in which the determining factors of psychosis are said to be primitively expressed and on the basis of which the delusion is said to be constructed according to

> secondary affective reactions and deductions that in themselves are rational.[34]

In *Seminar III* Lacan's task is to explain how these elementary phenomena result from the emergence of signifiers in the real. He claims that if they are to be called 'elementary' then this has to be understood in the sense that they contain all the elements of the fully developed psychois.[35] This approach is made possible by the recognition that all psychotic phenomena can in fact be analysed as phenomena of speech, rather than as a reaction by the subject, in the imaginary, to a lack in the symbolic.

In *On a Question Preliminary*, elementary phenomena (though no longer called this) are analysed as reflecting the structure of the signifier, resulting in an analysis of hallucinations that divides them into code phenomena and message phenomena.[36]

The code phenomena include Schreber's *Grundsprache* or basic language and its neologisms and 'autonyms.' 'Autonymous' is Roman Jakobson's term for contexts in which expressions are mentioned rather than used — the first word in this sentence is an example. Jakobson describes this as a case of a message referring to a code. It is a common occurrence in ordinary language, but in Schreber's case there is a highly developed code-message interaction; moreover, one that is also reflected in the relationships between the 'rays' or 'nerves' that speak (*Gottesstrahlen*). These rays, Lacan says, are nothing but a reification of the very structure and phenomenon of language itself.[37]

The code phenomena also include the frequently encountered phenomenon in psychosis of the enigma, along with psychotic certainty, which according to Lacan develops out of it.[38] Lacan claims that there is a temporal sequence between these phenomena. First, there is an initial experience of an enigma, arising from an absence or lack of meaning that occurs in the place where meaning should be. The enigma arises because the expectation of meaning that the signifier generates is radically disappointed. An enigma is not just the absence of meaning, but its absence there where meaning should be present. Thus, in a second stage, what was already implicit in the first comes to the fore, namely the conviction, which by its very nature the signifier generates, that there is a meaning, or as Schreber's rays put it, that 'all nonsense cancels itself out' (*aller Unsinn hebt sich auf*).[39]

One should note that in both cases there is effectively a failure of language ('the code'), to produce meaning ('the message'): in the first there is a communication of the structure of language but no meaning is conveyed; in the second the absence of meaning gives rise to the conviction of the psychotic.

As examples of message phenomena Lacan gives the interrupted messages which Schreber receives from God and to which he is called upon to give a reply that completes the message. For instance, 'Now I will myself...' (*Nun will ich mich...*), to which Schreber replies, '... face the fact that I am an idiot' (*darein ergeben, daß ich dumm bin*). In calling these 'message phenomena,' on the grounds that the sentence is interrupted at a point at which the indexical elements of the sentence have been uttered, Lacan appears to have in mind Jakobson's observation that the 'general meaning of a shifter cannot be defined without a reference to the message.'[40]

Both types of phenomena are examples of the return of the signifier in the real. Both indicate the appearance, in the real, of the signifier cut off from its connections with the signifying chain, that is, S_1 appears in the real without S_2, and as a consequence the 'quilting' that would normally produce meaning cannot occur. However, this does not result in the complete extinguishment of meaning, but rather in the proliferation of a meaningfulness that manifests itself in the real in the form of verbal hallucinations, as well as in the enigma and the conviction the psychotic experiences.

Of special note as examples of the return of the signifier in the real are those verbal hallucinations, often persecutory, of the psychotic, such as the case of the hallucinated insult 'Sow!,' discussed in both *Seminar III* and *On a Question Preliminary*, where both imaginary and symbolic disturbances can be detected.[41] On Lacan's analysis the example displays disturbances of the code. But it also reveals the appearance in psychotic form of the same content one finds expressed in different ways in neurotic formations of the unconscious — the utterance expresses the imaginary meaning of fragmentation of the body. What is perhaps different is that this emerges in the place from which phallic meaning has been foreclosed.

Given that the foreclosure of the signifier of the Name-of-the-Father entails the corresponding absence of phallic meaning, it is to be expected that this will have particular consequences for the psychotic subject's sexual identity. Lacan speaks of a 'push towards woman' to describe the gradual transformation of sexuality in Schreber's delusion as well as in other cases of psychosis. Prior to his psychosis Schreber lived as a heterosexual man with no apparent trace of feminization. The first intimation of this push towards woman is given in Schreber's conscious fantasy just prior to the onset of his psychosis: 'How beautiful it would be to be a woman undergoing sexual intercourse.' Subsequently Schreber's 'manly honour' struggles against the increasingly desperate attempts by God to 'unman' him and transform him into a woman. But he finally becomes reconciled to this transformation, recognizing that his emasculation is necessary if one day he is to be fertilised by God and repopulate the world with new beings. In the meantime he will adorn his naked body with trinkets and cheap jewellery to enhance and promote this unavoidable feminization.

Lacan sees in this development two separate aspects to the restoration of the imaginary structure. Both were detected by Freud and both are, for Lacan, linked either directly or indirectly to the absence of phallic meaning in the imaginary. The first aspect has already been mentioned; it is Schreber's 'transsexualism.' The second aspect links 'the feminization of the subject to the co-ordinate of divine copulation.'[42] This psychotic drive to be transformed into a woman is an attempt to embody the woman in the figure of the wife of God. Lacan notes that transsexualism is common in psychosis and that it is normally linked to the demand for endorsement and consent from the father.[43]

What triggers a psychosis? Lacan argues that even though the onset of psychosis is largely unforeseeable, the psychotic structure will have been there all along — like an invisible flaw in the glass — prior to the appearance of the clinical psychosis, when it suddenly and dramatically manifests itself. And we can see this in Schreber, who had up until the age of 51 led a relatively normal life, enjoying a successful career, and carrying out the demanding duties of a senior position in the judiciary.

Lacan holds that it is a certain type of encounter, in which the Name-of-the-Father is 'called into symbolic opposition to the subject,' that is the trigger, the precipitating cause of a psychosis.[44] What does this 'called into symbolic opposition to the subject' mean? The issue is explored in *Seminar III* in a lengthy discussion that continues over a number of sessions concerning the function of what Lacan calls *l'appel*, the 'call,' the 'calling,' the 'appeal' or even the 'interpellation.' The discussion is not related specifically to psychosis but rather to a quite general function of language.[45]

Lacan takes a number of examples from everyday French which draw on the difference between *Tu es celui qui me suivras* and *Tu es celui qui me suivra*, where the subordinate clause is in the second and third person respectively.[46] The same basic idea may be expressed in the English distinction between 'shall' and 'will.' Consider the two statements: 'You are the one who will follow me,' and 'You are the one who shall follow me.' It is possible to take the first as a description of or prediction about something that will come to pass: I predict that you will follow me. The second, on the other hand, can serve as an appeal, where the interlocutor, the one who is being addressed, is called upon to make a decision, to pursue a course of action which he or she must either embrace or repudiate. This latter case is, for instance, exemplified by Jesus of Nazareth's invocation, his appeal, to his disciples-to-be: 'I say to you: "You are the ones who shall follow me." Now, tell me, what is your reply, what do you say to this? Give me your answer, for now is the time to choose.' In this example we could say that Jesus is 'in symbolic opposition' to his disciples, or we could equally well say that he is asking them for 'symbolic recognition,' for his speech calls upon them to respond in a way that engages them in, commits them to, a decision, one loaded with practical consequences, as to whether they are to recognize him as the Messiah. For Schreber, then, there is a moment when he is called, interpellated, by — or perhaps better 'in' — the Name-of-the-Father. This is when the lack of the signifier declares itself, and it is sufficient to trigger the psychosis.

How is this symbolic opposition, this call for symbolic recognition, brought about in psychosis? Lacan gives this response: by an encounter with 'a real father, not necessarily by the subject's own father, but by A-father' (*Un-père*).[47] This is a situation that arises under two conditions: when the subject is in a particularly intense relationship involving a strong narcissistic component; and when, in this situation, the question of the father arises from a third position, one that is external to the erotic relation. For instance, and the examples are Lacan's, it may occur:

> for the woman who has just given birth, in her husband's face, for the penitent confessing his sins in the

> person of his confessor, for the girl in love in her meeting with 'the young man's father.'[48]

And, as is well known, it can also occur in analysis, where the development of the transference can sometimes precipitate a psychosis. Lacan puts it thus:

> It sometimes happens that we take prepsychotics into analysis, and we know what that produces — it produces psychotics. The question of the contraindications of analysis would not arise if we didn't all recall some particular case in our practice, or in the practice of our colleagues, where a full-blown psychosis . . . is triggered during the first analytic sessions in which things heat up a bit . . .[49]

Indeed, at issue in the suitability or not of a subject for analysis is the unpredictability of psychosis, the uncertainty of knowing in whom a psychosis may be triggered, and the lack of diagnostic criteria for psychosis prior to its onset. And yet, if Lacan's views on the structure of psychosis are right, it makes sense to speak of 'prepsychosis' in the case of subjects with a psychotic structure who are not clinically psychotic.

Once the psychosis is triggered, everything will have changed for good, but what about before the onset? It is in pursuing this question that the work of Maurits Katan on prepsychosis and that of Helene Deutsch on the 'as if' phenomenon is discussed.[50] Lacan finds Katan's characterization of the prepsychotic period unconvincing, facetiously remarking that nothing resembles a prepsychosis more than a neurosis does.[51] He finds more of interest in Deutsch's work, and especially in what she refers to as the 'as if' phenomenon, where, for example, an adolescent boy identifies with another youth in what looks like a homosexual attachment but turns out to be a precursor of psychosis.[52] Here there is something that plays the role of a *suppléance*, a suppletion, that is a substitute or a stand-in for what is missing at the level of the symbolic.[53] Lacan uses the analogy of a three-legged stool:

> Not every stool has four legs. There are some that stand upright on three. Here, though, there is no question of their lacking any, otherwise things go very badly indeed . . . It's possible that at the outset the stool doesn't have enough legs, but that up to a certain point it will nevertheless stand up, when the subject, at a certain crossroads of his biographical history, is confronted by this lack that has always existed.[54]

Suppletion can take various forms. The case of Deutsch's is a good example of imaginary suppletion, where the support derived from an identification with the other is sufficient to compensate for the absence of the signifier. The psychosis is thus triggered at the moment at which the imaginary suppletion, with which the subject has until then been able to make do, proves inadequate. It is not uncommon for this to occur at the beginning of adult life when the subject loses the protective support of the family network. Indeed, Lacan even goes so far as to evoke the imaginary identification with the mother's desire as a means of maintaining the stability of the 'imaginary tripod.'

Lacan also considers that the delusion itself can provide the psychotic with a degree of stability in the form of a 'delusional metaphor,' which can be regarded as a second form of suppletion.[55] Considered by Freud as an attempt at cure, the stability of the delusional metaphor is seen by some in Lacan's school as the aim of the treatment of psychotics — an important consideration in the light of the claim that psychosis is a discrete subjective structure that no treatment will cure.

A third form of suppletion is, despite the air of paradox, best called symbolic suppletion. It is an intriguing fact that some psychotics have been capable of making important scientific or artistic contributions. The mathematician Georg Cantor is a famous example, but there are numerous such cases. We know about them because of the documented psychotic episodes these people underwent. But it is also interesting to speculate that there may be cases where the psychosis never declares itself and the clinical phenomena never eventuate. Perhaps in these cases the (pre)psychotic subject may find a form of substitute for the foreclosed signifier that enables him or her to maintain the fewest symbolic links necessary for normal, even for highly original and creative, functioning. In his *Seminar XXIII*, *Le sinthome* of 1975-76

Lacan argues that James Joyce was such a case. And indeed, there are a number of indications that one can point to in support of the claim that Joyce was probably a psychotic who was able to use his writing as an effective substitute to prevent the onset of psychosis. This is an interesting thought, and I return to it below. There is something necessarily speculative about such cases, and Joyce himself is obviously such a special case that he can hardly serve as a model for others. Still, there are important issues here concerning the diagnosis of psychosis. Could, for example, the so-called borderlines be situated here? Are they to be regarded as undeclared psychoses? Clearly, the Lacanian model implies a search for indications of psychosis independent of and prior to the onset of a full-blown clinical psychosis.

What causes foreclosure of the Name-of-the-Father? Assuming the psychotic structure is laid down at the moment of the Oedipus complex, under what conditions is this foreclosure produced? Lacan does not have much to say about this issue, though he does make a criticism of certain views and offers some positive observations of his own. The criticism is that it is not enough to focus on the child-mother or child-father relationship alone; one must look at the triadic, Oedipal structure. Thus, in looking at child, mother and father, it is not enough to think in terms of 'frustrating' or 'smothering' mothers, any more than in terms of 'dominating' or 'easygoing' fathers, since these approaches neglect the triangular structure of the Oedipus complex. One needs to consider the place that the mother, as the first object of the child's desire, gives to the authority of the father, or as Lacan puts it, one needs to consider 'the place that she reserves for the Name-of-the-Father in the promulgation of the law.'[56] Lacan adds (and this is the second point) that one also needs to consider the father's relation to the law in itself. The issue here is whether or not the father is himself an adequate vehicle of the law. There are circumstances, he says, that make it easier for the father to be found undeserving, inadequate or fraudulent with respect to the law and therefore found to be an ineffective vehicle for the Name-of-the-Father. This leads him to remark that psychosis occurs 'with particular frequency' when the father 'has the function of a legislator,' whether as one who actually makes the laws or as one who poses as the incarnation of high ideals.[57]

V. Heavenly Joyce

Lacan's discussion of Joyce, some twenty years after the seminar on Schreber, was not as it happens merely an occasion to explore further the issue of suppletion in relation to foreclosure. It resulted in nothing less than a reformulation of the way in which the differences between neurosis and psychosis should be approached and also contributed to an understanding of the difference between paranoia and schizophrenia.

From the discussion so far it can be seen that initially neurosis is taken as the model for the formation of symptoms and the construction of the subject. When, in *On a Question Preliminary*, Lacan writes that 'the condition of the subject . . . is dependent on what is being unfolded in the Other,' it is clear that the structure of psychosis is conceptualised as a variant of the structure of neurosis.[58] One only needs to compare Schema R and Schema I, for instance, where the psychotic structure of Schema I is a transformation — produced by the foreclosure of the Name-of-the-Father and the corresponding lack of phallic meaning — of the neurotic structure in Schema R.

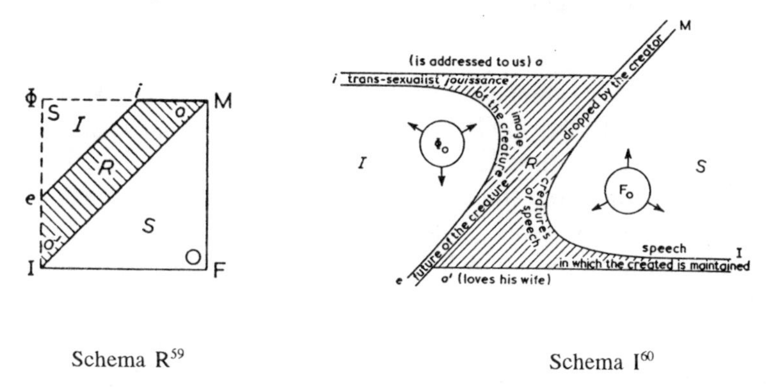

Schema R[59]

Schema I[60]

Lacan's approach in his seminar on James Joyce offers a different perspective, from which what Colette Soler has called a 'general theory of the symptom' can be extracted.[61] This general theory is applicable to both neurosis and psychosis, whereas the theory of neurotic metaphor becomes a special case, created by the addition of the function of the Name-of-the-Father. Thus, rather than taking neurosis as the primary structure and considering psychosis to be produced by the foreclosure of the Name-of-the-Father, neurosis is henceforth considered as a special case created by the introduction of a specific signifier. This step effectively generalizes the concept of foreclosure. The delusional metaphor of psychosis is *one* response to this foreclosure; the symptom-metaphor of neurosis is another.

Developing these views by way of topology, Lacan revises his earlier thesis that the symbolic, the imaginary and the real are linked like the rings of a Borromean knot, i.e. in such a way that severing any one link will untie the other two.

The Borromean knot[62]

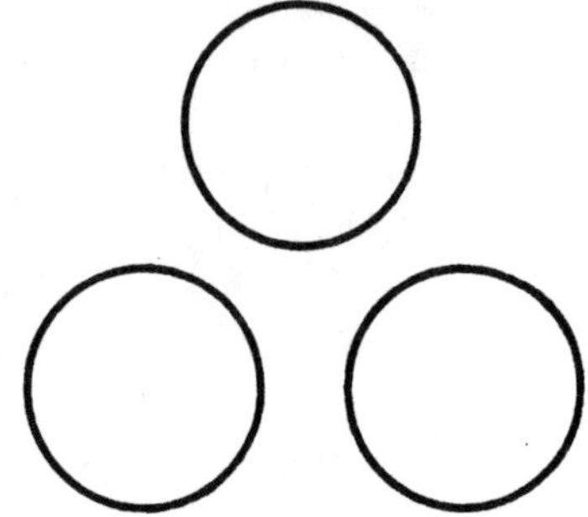

Three separate rings

However, in the seminar on Joyce, Lacan declares that it is incorrect to think that the three-ring Borromean knot is the normal way in which the three categories are linked. It is therefore not the case that the separation of the three rings is the result of some defect, because the three are already separate. Where they are joined together, they are joined by a fourth link, which Lacan calls the *sinthome* and which he writes as Σ.

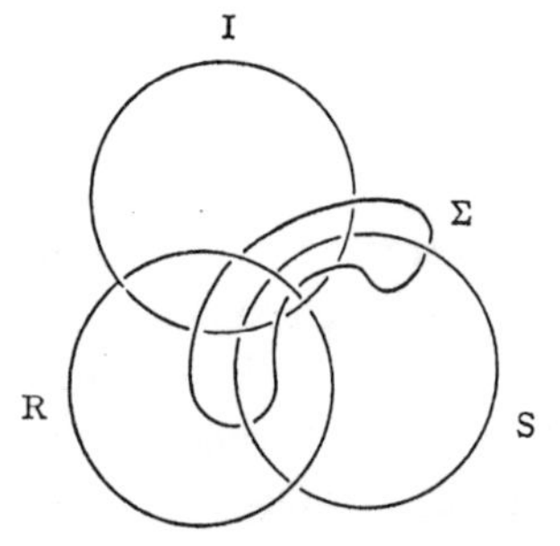

The Borromean knot with four rings[63]

The Name-of-the-Father is henceforth only a particular form of the *sinthome*:

> The Oedipus complex is, as such, a symptom. It is in so far as the Name-of-the-Father is also the Father of the name that everything hangs together, which does not make the symptom any the less necessary.[64]

In *Ulysses* this father has to be 'sustained by Joyce in order for the father to subsist.'[65]

Lacan's thesis, then, is that although Joyce was psychotic, he succeeded in avoiding the onset of psychosis through his writing, which thus plays the role for Joyce of his *sinthome*. Indeed, Lacan says, through his writing Joyce went as far as one can in analysis.[66] Joyce's achievement in preventing his own psychosis means that in him the psychotic phenomena appear in a different form both from neurosis and from a declared psychosis. Lacan locates the elementary phenomena and the experience of enigma, for instance, in Joyce's 'epiphanies,' fragments of actual conversations overheard, extracted from their context, and carefully recorded on separate sheets.[67] All this was completed even before Joyce's first novel, and many of the fragments were subsequently reinserted unannounced into later texts. Torn from their context, the epiphanies remain nonsensical or enigmatic fragments and are striking for their qualities of incongruity and insignificance:

> Joyce — I knew you meant him. But you're wrong about his age.
> Maggie Sheehy — (*leans forward to speak seriously*). Why, how old is he?
> Joyce — Seventy-two.
> Maggie Sheehy — Is he?[68]

What is so striking is not so much that the epiphanies do not make much sense, which is what one might expect of such fragments taken out of their context, but rather that Joyce, or Stephen, should describe these meaningless and enigmatic fragments, outside of discourse and cut off from communication, as a 'sudden spiritual manifestation.' Lacan claims that this process in which the absence of meaning of the epiphany is transformed into its opposite, the certainty of an ineffable revelation, is comparable to the enigmatic experience and its conversion into psychotic conviction in Schreber. Of course, Joyce differs from Schreber in that he cultivates the phenomenon and transforms it into a creative work. In *Finnegan's Wake* Joyce the craftsman transforms linguistic meaning into nonsense and vice versa, so that what corresponds to the enigmatic experience of a Schreber is thereby raised to the level of an artistic process.

It is therefore to be expected that the question of jouissance in psychosis should be treated somewhat differently in the seminar on Joyce. In the case of Schreber the foreclosure of phallic meaning leads to homosexual and transsexual impulses. For Freud, as we have seen, this is to be regarded as the consequence of a repressed passive homosexuality, whereas Lacan does not think that this will adequately account for the psychosis. It is more accurate to say that Schreber's virility itself is attacked by the return in the real of the castration that is foreclosed from the symbolic. In Schreber the barrier to jouissance is surmounted and jouissance is no longer located outside the body. Schreber's body is thus no longer the desert it is for the neurotic and is therefore besieged by an ineffable, inexplicable jouissance, which is ascribed to the divine Other who seeks his satisfaction in Schreber.[69]

Joyce's writing transforms the 'enjoy-meant' (*jouis-sens*) that literature normally conveys into jouissance of the letter, into an enjoyment that lies outside of meaning. But what is even more astonishing is that in a secondary way, through imposing or introducing this strange literature that is outside of discourse, he manages to restore the social link that his writing abolishes, and to promote himself to the place of the exception. Furthermore, he has the responsibility, which is usually assumed by the work of the delusion, for producing sense out of the opaque work, passed down to his commentators, thereby assuring the survival of his name.

One final important consideration is the particular prominence Lacan gives in *Seminar XXIII* to the function of the letter in psychotic experience. In his earlier work, in which he spoke of the symptom as a formation of the unconscious on a par with dreams, jokes and parapraxes, the symptom is taken to be a knot of signifiers excluded from discourse and therefore unable to be included in any circuit of communication. However, alongside this emphasis placed upon the signifier as such there are a number of important observations on the function of the letter. In fact, as early as 1957 Lacan stated that the symptom 'is already inscribed in a process of writing.'[70] The materiality of the letter was further discussed in *The Agency of the Letter*, while an important thesis of the *Seminar on 'The Purloined Letter,'* in which Lacan made his first reference to Joyce's 'a letter, a litter,' is that the letter is not just a signifier but also an object.[71] As such it may become a remainder, a remnant, a vestige left in the wake of the message it conveys. The letter may occupy a status not unlike a fetish object, as was the case with André Gide, whose letters were burnt by his wife when confronted with evidence she could no longer ignore of his sexual exploits with young boys. Gide's collapse belies the fact that the letters were the vehicle of a jouissance supplementary to the message they conveyed.[72] Similarly, the assumption in the seminar on Joyce is that the symptom is no longer to be regarded simply as a message excluded from the circuit of communication but also as a site of jouissance. While this does not make the theory of the signifier redundant, nevertheless it stresses the localised effects of the materiality of the letter.

VI. Conclusion

The thought that something fundamental may be excluded from the symbolic, and the role that this may play in understanding psychosis, was immediately grasped by Lacan, even prior to the discussion of Schreber in *Seminar III*, as a corollary of the thesis that the unconscious is structured like a language. Not only did this thought offer Lacan, with his psychiatric grounding, the means to develop a better theory of psychosis than psychoanalysis had previously managed to do, but the detailed work on the Schreber case can also be seen as a verification of the theoretical position Lacan had until then been developing in the context of neurosis alone. The Schreber case highlighted the nature of what it was that was foreclosed: the Name-of-the-Father. But it also brought the category of the real into much sharper focus than was apparent in earlier seminars, where the demarcation between the imaginary and the symbolic was more pressing, no doubt as the result of a focus on neurotic structures. In this context, the return to a discussion of psychosis and foreclosure in the seminar on Joyce is quite important, with the real taking on a new and more ramified role in the overall explanation of psychosis. What is of particular interest in the discussion of Joyce is that it presents a new theory, according to which foreclosure is the universal condition of the symptom.

Notes

1. J. Damourette & E. Pichon, *Des mots à la pensée: Essai de grammaire de la langue française* (7 vols.), Paris, d'Artrey, 1911-1940. See also: J. Damourette & E. Pichon, Sur la signification psychologique de la négation en français, *Journal de psychologie normale et pathologique*, 1928, XXV, pp. 229-253. Pichon was also a psychoanalyst and senior colleague of Lacan's in the *Société Psychanalytique de Paris*.

2. J. Damourette & E. Pichon, Sur la signification psychologique de la négation en français, *o.c.*, p. 245. 'Scotomisation' is a term they adopt from René Laforgue. See: R. Laforgue, Verdrängung und Skotomisation, *Internationale Zeitschrift für Psychoanalyse*, 1926, XII, pp. 54-65.

3. J. Damourette & E. Pichon, Sur la signification psychologique de la négation en français, *o.c.*, p. 243.

4. See: S. Freud, The Interpretation of Dreams (1900*a*), *Standard Edition*, IV & V; S. Freud, The Psychopathology of Everyday Life (1901*b*), *Standard Edition*, VI; S. Freud, Jokes and their Relation to the Unconscious (1905*c*), *Standard Edition*, VIII.

5. For 'the unconscious structured like a language,' see for example: J. Lacan, *The Seminar. Book VII: The Ethics of Psychoanalysis* (1959-60) (trans. with notes D. Porter), Edited by J.-A. Miller, New York NY-London, W.W. Norton & Company, 1992, p. 32.

6. See: S. Freud, From the History of an Infantile Neurosis (1918*b*[1914]), *Standard Edition*, XVII, pp. 79-80.

7. For *rejet*, see for example: J. Lacan, *The Seminar. Book I: Freud's Papers on Technique* (1953-54) (trans. with notes J. Forrester), Edited by J.-A. Miller, New York NY-London, W.W. Norton & Company, 1989, p. 43. For *retranchement*, see: J. Lacan, Réponse au commentaire de Jean Hyppolite sur la 'Verneinung' de Freud (1954), *Ecrits*, Paris, du Seuil, 1966, pp. 381-399 and p. 386 in particular.

8. J. Lacan, *The Seminar. Book III: The Psychoses* (1955-56) (trans. with notes R. Grigg), Edited by J.-A. Miller, London-New York NY, Routledge, 1993, p. 321.

9. See, for example: S. Freud, The Loss of Reality in Neurosis and Psychosis (1924*e*), *Standard Edition*, XIX, pp. 181-187.

10. See: J. Lacan, Ouverture de la section clinique, *Ornicar ?*, 1977, no. 9, pp. 7-14.

11. See: J. Lacan, *The Seminar. Book III: The Psychoses, o.c.*, p. 10; S. Freud, Psycho-Analytic Notes Upon an Autobiographical Account of a Case of Paranoia (*Dementia Paranoides*) (1911*c*[1910]), *Standard Edition*, XII, pp. 3-82; D.P. Schreber, *Memoirs of My Nervous Illness* (1903) (trans. I. Macalpine & R.A. Hunter), with a new introduction by S.M. Weber, Cambridge MA-London, Harvard University Press, 1988.

12. See: J. Lacan, *The Seminar. Book III: The Psychoses, o.c.*, p. 10.

13. See: S. Freud, Psycho-Analytic Notes Upon an Autobiographical Account of a Case of Paranoia (*Dementia Paranoides*), *o.c.*, pp. 41-48.

14. See: S. Freud, Neurosis and Psychosis (1924*b*[1923]), *Standard Edition*, XIX, pp. 147-153; S. Freud, The Loss of Reality in Neurosis and Psychosis, *o.c.*, pp. 181-187.

15. J. Lacan, *The Seminar. Book III: The Psychoses, o.c.*, pp. 85-86.

16. See: J. Lacan, Réponse au commentaire de Jean Hyppolite sur la 'Verneinung' de Freud, *o.c.*, pp. 385-393. See also: J. Lacan, *The Seminar. Book I: Freud's Papers on Technique, o.c.*, pp. 52-61 & 289-297. This seminar includes Lacan's original discussion and Hyppolite's article, *A spoken commentary on Freud's* Verneinung.

17. S. Freud, From the History of an Infantile Neurosis, *o.c.*, pp. 79-80. Translation modified. This passage illustrates the difficulty of tracking the term *Verwerfung* through the *Standard Edition*. Freud's '*Eine Verdrängung ist etwas anderes als eine Verwerfung*' is rendered as 'A repression is something very different from a condemning judgement.'

18. *Ibid.*, p. 84. Again, I have modified the English version, but this time by restoring Freud's punctuation.

19. J. Lacan, Réponse au commentaire de Jean Hyppolite sur la 'Verneinung' de Freud, *o.c.*, p. 388. My translation.

20. S. Freud, Negation (1925*h*), *Standard Edition*, XIX, pp. 233-239.

21. J. Lacan, Réponse au commentaire de Jean Hyppolite sur la 'Verneinung' de Freud, *o.c.*, p. 388.

22. *Ibid.*, p. 389. See also: S. Freud, Project for a Scientific Psychology (1950*c*[1895]), *Standard Edition*, I, pp. 295-343 & pp. 347-387.

23. J. Lacan, Réponse au commentaire de Jean Hyppolite sur la 'Verneinung' de Freud, *o.c.*, p. 389.

24. *Ibid.*, p. 388. My translation. Compare with Freud's observations on the mechanism of paranoia in the Schreber case: 'It was incorrect to say that the perception which was suppressed internally is projected outwards; the truth is rather, as we now see, that what was abolished internally [*das innerlich Aufgehobene*] returns from without.' S. Freud, Psycho-Analytic Notes Upon an Autobiographical Account of a Case of Paranoia (*Dementia Paranoides*), *o.c.*, p. 71.

25. J. Lacan, *The Seminar. Book III: The Psychoses, o.c.*, p. 150.

26. For the foreclosure of femininity, see: J. Lacan, *The Seminar. Book III: The Psychoses, o.c.*, p. 86. For the foreclosure of the subject of science, see: J. Lacan, Science and Truth (1965) (trans. B. Fink), *Newsletter of the Freudian Field*, 1989, no. 3, pp. 4-29 and p. 22 in particular.

27. For the notion of 'quilting point' (*point de capiton*), see: J. Lacan, *The Seminar. Book III: The Psychoses, o.c.*, pp. 258-270.

28. The first use in writing of this term, which occurs in the so-called 'Rome Report' published in 1956, links the symbolic father to the law: 'It is in the *name of the father* that we must recognize the support of the symbolic function which, from the dawn of history, has identified his person with the figure of the law.' J. Lacan, The Function and Field of Speech and Language in Psychoanalysis (1953), *Ecrits: A Selection* (trans. A. Sheridan), London, Tavistock, 1977, p. 67.

29. See: J. Lacan, L'étourdit, *Scilicet*, 1973, no. 4, p. 22.

30. J. Lacan, On a Question Preliminary to Any Possible Treatment of Psychosis (1957-58), *Ecrits: A Selection, o.c.*, p. 200. In the formula, I have modified Alan Sheridan's translation of Lacan's *signifié au sujet* (signified to the subject) to 'signified for the subject.'

31. For 'topographical regression,' see: J. Lacan, *The Seminar. Book III: The Psychoses, o.c.*, pp. 154-155; J. Lacan, On a Question Preliminary to Any Possible Treatment of Psychosis, *o.c.*, p. 209.

32. See: J. Lacan, The Mirror Stage as Formative of the Function of the I as Revealed in Psychoanalytic Experience (1949), *Ecrits: A Selection, o.c.*, pp. 1-7.

33. See: J. Lacan, *The Seminar. Book III: The Psychoses, o.c.*, p. 19.

34. J. Lacan, *De la psychose paranoïaque dans ses rapports avec la personnalité* (1932), Paris, du Seuil, 1975, p. 207.

35. '[T]he elementary phenomena are no more elementary than what underlies the entire construction of a delusion. They are as elementary as a leaf is in relation to the plant, in which a certain detail can be seen of the way in which the veins overlap and insert into one another — there is something common to the whole plant that is reproduced in certain of the forms that make it up . . . A delusion isn't deduced. It reproduces its same constitutive force, It, too, is an elementary phenomenon. This means that here the notion of element is to be taken in no other way than as structure, differentiated structure, irreducible to anything other than itself.' J. Lacan, *The Seminar. Book III: The Psychoses, o.c.*, p. 19.

36. In Schreber's verbal hallucinations we can recognize 'quite other differences than those into which they are 'classically' classified . . . namely, the differences that derive from their speech structure, in so far as this structure is already in the *perceptum*.' J. Lacan, On a Question Preliminary to Any Possible Treatment of Psychosis, *o.c.*, p. 184, translation modified. The original translation is quite misleading. Lacan is following a distinction Jakobson draws between message and code. See: R. Jakobson, Shifters, Verbal Categories, and the Russian Verb, *Selected Writings*, Vol. II, The Hague, Mouton, 1971, pp. 130-147.

37. J. Lacan, On a Question Preliminary to Any Possible Treatment of Psychosis, *o.c.*, p. 185.

38. *Ibid.*, p. 185. 'What is involved here, in fact is an effect of the signifier, in so far as its degree of certainty (second degree: signification of signification) assumes a weight proportional to the enigmatic void that first presents itself in the place of the signification itself.'

39. D.P. Schreber, *Memoirs of My Nervous Illness, o.c.*, pp. 182-183.

40. R. Jakobson, Shifters, Verbal Categories, and the Russian Verb, *o.c.*, p. 131.

41. See: J. Lacan, *The Seminar. Book III: The Psychoses, o.c.*, pp. 47-53; J. Lacan, On a Question Preliminary to Any Possible Treatment of Psychosis, *o.c.*, pp. 182-183.

42. J. Lacan, On a Question Preliminary to Any Possible Treatment of Psychosis, *o.c.*, p. 210.

43. *Ibid.*, p. 209.

44. *Ibid.*, p. 217.

45. See: J. Lacan, *The Seminar. Book III: The Psychoses, o.c.*, pp. 247-309.

46. *Ibid.*, pp. 271-294.

47. J. Lacan, On a Question Preliminary to any Possible Treatment of Psychosis, *o.c.*, p. 217.

48. *Ibid.*, p. 217.

49. J. Lacan, *The Seminar. Book III: The Psychoses, o.c.*, p. 251.

50. See: M. Katan, Schreber's Prepsychotic Phase, *International Journal of Psycho-Analysis*, 1953, XXXIV, pp. 43-51; M. Katan, Structural Aspects of a Case of Schizophrenia, *The Psychoanalytic Study of the Child*, 1950, V, pp. 175-211; H. Deutsch, Some Forms of Emotional Disturbance and their Relationship to Schizophrenia, in J.D. Sutherland & M. Masud R. Khan (Eds.), *Neuroses and Character Types: Clinical Psychoanalytic Studies*, London, The Hogarth Press and the Institute of Psycho-Analysis, 1963, pp. 262-281.

51. See: J. Lacan, *The Seminar. Book III: The Psychoses, o.c.*, p. 191.

52. *Ibid.*, pp. 192-193.

53. It should be noted that the actual term suppletion (*suppléance*) does not appear in Lacan's work until 1975. See: J. Lacan, Le Séminaire XXIII, Le sinthome (1975-76), texte établi par J.-A. Miller, *Ornicar ?*, 1976, no. 6, p. 6 (seminar of 18 November 1975).

54. *Ibid.*, p. 203.

55. J. Lacan, On a Question Preliminary to Any Possible Treatment of Psychosis, *o.c.*, 217.

56. *Ibid.*, p. 218.

57. *Ibid.*, pp. 218-219.

58. *Ibid.*, p. 193.

59. *Ibid.*, p. 197.

60. *Ibid.*, p. 212.

61. See: C. Soler, L'expérience énigmatique du psychotique, de Schreber à Joyce, *La Cause freudienne*, 1993, no. 23, pp. 50-59.

62. J. Lacan, *Le Séminaire, Livre XX, Encore* (1972-73), texte établi par J.-A. Miller, Paris, du Seuil, 1975, p. 112.

63. J. Aubert (Ed.), *Joyce avec Lacan*, Paris, Navarin, 1987, p. 45.

64. J. Lacan, Le Séminaire XXIII, Le sinthome, seminar of 18 November 1975, *o.c.*, p. 9. My translation.

65. *Ibid.*, p. 9.

66. J. Lacan, Lituraterre, *Littérature*, 1971, no. 3, p. 3.

67. 'By an epiphany he meant a sudden spiritual manifestation, whether in the vulgarity of speech or of gesture or in a memorable phase of the mind itself. He believed that it was for the man of letters to record these epiphanies with extreme care, seeing that they themselves are the most delicate and evanescent of moments.' *Stephen Hero*, London, Jonathan Cape, 1956, p. 216.

68. R. Scholes & R.M. Kain (Eds.), *The Workshop of Daedalus: James Joyce and the Raw Materials for 'A Portrait of the Artist as a Young Man,'* Evanston IL, Northwestern University Press, 1965, p. 21.

69. This explains Lacan's 1966 comment that in paranoia jouissance is identified as located in the place of the Other as such. See: J. Lacan, Présentation des *Mémoires* du président Schreber en traduction française (1966), *Ornicar ?*, 1986, no. 38, p. 7.

70. J. Lacan, La psychanalyse et son enseignement (1957), *Ecrits*, *o.c.*, pp. 444-445.

71. See: J. Lacan, The Agency of the Letter in the Unconscious or Reason since Freud (1957), *Ecrits: A Selection, o.c.*, pp. 146-178; J. Lacan, Seminar on 'The Purloined Letter' (1956) (trans. J. Mehlman), *Yale French Studies*, 1972, no. 48, pp. 39-72; J.-A. Miller, Préface, in J. Aubert (Ed.), *Joyce avec Lacan, o.c.*, pp. 9-12.

72. See: J. Lacan, Jeunesse de Gide ou la lettre et le désir (1958), *Ecrits, o.c.*, pp. 739-764 and pp. 760-761 in particular.

CHAPTER 4

The Original Sin of Psychoanalysis: On the Desire of the Analyst

Katrien Libbrecht

I. Introduction

Lacan's concept of the desire of the analyst is both very specific and highly hybrid. On the one hand, it refers to the *function* of the desire of the analyst as an enigma, *x*, which is considered to be the driving force of the analytic treatment for the analyst. As a function, this desire of the analyst is explicitly related to the outcome of his or her training analysis. Since this concept does not stem from Lacan's 'return to Freud,' it substantiates the specificity of Lacan's position regarding psychoanalytic praxis. However, on the other hand, the desire of the analyst only derives its meaning from a series of other concepts in Lacan's theory. It touches for instance on the conception and handling of transference, on the direction of the treatment, on the position and the act of the analyst, and on the ethics of psychoanalysis. Since it refers to the training of the analyst, it also relates to the definition of the conclusion of the treatment and to the procedure of the pass from analysand to analyst, which Lacan formalised in his *Proposition of 9 October 1967 on the Psychoanalyst of the School.*[1]

There are at least two starting-points for a discussion of the desire of the analyst. Firstly, one can examine it as that which results from the training analysis and secondly, it can be apprehended as the driving force of an analysis on the part of the analyst. Both lines of thought can be inferred from the first two sections of Lacan's *Founding Act* of the *Ecole française de Psychanalyse* (EFP) of 1964.[2] The first section of this *Act*, dealing with pure psychoanalysis, is specified by Lacan as encompassing 'all the issues of the training analysis.'[3] It highlights questions such as: 'How to define an analyst?' and 'At what stage does one become an analyst?' Here, the desire of the analyst is Lacan's alternative for the demand *to be* an analyst. The latter expression locates the conclusion of the training analysis within the field of identification and ideal; the trainee is brought to 'being' an analyst by means of identifying with the (image of the) ideal analyst. In contrast to the dominant trend within the psychoanalytic associations residing under the International Psychoanalytic Association (IPA), Lacan — taking the unconscious rather than the ego as his point of departure — strove towards a definition of the conclusion of the training analysis beyond the realm of the ego and the ego ideal. For him, the result of a training analysis ought to be comprehended in terms of the unconscious, more specifically in terms of unconscious desire. In short, 'What is the result of an analysis carried through till its end?' is the query around which this first line of enquiry revolves.

The second reading of the desire of the analyst is closely related to both the first and the second section of the *Founding Act*. The second section, dealing with applied psychoanalysis, comprises the doctrine of the treatment and its variations, and also concerns the direction of psychoanalytic treatment. The second reading therefore addresses the position and the function of the analyst within the analytic process. Here, related topics are the handling of transference and the ethics of psychoanalysis. The following themes emerge: 'What is the desire of an analyst?' and 'What does an analyst want in the treatment?' An indication of the importance of this second reading is that Lacan first alluded to the desire of the analyst in his article on *The Direction of the Treatment and the Principles of its Power* of 1958.[4]

The above two readings of the desire of the analyst — firstly, as that which stems from the training analysis and secondly, as the driving force of an analysis on the part of the analyst — are in at least one distinctive way related to one another. The desire of the analyst during psychoanalysis is supposed to be the result of an analysis that proved to be didactic. Yet, how does this desire of the analyst relate to the demand of an analysand to become an analyst? In *The Direction of the Treatment*, Lacan dealt with this issue in a remark addressed at the so-called 'training analysts':

> Whoever cannot carry his training analyses to the turning-point at which it is proved with fear and trembling that all the demands that have been articulated in the analysis, and more than any other the original demand to become an analyst, which is now about to be fulfilled, were merely transferences intended to maintain in place a desire that was unstable or dubious in its problematic — such a person knows nothing of what must be obtained from the subject if he is to be able to assume the direction of an analysis, or merely offer an accurate interpretation of it.[5]

What Lacan stressed here, is that a 'training analysis' can only be 'successful' if the analysis shows that, beyond the demands of the analysand (which Lacan links to the transference), there is also a desire at work. In order to certify the passage from the position of analysand to the position of analyst, Lacan eventually installed the procedure of the pass as a means to verify the effects of a training analysis on the level of the trainee's desire.

II. The Desire of the Analyst as Desire of the Other

An exploration of the desire of the analyst first of all brings us to Freud's desire.[6] When we consider Freud as the founder of psychoanalysis, and hence as the 'first' analyst, then his desire can be regarded as the cause of psychoanalysis.

From the very start, Lacan's teachings were dominated by a return to Freud. This return was governed by an explicit interrogation of the nature of psychoanalysis, which pervaded his teachings during the 1950's, prior to the installation of the notion of the desire of the analyst. It involved both the origin of psychoanalysis (the discovery of the field of the unconscious) and its transmission as a theory and praxis, including the training of an analyst.

In *The Direction of the Treatment*, Lacan praised Freud as:

> A man of desire, of a desire that he followed against his will into ways in which he saw himself reflected

> in feeling, domination and knowledge, but of which he, unaided, succeeded in unveiling, like an initiate at the defunct mysteries, the unparalleled signifier . . .[7]

This citation illustrates the centrality of the notion of desire for Lacan in his attempt to grasp what was driving Freud.

During the 1950's, Lacan's references to Freud's original desire can be interpreted in terms of the formula — derived from Kojève's reading of Hegel — 'the desire of a human being is the desire of the Other.'[8] This formula has several meanings. In reference to Hegel, it signifies that human desire is essentially directed at the desire of an other. One's desire is marked by the desire of an other in the sense that one always desires what is desired by an other, or that no human being desires what no other human being desires. In Hegelian terms, this also comprises that human desire is fundamentally a desire for recognition. Applying the Hegelian formula to the unconscious as Other scene, human desire is then defined as being determined by the desire that unfolds itself on the Other scene. Inasmuch as Lacan's references to Freud's desire can be apprehended through this Hegelian formula, it appears that he is interested in the desire of Freud in its status of desire of the Other.[9] Viewed from this angle, the meaning of the return to Freud, which Lacan reformulated as a return to the meaning of Freud, can be further comprehended as including a decipherment of Freud's desire.[10]

According to Lacan, Freud's desire is a particular desire to know about unconscious desire.[11] In more general terms, Freud's desire entails a specific subjective position with regard to truth. His desire is a desire to know the truth (about unconscious desire). This position was evoked by Lacan in his article *The Freudian Thing*.

> And the meaning of what Freud said may be conveyed to anyone because addressed as it is to all, it concerns each individual: to make this clear, one has only to remember that Freud's discovery puts truth into question, and there is no one who is not personally concerned by the truth.[12]

During the 1960's, Lacan became more critical about Freud's quest for knowledge. This critique was refined as a critique of Freud's conception of the relation between knowledge and truth, including Freud's stance with regard to science, and coincided with a change in Lacan's own attitude towards knowledge and truth.[13] Yet the object of Freud's desire to know, namely the realm of desire itself, remained paramount in Lacan's elaborations of the function of the desire of the analyst. For Lacan, the desire of the analyst is not a desire to know, but nevertheless a desire which has desire itself as its object.

Lacan's concept of the desire of the analyst is thus at once reminiscent of and running counter to Freud. In the very act of turning to Freud's desire in order to explore unconscious desire, Lacan situated the nature of psychoanalysis within the domain of desire for desire, stipulating that desire is always related to the Other (the unconscious as Other scene). But in criticizing Freud's stance with regard to knowledge and truth, he also disqualified Freud's desire to know the truth, suggesting that the psychoanalyst is only concerned with desire for desire and not with desire for truth through knowledge. The desire of the analyst has only one object, namely desire itself. Therefore, Lacan's reference to Freud's search for desire (Freud's desire to investigate desire) constitutes the only Freudian source of the 'desire of the analyst.'[14]

A second 'significant Other' in Lacan's conceptualization of the desire of the analyst is Sándor Ferenczi. Lacan referred to him on several occasions, especially with regard to his views on the training of the analyst. In his 1955 article *Variantes de la cure-type*, in which he argued against the centrality of the ego in analysis and for the foundation of analysis on the power of speech, Lacan paused to examine what should become of the ego of the analyst during analysis. He referred to Ferenczi as the analyst of the first generation who most emphatically examined what is required from the analyst at the end of the treatment.[15] Ferenczi had underscored the necessity of a training analysis as the second fundamental rule of psychoanalysis, the first one being the rule of free association. In *Variantes de la cure-type*, Lacan discussed Ferenczi's 1928 article on the elasticity of psychoanalytic technique, in which he had talked about a 'special hygiene' for the analyst.[16] Lacan extracted from Ferenczi's suggestions that the analyst's ego has to erase itself in favour of the subject-point (*point-sujet*) of interpretation.[17] The end of the ego in analysis is marked by 'the subjectivation of its death.'[18] This implicates that at the end of the training analysis the analysand must have stripped the narcissistic image of his ego of the various forms of desire by which that image had been constituted. The narcissistic image of the ego should be reduced to the sole figure which sustains it behind the masks of those desires and which is nothing less than the absolute master, death.[19] Lacan linked this particular condition of the analysand's ego at the end of his or her training analysis to how an analyst is required to handle knowledge during analysis. The analyst needs to suspend all objective knowledge that is, all knowledge about the object of desire. Furthermore, Lacan explained the figure of death with the idea that the analyst, as every human being, knows nothing about death except that every human being is destined to it (Heidegger's notion of *Sein zum Tode*). This knowledge of the imminence of death is the only knowledge the analyst can maintain.

Henceforth, Lacan translated Ferenczi's ideas about a special hygiene for the analyst into the formulation that the analyst's ego needs to be replaced by the analyst's 'being for death.' In *Seminar VII, The Ethics of Psychoanalysis*, this being for death shifted to the notion of living 'between two deaths' (*entre deux morts*).[20] This expression, which refers to the zone between the symbolic death (effected by the signifier) and the real death, was presented by Lacan to describe the position of the eponymous heroine (who is condemned to the sealed chamber of the tomb) in Sophocles' *Antigone*.

> Her punishment will consist in her being shut up or suspended in the zone between life and death. Although she is not yet dead, she is eliminated from the world of the living . . . From Antigone's point of view life can only be approached, can only be lived or thought about, from the place of that limit where her life is already lost, where she is already on the other side.[21]

Lacan developed the intricate relation between desire and death more fully in his *Seminar VIII, Transference*, in the course of an extensive commentary on Plato's *Symposium*.[22] In his reading of Plato, Lacan put forward a third significant source for the desire of the analyst: the nature and the function of the desire of Socrates. Lacan's glosses on the position of Socrates in Plato's *Symposium* provide two indications for the position of the analyst: the atopic nature of desire and the desire for/of death.

In the lesson entitled 'The atopia of Eros,' Lacan talked about the vigour with which Socrates defends the idea of immortality, and he used this as an entry to question the very foundation of Socrates' desire. Lacan firstly emphasized the ἀτοπία (atopia) of Socrates' desire: it is unclassifiable, it cannot be situated (*est nulle part*). Secondly, he suggested that this atopia of desire coincides with a topical purity, in the sense that it flags the pure space 'between two deaths' and the empty place of desire. Put differently, Socrates' desire is purified to such an extent that all that is left of it is its place. Yet Lacan added that it is not sufficient, in the case of the analyst, to speak about a purification of his/her unconscious; a more suitable phrase would be 'What is left of the fantasy of the analyst?'[23] This provides a first indication of what Lacan called the 'coordinates' an analyst must attain in order to occupy the position of an analyst. These are defined as: 'being open to the desire of the patient so that the patient's desire can be realized as desire of the Other.'[24] This means that the analyst has to refrain from filling in his or her position for the analysand, in order to create the possibility that the analysand realizes his/her own desire, with the restriction that this desire is inevitably marked by the Other.

A further elaboration of the link between Socrates' desire and the desire of the analyst during the treatment can be found in the lesson entitled 'Critique of countertransference.'[25] Here, Lacan considered the 'stoic ideal' in analysis, which prescribes that the analyst has to remain indifferent (apathetic) to imaginary seductions. Examining the basis of this apathy, Lacan claimed that the analyst must be possessed by a desire which is 'stronger' than the desires involved in the imaginary seductions, implying that through training analysis a mutation should take place in the economy of the analysand's desire. Lacan related this 'stronger' desire to Socrates' claim that the desire for death is really the strongest desire, thus indicating how the reorganisation of the desire in the analyst must be conceived.

Here, Lacan also developed a comparison between analysis and the game of bridge.[26] The analyst functions as the player in the game of bridge, whereas the analyst's ego is the dummy, i.e. the associate of the player. The dummy does not enter the play, nor can s/he influence the game. The analyst only brings the dummy to his/her aid, in order to introduce the partner of the analysand — the analysand's ego — as the fourth player. As such, Lacan specified that in analysis the analyst does not play with death (*la mort*), but with a dummy (*un mort*). This phrase can be interpreted in the light of what becomes of the analysand's ego at the end of training analysis, and hence of how the analyst's ego functions in analysis: 'there must be something capable of playing dead (*jouer le mort*) in this small other [ego] which is in him [the analyst].'[27]

Thus far, we have dealt with three significant Others in Lacan's development of the desire of the analyst during psychoanalytic treatment. However, the desire of the Other is also relevant for another reason, internal to the process of analysis. Until the end of the 1950's, Lacan not only identified the position of the analyst with the position of the Other, but he formulated the aim of analysis as the realization of the desire of the analysand as desire of the Other. This underscores the importance of the position of the analyst in this process, as well as the essential condition of desire as such. Desire always includes the Other.

III. The Desire of the Analyst as an Alternative for the Demand to Be an Analyst

When Lacan talked about analytic treatment, it was always with reference to the training of the analyst and thus to training analysis. However, strictly speaking, for Lacan there is only one kind of analysis, the didactic character of which can only be established afterwards, i.e. after the analysis is concluded.

The major consequence of this principle is that trainees (those who enter analysis with the demand to become an analyst) are not treated differently from common analysands (who enter analysis with a demand to be freed of a particular symptom). Lacan considered the demand to be an analyst, or rather the object of this demand (to be an analyst), as the prime symptom of the trainee.[28] This means that a trainee can enter analysis with the demand to become an analyst, and, in the event, end his/her analysis with a desire that does not imply functioning as an analyst.

At first glance, this statement generates a paradox. On the one hand, those people who engage in a training analysis as a precondition of becoming an analyst can end up with a different desire, and thus no longer want to become an analyst. On the other hand, someone can enter analysis with a 'regular' symptom, ending the treatment with the desire to function as an analyst. Yet the fact that a so-called trainee can end his/her analysis with another desire than the one to become an analyst, is only a paradox within an 'orthodox' view of psychoanalytic training, in which there is a strict difference between a regular analysis and a training analysis from the very start. A training analysis in this sense is formalised in terms of a fixed number of sessions per week, a fixed term, a fixed training analyst, etc. Lacan's conception of the training of the analyst does not start with an a priori differentiation — 'Is this a training analysis or not?' Not the entry, but the conclusion of the treatment (and eventually the procedure of the pass) is decisive for whether an analysand will function as an analyst or not.[29] Therefore, the issue of what should become of the symptom of wanting to be an analyst shifts to queries about the end of the treatment: 'What does analysis aim at?' and 'How should the end of a training analysis be articulated and formalised?' Lacan's concept of the desire of the analyst can be regarded as his alternative for the demand to become an analyst.

Elaborating this interpretation of the desire of the analyst — as the end of the training analysis — requires an investigation of the function of desire in Lacan's theory. Lacan considered desire as the fundamental driving force of the human subject, and from the very start of his teachings it occupied a special place in his theory. Until the late 1950's, Lacan was interested foremost in the vicissitudes of the desire of the analysand. Indeed, his seminar on *Desire and its Interpretations* (1958-59) was to a large extent devoted to the desire of the analysand.[30] The decisive role of desire on the part of the analyst was only established from the late 1950's onwards. Furthermore, until the mid 1950's, Lacan viewed desire primarily as a desire for recognition, bound up with the dialectics of intersubjectivity as laid down in the L schema, first presented in *Seminar II* (1954-55).[31]

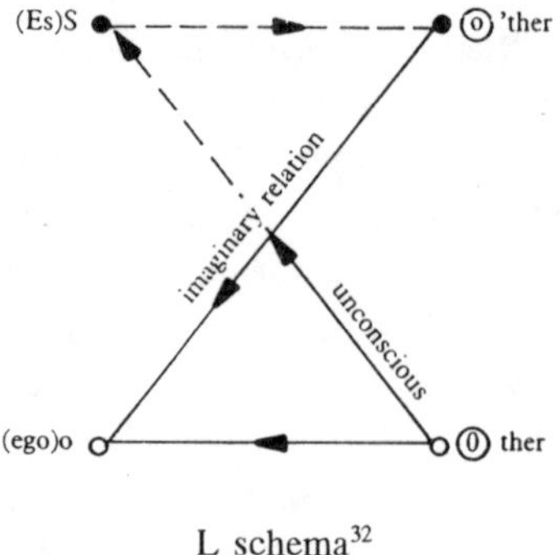

L schema[32]

The symbolic relation between the subject (S) and the Other (O) is mediated and obstructed by the imaginary relation between the ego (o) and its specular other (o′). Lacan called this the 'symmetrical world of the *egos* and of the homogenous others.'[33] The imaginary (o-o′ in the schema) gains its (false) reality from the symbolic order or the 'wall of language.'[34] The Other, where speech originates, is presented here as an authentic Other or a true subject.[35] Lacan defined the role of language as follows:

> [L]anguage is as much there to found us in the Other as to drastically prevent us from understanding him. And that is indeed what is at stake in the analytic experience. The subject doesn't know what he is saying, and for the best of reasons, because he doesn't know what he is.[36]

At this stage, analysis is a dialectical, intersubjective experience, in which desire is implied insofar as the field of the subject is the field of desire.[37] In analysis, the subject is constituted through a discourse to which the presence of the analyst, in the position of Other, brings the dimension of dialogue.[38] To be capable of sustaining the analytic dialogue (*porter la parole*) from the position of Other is what the training analysis is directed at.[39] This depends on what Lacan described as a decline of the trainee's imaginary world, in favour of a symbolic realization of the subject. The final relation of the subject of the patient to a genuine Other, who gives the answer one does not expect, defines the end of analysis. The conclusion of the treatment, as contained in Freud's phrase *Wo Es war, soll Ich werden*, is interpreted as 'the subject taking the place of the ego in speech.'[40]

In his 1957 article *The Agency of the Letter in the Unconscious or Reason since Freud*, Lacan distinguished metaphor from metonymy as the two sides of the signifier, positioning desire on the side of metonymy. Desire is defined as a metonymical process, more precisely as the metonymy of the lack of being (*manque à être*). The relation between two signifiers installs this lack of being, which in turn installs a human being's desire as always a desire for something else (the metonymical dimension). As a corollary to this movement, the divided subject ($) emerges.[41] This shift from the subject as constituted through discourse to the divided subject, and from the desire for recognition to the metonymy of desire, has an impact on how desire is treated in the course of analysis. Desire (or rather the desiring subject) no longer needs to be recognized, the major aim of analysis being the decipherment and thus the interpretation of desire. This is rendered all the more difficult by the 'incompatibility of desire and speech.'[42] Speech can never fully grasp, nor articulate desire, if only because desire as such is not said, but merely found in the gap opened by the effect of the signifier.[43] This emphasis on the interpretation of desire is present in the article *The Direction of the Treatment*. There, Lacan stated that the analysand should be brought to the avowal of his/her desire, which bears witness to his/her assimilation of symbolic castration. This means that the subject must acknowledge that his/her desire is subordinate to the law of the symbolic.

Whilst adducing the split subject, the lack of being, the importance of desire in the direction of the treatment, and the interpretation of desire, Lacan for the first time alluded to the nature of the desire of the analyst: 'Let us question what part it [the importance of the "literary" element in analysis] should play for the analyst (in the analyst's being), as far as his own desire is concerned.'[44]

In *The Ethics of Psychoanalysis* (1959-60), Lacan specified that the desire of the analyst is an *experienced* desire.[45] The experience alluded to is the encounter, at the end of the training analysis, with the problematic of desire: 'To have carried an analysis through to its end is no more nor less than to have encountered that limit in which the problematic of desire is raised.'[46] The 'limit' referred to is the acknowledgement, by the analysand, that the analyst not only lacks the 'Sovereign Good' asked of him/her but, moreover, that there is no such thing which can provide timeless 'happiness.' How does this relate to the problem of desire? In the final paragraphs of *The Direction of the Treatment*, Lacan declared that Freud had shown that life has only one meaning, namely 'that in which desire is borne by death' (*porté par la mort*).[47] In the seminar on ethics he underscored that 'the function of desire must remain in a fundamental relationship to death.'[48] Therefore, the problem of desire at the end of the training analysis embraces the relation between desire and death. The end of the training analysis is the acceptance of the human condition, the fundamental helplessness of any human being in relation to death, especially his/her own death.[49] Helplessness implies that there is no help to be expected from anybody at this level. 'At the end of a training analysis the subject should reach and should know the domain and the level of the experience of absolute disarray.'[50] It is this to which Lacan referred when he typified the desire of the analyst as an experienced desire.

In the penultimate lesson of the seminar on ethics, Lacan announced his following seminar, on *Transference*, as 'outlining the ends and the means of analysis in relation to each other.'[51] This seminar proved indeed crucial for the definition of the desire of the analyst. Lacan started off by claiming that the conclusion of a training analysis had hardly been elaborated nor articulated within the psychoanalytic field. What has to be established in order for someone to adopt the analyst's position? Gradually refining this question, Lacan indicated that the answer resides in a movement away from the topic of transference and the so-called countertransference. Of importance here is that Lacan conceived the desire of the analyst as different from that of the analysand. Whereas the analysand's desire is the desire of the Other (analyst), the analyst's situation is different. The distinction emerges in Lacan's use of terms such as 'purified' and 'changed economy' in order to qualify the desire of the analyst. The desire of the analyst differs from that of the analysand inasmuch as the former rests on a mutation of the economy of desire itself, which is produced within the training analysis.[52] Moreover, the necessity of desire on the side of the analyst is borne out in Lacan's statement that desire is a remedy against anxiety. To ascertain that the analyst does not initiate anxiety on the part of the analysand in the treatment, s/he ought to have 'some' desire at his/her disposal.[53]

In *Transference* Lacan also examined the role of the fundamental fantasy at the end of analysis: 'What is left of the (fundamental) fantasy of the analyst at the end of the training analysis?'[54] This conjures up the analyst's relation to the partial object — identified as 'petit *a*,' or *agalma* in reference to the *Symposium* — which, in turn, leads to his/her stance vis-a-vis the drive.[55]

Desire, the fundamental fantasy, the object *a* and the drive became more differentiated in Lacan's works from 1964 onwards. The disjunction of desire, which regards the Other, and the drive, pertaining to the Thing (*Ding*), is for example explicit in Lacan's 1964 article *On Freud's 'Trieb' and the Psychoanalyst's Desire*.[56]

> Desire is desire for desire, the Other's desire, as I have said, in other words, subjected to the Law . . . for desire comes from the Other, and jouissance is on the side of the Thing.[57]

In this article, the aim of psychoanalysis is also linked to the register of the desire of the analyst.[58] This is equally present in the seminar on *The Four Fundamental Concepts of Psychoanalysis*, which Lacan was giving at the time.[59]

> The training of the psycho-analyst requires that he should know, in the process through which he guides his patient, what it is around which the movement turns. *He* must know, to him must be transmitted, through actual experience, what it is all *about*. This pivotal point is what I designate — in a way, which, I think, will seem to you sufficiently justified, but which, I hope, as we progress, will appear more and more clear to you, more and more necessary — it is what I designate under the term *the desire of the psycho-analyst*.[60]

'What is left of the analyst's fantasy?' is answered in this seminar through the notion of the 'traversing' (*traversée*) of the fundamental fantasy.

In order to elucidate the meaning of this 'traversing' of the fantasy, we must first examine what is meant by 'fundamental fantasy' and what place it is granted in the treatment. According to Lacan, the fundamental fantasy (and not the object) functions as the support of desire. This fantasy takes the form of a scenario which governs the subject in his/her relation to the object *a*. Hence, the fantasy serves both the function of supporting desire and of sustaining the subject at the level of his/her vanishing desire.[61]

> The subject sustains himself as desiring in relation to an ever more complex signifying ensemble. This is apparent enough in the form of the scenario it assumes, in which the subject, more or less recognizable, is somewhere, split, divided, generally double, in his relation to the object, which usually does not show its true face either.[62]

But the fundamental fantasy also expresses the subject's particular mode of jouissance. Hence, the fantasy can be considered as having at least two sides. The first side is the side of the subject, which is also the side of speech and of (unconscious) desire. The second side is the side of the object *a*, which is also the side of jouissance, leading to the experience of the drive.

The analytic process aims at the construction of this fundamental fantasy, i.e. the mapping of the subject in relation to the object *a*. Lacan also called this the loop of the subject $\$$ to *a*. This loop is conceptualized by means of the operations of alienation and separation and it should be run through several times in the course of an analysis, until the point where 'the experience of the fundamental fantasy becomes the drive.'[63] It is at this moment of the separation or the destitution of the subject, that the 'traversing' of the fantasy takes place. Here, the end of analysis comprises both desire and the drive.[64]

What is left of the fantasy of the analyst is the experience of the drive and/or the destitution of the subject. What does this mean? For Lacan, the end of analysis is the return to 'the real lack,' which he described as the 'advent' of the living being and sexual reproduction: 'This lack is real because it relates to something real, namely, that the living being, by being subject to sex, has fallen under the blow of individual death.'[65] In this sense, the end of analysis as 'the destitution of the subject' is a further elaboration of the confrontation with the human condition, the loss of immortality.

> What, then, does he who has passed through the experience of this opaque relation to the origin, to the drive, become? How can a subject who has traversed the radical fantasy experience the drive? This is the beyond of analysis . . . Up to now, it has been approachable only at the level of the analyst, in as much as it would be required of him to have specifically traversed the cycle of the analytic experience in its totality.[66]

In order to evaluate the analytic experience and the outcome of the training analysis, Lacan finally invented the procedure of the pass.[67] Basic to this procedure is that the analysand testifies to the end of his or her analysis. As a means of controlling the passage from analysand to analyst, it amounts to a formalisation of the end of a training analyis.[68]

In 1969, Lacan installed the discourse of the analyst — one of four social bonds founded in language, each of which is determined by and named after its 'dominant,' i.e. the agent of the discourse — as a further formalisation of the analytic process.

$$\frac{a}{S_2} \rightarrow \frac{\$}{S_1}$$

The discourse of the analyst[69]

This discourse of the analyst must not be confused with the analyzing discourse that is, with what is actually said by the analysand in analysis.[70] The position of the analyst is delineated in the discourse of the analyst as a semblance of a. The a refers both to the object as cause of the desire of the analysand ($\$$), and to the *plus-de-jouir*, the surplus jouissance (of the analysand). In terms of the training analysis, this amounts to the fact that the analyst has to be able to take this position of a semblance of a.

In the discourse of the analyst, knowledge (S_2) functions on the place of truth. This does not mean that the analyst uses his/her knowledge as truth, but that knowledge functions in the same way as truth, namely as half-saying (*mi-dire*).[71] This type of knowledge is also derived from the training analysis. Therefore, the outcome of the training analysis (and thus the desire of the analyst) should not only imply a change in the subject's relation to desire and jouissance (the construction of the fantasy and the destitution of the subject); the position of the analyst also requires a special relation to truth and knowledge.[72] How can this be comprehended?

In the mid 1950's, Lacan indicated that the analyst can have no preference for any specific knowledge. In his 1967 *Proposition*, he further contended that although the analyst knows nothing of the knowledge the patient supposes s/he possesses, this in no way authorizes her/him to be satisfied with the fact that s/he knows nothing.

In *Seminar XVII*, Lacan further specified that the way knowledge functions in the discourse of the analyst is comparable to how a myth functions, i.e. as a statement about the impossible.[73]

IV. From Subjective to Enigmatic Desire

In *The Direction of the Treatment*, Lacan wrote: 'An ethic is yet to be formulated that integrates the Freudian conquests in the realm of desire: one that would place in the forefront the question of the analyst's desire.'[74] Yet, what is the function of the psychoanalyst, what does s/he want in the treatment? Now that the desire of the analyst as the possible outcome of (training) analysis has, to some extent, been clarified, these questions can be answered more thoroughly.

Again, a certain evolution in Lacan's answer is evident. This evolution can be characterized as a shift from the subjective position of the analyst to the position of the analyst as object *a*, cause of desire and *plus-de-jouir* (surplus jouissance) of the analysand.[75] The latter no longer refers to the subjectivity of the analyst or, more generally speaking, to the analyst as a person. On the contrary, the function of the analyst's desire essentially requires a desubjectivation of the analyst, in favour of his/her position as object. This can undoubtedly be termed the true Lacanian position of the analyst.[76] Lacan's installation of this position dates from 1964 and it is a truly Lacanian stance because it goes beyond Freud's indications concerning the place of the analyst in the treatment.[77] More particularly, it goes beyond the dynamics of transference and countertransference. In order to understand the difference between the analyst as a subject and the analyst as a pure function (of object), we must therefore also take Lacan's view on (counter)transference into account.

The subjectivity of the analyst is present in Lacan's glosses on the the analyst as a person in the analytic process: the necessary engagement of the analyst in the transference.[78] This engagement is intricately related to the notion of countertransference as it was conceived and handled in the psychoanalytic circles of the 1950's. Lacan spent a considerable amount of time theorizing countertransference as something beyond the subjective dimension of the analyst in the analytic process. Of special interest in this regard are Lacan's article on *The Direction of the Treatment*, his seminar on *Transference* and the 1964 seminar on the *Four Fundamental Concepts of Psychoanalysis*.

Lacan began his seminar on transference with the statement that the notion of intersubjectivity is not sufficient to deal with transference.[79] Transference is no longer comprehended as the relation of one subject (analysand) to another subject (analyst), but as the relation of the subject of the analysand to the other as a loved object. Desire is the key concept of transference.[80] When discussing the notion of countertransference, Lacan explicitly distanced himself from what was generally accepted: firstly, that countertransference is an imperfection of the purification of the analyst's unconscious in his/her relation to the analysand, and secondly, that countertransference concerns the sentiments the analyst experiences in the treatment, as determined by the analyst's relation to the analysand. For Lacan, countertransference is the unavoidable subjective implication of the analyst in the transference situation.[81] This signifies that the analyst must be truly engaged in the transference situation.[82]

However, Lacan's seminar on transference also embodied another important shift. Apart from the analyst's subjective implication, Lacan indicated that something else should also be in play: a third position, functioning as a kind of a partner of the analyst. This two-sidedness was further elaborated in *The Four Fundamental Concepts of Psychoanalysis*, where the object *a* as cause of desire was inserted into the movement of transference. Whereas the transference operates, according to Lacan, in the direction of identification, the desire of the analyst aims at its exact opposite, namely the fundamental lack and the 'insatisfaction' of desire.

> [T]he operation and manipulation of the transference are to be regulated in a way that maintains a distance between the point at which the subject sees himself as lovable [Identification] — and that other point where the subject sees himself caused as a lack by *a*, and where *a* fills the gap constituted by the inaugural division of the subject [$]. [83]

The analytic process is not directed towards a *re*stitution of the subject, completing it by means of an identification, but towards a *de*stitution of the subject, in the form of the patient's acceptance of the fundamental lack.

To grasp fully the differences between Lacan's position in 1964 and what he developed in *Transference*, we should take into account his thesis in *On Freud's 'Trieb' and the Psychoanalyst's Desire*. Two ideas are involved. Firstly, there is the desire of the analyst as that which falls outside of the dynamics of transference. Secondly, there is the disentanglement of the desire and the drive, or the disjunction of the subject's relation to desire (transference) and the subject's relation to the drive. From this moment on, the latter is paramount in the direction of the treatment.[84] Both elements pave the way for a positioning of the analyst as object *a* in the treatment. The desire of the analyst is to install and maintain this position of object and cause of desire:

> [I]f transference is what separates demand from the drive, the analyst's desire is that which brings it back. And in this way, it isolates the *a*, places it at the greatest possible distance from the I that he, the analyst, is called upon by the subject to embody [in the transference]. It is from this idealization that the analyst has to fall in order to be the support of the separating *a* . . .[85]

This separation is linked to the desire of the analyst:

> [T]ransference operates in the direction of bringing demand back to identification. It is in as much as the analyst's desire, which remains an *x*, tends in a direction that is the exact opposite of identification, that the crossing of the plane of identification is possible, through the mediation of the separation of the subject in experience. The experience of the subject is thus brought back to the plane at which, from the reality of the unconscious, the drive may be made present.[86]

Thus, the desire of the analyst as enigma, *x*, opens the door to the experience of the drive, which is beyond the fundamental fantasy and which is related to the desubjectivation of the analysand or the operation of separation. This conceptualization is in keeping with Lacan's articulation of the desire and the fantasy in relation to the drive and jouissance. Desire is both subjected to and instituted by the Law (of the symbolic), whereas the drive, as the beyond of desire, is not tied to any prohibition. The drive always obtains jouissance.[87] The object *a* is situated on the side of the drive and of jouissance.

The disjunction of desire and drive sheds a clear light on the nature of the desire of the analyst as a desire which, firstly, directs the treatment away from identification, and secondly, conducts it towards the traversing of the fantasy and the laying bare of jouissance. In order to avoid identification, the analyst's desire should remain enigmatic in nature. This means that what the analyst wants is devoid of any subjective or particular implication.

In contrast to the particularity of the analyst as a subject, the desire of the analyst as a function is taken in its universality.[88] In his 1967 *Proposition*, Lacan described this function in mathematical terms as the '*x*' of an equation.[89] The desire of the analyst can only operate when it comes in the position of the '*x*'.

How can we link this statement to the position of the analyst as object *a*? In our opinion, to speak of the position of the analyst in the treatment as object *a*, i.e. as cause of the desire of the analysand, refers to the analyst's position in the transference relation. In addition, the desire of the analyst as the enigmatic motor of the treatment (the '*x*') refers to the desire which has as its object psychoanalysis itself. The object of the desire of the analyst in the treatment is the direction of the treatment towards its end, the limit where the analysand's being as *désêtre* — the destituted subject — is delivered. Thus, what the analyst desires, is psychoanalysis.

How can we relate this to Lacan's formalisation of the discourse of the analyst? In our opinion, the discourse of the analyst is analogous to the desire of the analyst. The installation of the discourse of the analyst is not a function of subjective desire (as was the case with Freud). The introduction of the psychoanalytic setting, i.e. analysis as a 'social bond,' *is* the desire of the analyst.

V. Conclusion

In retrospect, we can highlight three major themes, including one decisive turn, in our itinerary from Freud's desire *as an* analyst to Lacan's desire *of the* analyst.

The first theme is germane to Freud's desire as the original subjective implication in the discovery of psychoanalysis. Lacan commenced his teachings by positioning Freud as the original explorer of unconscious desire, thereby putting him in the position of Ideal Analyst. However, Lacan's subsequent inquiry into the post-Freudian development of psychoanalysis, in which he especially criticized the impact of identification on the direction of the treatment, effected an important change. Lacan no longer stressed Freud's desire as original desire, but underscored Freud's desire to reveal an unconscious desire in the patient as the essential concern of psychoanalysis. According to Lacan, the object of psychoanalysis is desire. Parallel to this movement, he emphasized the importance of formalising the end of the treatment as the avowal of unconscious desire. Within this line of thought, the desire of the analyst, first mentioned in the late 1950's, detaches itself from Freud's desire. Exemplary of Lacan's changed position with regard to Freud (who is no longer considered as Ideal) is his statement in the 1964 seminar, *The Four Fundamental Concepts of Psychoanalysis*, that something in the desire of Freud was never analyzed:

> So hysteria places us, I would say, on the track of some kind of original sin in analysis. There has to be one. The truth is perhaps simply one thing, namely,

> the desire of Freud himself, the fact that something, in Freud, was never analyzed.[90]

The year 1964 marked a major turn in Lacan's conceptualization of psychoanalytic praxis, which is the second theme of our itinerary. Here, the desire of the analyst is conceived as a force operating beyond the transference relation, which conducts the treatment towards a destitution of the subject and the experience of the drive. Lacanian psychoanalysis is directed at laying bare the patient's jouissance, beyond his/her avowal of unconscious desire. The analyst's desire must remain enigmatic to the analysand in order to cross the plane of identification and achieve 'absolute difference.' Nowadays, when Lacanian analysts refer to the desire of the analyst, it is usually in reference to this typification of the desire of the analyst, as an enigma or '*x*'.

The third and final theme epitomizes the articulation of the desire of the analyst and the discourse of the analyst, which Lacan introduced in 1969. Our interpretation of this articulation is that the desire of the analyst — operating as an '*x*' for the analysand — is reduced to the introduction of psychoanalysis, i.e. the discourse of the analyst as such. The only thing an analyst 'desires' is to create the conditions for analysis to 'happen.' In this respect, Lacan eventually returned to Freud's desire as the very condition for psychoanalysis, for this view on the desire of the analyst strongly resembles Freud's opinion regarding the position of the analyst at the beginning of treatment: the analyst has to take on each analysis as if it were his/her first one. And indeed, for every single case, the analyst has to make analysis happen anew, which constitutes the major challenge for each analyst: an endless repetition of the 'original sin.'

Notes

1. See: J. Lacan, Proposition of 9 October 1967 on the Psychoanalyst of the School (trans. R. Grigg), *Analysis*, 1995, no. 6, pp. 1-13.

2. See: J. Lacan, Founding Act (June 21, 1964) in J. Lacan, *Television/A Challenge to the Psychoanalytic Establishment* (1973) (trans. D. Hollier, R. Krauss & A. Michelson), Edited by J. Copjec, New York NY-London, W.W. Norton & Company,

1990, pp. 97-106. Three months later the EFP was renamed the *Ecole freudienne de Paris*.

3. *Ibid.*, p. 98.

4. See: J. Lacan, The Direction of the Treatment and the Principles of its Power (1958), *Ecrits: A Selection* (trans. A. Sheridan), London, Tavistock, 1977, p. 276.

5. *Ibid.*, p. 271.

6. For an extensive interpretation of this issue from a Lacanian point of view, see: S. Cottet, *Freud et le désir du psychanalyste* (1982), Paris, du Seuil, 1996.

7. J. Lacan, The Direction of the Treatment and the Principles of its Power, *o.c.*, p. 277.

8. J. Lacan, *The Seminar. Book I: Freud's Papers on Technique* (1953-54) (trans. with notes J. Forrester), Edited by J.-A. Miller, New York NY-London, W.W. Norton & Company, 1988, pp. 146-147. Here, Lacan still talked about a 'desire of the other' (small o), the Other (capital O) not appearing in the formula until *Seminar II*.

9. One could even go a step further and state that the condition for desire as such — including Freud's desire — is the reference to an Other. Forrester argues that: 'To establish the position of analyst, [Freud] made Breuer the founder of psychoanalysis, the first analyst.' The reference to the Other also evokes transference as the driving force of psychoanalysis, in its praxis as well as in its development. See: J. Forrester, *The Seductions of Psychoanalysis: Freud, Lacan and Derrida*, Cambridge, Cambridge University Press, 1990, p. 236.

10. See, for instance: J. Lacan, The Freudian Thing, or the Meaning of the Return to Freud in Psychoanalysis (1955), *Ecrits: A Selection*, *o.c.*, p. 117: 'The meaning of a return to Freud is a return to the meaning of Freud.'

11. See, for instance, Lacan's comments on Freud's dream of Irma's injection (from *The Interpretation of Dreams*) in: J. Lacan, *The Seminar. Book II: The Ego in Freud's Theory and in the Technique of Psychoanalysis* (1954-55) (trans. S. Tomaselli, notes J. Forrester), Edited by J.-A. Miller, Cambridge, Cambridge University Press, 1988, especially p. 151.

12. J. Lacan, The Freudian Thing, or the Meaning of the Return to Freud in Psychoanalysis, *o.c.*, pp. 117-118.

13. In his seminar *L'envers de la psychanalyse* (1969-70), for instance, Lacan questioned Freud's use of myths (i.e. the Oedipus myth and the myth of the primal father) in connection with the relation between knowledge and truth. Lacan's alternative was the formalisation of the discourse of the analyst as counterpart of the discourse of the master. See: J. Lacan, *Le Séminaire, Livre XVII, L'envers de la psychanalyse* (1969-70), texte établi par J.-A. Miller, Paris, du Seuil, 1991, especially pp. 99-115.

14. J. Lacan, *The Four Fundamental Concepts of Psychoanalysis* (1964) (trans. A. Sheridan), Edited by J.-A. Miller, Harmondsworth, Penguin Books, 1979, p. 13: 'I have said that the Freudian field of analytic practice remained dependent on a certain original desire, which always plays an ambiguous, but dominant role in the transmission of psychoanalysis . . . Well! Freud, too, is concerned with desire as an object.'

15. J. Lacan, Variantes de la cure-type (1955), *Ecrits*, Paris, du Seuil, 1966, pp. 339-341.

16. The article in question is: S. Ferenczi, Die Elastizität der psychoanalytischen Technik, *Internationale Zeitschrift für Psychoanalyse*, 1928, XIV, no. 2, pp. 197-209. An English translation of this article is included in: S. Ferenczi, *Final Contributions to the Problems and Methods of Psycho-Analysis* (trans. E. Mosbacher et al.), Edited by M. Balint, London, The Hogarth Press and the Institute of Psycho-Analysis, 1955, pp. 87-101.

17. J. Lacan, Variantes de la cure-type, *o.c.*, p. 341: '*[E]n toutes ces consignes, n'est-ce pas le Moi qui s'efface pour laisser place au point-sujet de l'interprétation. Aussi bien ne prennent-elles vigueur de l'analyse personnelle du psychanalyste, et spécialement de sa fin.*'

18. *Ibid.*, p. 348.

19. *Ibid.*, p. 348.

20. J. Lacan, *The Seminar. Book VII: The Ethics of Psychoanalysis* (1959-60) (trans. with notes D. Porter), Edited by J.-A. Miller, New York NY-London, W.W. Norton & Company, 1992, pp. 270-283.

21. *Ibid.*, p. 280. For an extensive comment on the notion of 'between two deaths,' see: S. Žižek, *The Sublime Object of Ideology*, New York NY-London, Verso, 1989, pp. 131-149.

22. J. Lacan, *Le Séminaire, Livre VIII, Le transfert* (1960-61), texte établi par J.-A. Miller, Paris, du Seuil, 1991, pp. 17-19.

23. *Ibid.*, pp. 125-127.

24. *Ibid.*, p. 128. My translation.

25. *Ibid.*, pp. 215-231, especially pp. 221-222.

26. See also: J. Lacan, The Direction of the Treatment and the Principles of its Power, *o.c.*, pp. 229-230.

27. Citation adopted from an unpublished translation of the seminar on *Transference* by C. Gallagher.

28. J. Lacan, Variantes de la cure-type, *o.c.*, p. 358. See also: J. Forrester, *The Seductions of Psychoanalysis: Freud, Lacan and Derrida*, *o.c.*, pp. 221-242, especially pp. 230-232.

29. From here onwards, the term 'training analysis' should be read as 'an analysis that proved to have training effects.'

30. See: J. Lacan, *Le Séminaire VI, Le désir et son interprétation* (1958-59), unpublished.

31. For a concise comment on the L schema, see: J.-A. Miller, Commentary on the graphs, in J. Lacan, *Ecrits: A Selection*, *o.c.*, pp. 332-333.

32. J. Lacan, *The Seminar. Book III: The Psychoses* (1955-56) (trans. with notes R. Grigg), Edited by J.-A. Miller, New York NY-London, W.W. Norton & Company, 1993, p. 14.

33. J. Lacan, *The Seminar. Book II: The Ego in Freud's Theory and in the Technique of Psychoanalysis*, *o.c*, p. 244.

34. *Ibid.*, p. 244.

35. *Ibid.*, p. 236: 'We must distinguish two *others*, at least two — an other with a capital *O*, and an other with a small *o*, which is the ego. In the function of speech, we are concerned with the *Other*.'

36. *Ibid.*, p. 244.

37. See, for instance: J. Lacan, Intervention on Transference (1951) (trans. J. Rose), in J. Mitchell & J. Rose (Eds.), *Feminine Sexuality: Jacques Lacan and the école freudienne*, London-New York NY, W.W. Norton & Company, 1982, p. 64.

38. *Ibid.*, p. 62.

39. J. Lacan, *The Seminar. Book I: Freud's Papers on Technique, o.c.*, p. 3; J. Lacan, Variantes de la cure-type, *o.c.*, p. 350.

40. J. Lacan, *The Seminar. Book II: The Ego in Freud's Theory and in the Technique of Psychoanalysis*, *o.c.*, p. 246.

41. See, for instance: J. Lacan, The Signification of the Phallus (1958), *Ecrits: A Selection*, *o.c.*, p. 285: 'If *it* speaks in the Other, whether or not the subject hears it with his ear, it is because it is there that the subject, by means of a logic anterior to any awakening of the signified, finds its signifying place. The discovery of what it articulates in that place, that is to say, in the unconscious, enables us to grasp at the price of what splitting (*Spaltung*) it has thus been constituted.'

42. J. Lacan, The Direction of the Treatment and the Principles of its Power, *o.c.*, p. 275.

43. See, for instance: J.-P. Klotz, Il faut prendre le désir à la lettre, in M.-H. Brousse, et al., *Commentaire de 'La direction de la cure et les principes de son pouvoir' de J. Lacan*, Lille, Association La Cause Freudienne, 1993, pp. 48-57. See also: J.P. Muller & W.J. Richardson, *Lacan and Language: A Reader's Guide to Écrits*, Madison CT, International Universities Press, 1982, p. 287.

44. J. Lacan, The Direction of the Treatment and the Principles of its Power, *o.c.*, p. 276.

45. J. Lacan, *The Seminar. Book VII: The Ethics of Psychoanalysis*, *o.c.*, pp. 303-304.

46. *Ibid.*, p. 300.

47. J. Lacan, The Direction of the Treatment and the Principles of its Power, *o.c.*, p. 277.

48. J. Lacan, *The Seminar. Book VII: The Ethics of Psychoanalysis*, *o.c.*, p. 303.

49. *Ibid.*, p. 303. Lacan referred to Freud's notion of *Hilflosigkeit* (helplessness), which he had introduced to describe the condition of the neonate. See for instance: S. Freud, Inhibitions, Symptoms and Anxiety (1926*d*[1925]), *Standard Edition*, XX, pp. 154-155.

50. J. Lacan, *The Seminar. Book VII: The Ethics of Psychoanalysis*, *o.c.*, p. 304.

51. *Ibid.*, p. 302.

52. J. Lacan, *Le Séminaire, Livre VIII, Le transfert, o.c.*, p. 221.

53. *Ibid.*, p. 430.

54. *Ibid.*, p. 127.

55. *Ibid.*, pp. 235-236.

56. J. Lacan, On Freud's 'Trieb' and the Psychoanalyst's Desire (1964) (trans. B. Fink), in R. Feldstein, B. Fink & M. Jaanus (Eds.), *Reading Seminars I and II: Lacan's Return to Freud*, Albany NY, State University of New York Press, 1996, pp. 417-421. See also J.-A. Miller's comment on this article in the same volume (pp. 422-426).

57. *Ibid.*, pp. 418-419.

58. *Ibid.*, p. 419.

59. According to Cottet, this seminar introduced a radical shift in Lacan's thinking about the desire of the analyst. Cottet argues that until 1964, Lacan conceived the desire of the analyst in terms of a 'purified' and a subjective desire, whereas, from 1964 onwards, Lacan no longer considered the analyst as a subject but as object *a*. See S. Cottet, *Freud et le désir du psychanalyste*, *o.c.*, Avant-propos de la seconde édition, pp. i-xii.

60. J. Lacan, *The Four Fundamental Concepts of Psychoanalysis*, *o.c.*, p. 230.

61. *Ibid.*, p. 185. See also: J. Lacan, The Direction of the Treatment and the Principles of its Power, *o.c.*, p. 272.

62. J. Lacan, *The Four Fundamental Concepts of Psychoanalysis, o.c.*, p. 185.

63. *Ibid.*, p. 273.

64. For a clinical elaboration and illustration of this thesis, see: B. Fink, *A Clinical Introduction to Lacanian Psychoanalysis: Theory and Technique*, Cambridge MA-London, Harvard University Press, 1997, pp. 205-217.

65. J. Lacan, *The Four Fundamental Concepts of Psychoanalysis, o.c.*, p. 205.

66. *Ibid.*, pp. 273-274.

67. J. Lacan, Proposition of 9 October 1967 on the Psychoanalyst of the School, *o.c.*, pp. 10-11.

68. From the moment it was introduced, the pass sparked off highly polemical discussions, which only exacerbated after the dissolution of the EFP in 1980. See, for instance: J. Lacan, Sur l'expérience de la passe, *Ornicar?*, 1977, no. 12/13, pp. 117-123; A. Levallois, Eléments de réflexion. Désaccord sur la passe, *Ornicar?*, 1977, no. 12/13, pp. 173-191; J.-A. Miller, Introduction aux paradoxes de la passe, *Ornicar?*, 1977, no. 12/13, pp. 105-112. Interesting sources on the problems of the pass, which played a role in the dissolution of the EFP and the subsequent creation of the ECF, are provided by the two series of *Delenda* (the first series of seven issues appeared between March and July 1980, i.e. after the dissolution of the EFP, and was followed by a second series of seven issues dating from September 1980 till June 1981 — the creation of the ECF). In 1991, the ECF organized a conference on the topic of the pass (*Revue de l'Ecole de la Cause freudienne*, 1991, no. 18), and in 1994 a whole issue of *La Cause freudienne* (the present journal of the ECF-ACF) was dedicated to the topic (no. 27).

69. J. Lacan, *Le Séminaire, Livre XVII, L'envers de la psychanalyse, o.c.*, p. 31.

70. *Ibid.*, p. 35.

71. *Ibid.*, p. 125.

72. *Ibid.*, p. 122; J. Lacan, Proposition of 9 October 1967 on the Psychoanalyst of the School, *o.c.*, p. 5.

73. J. Lacan, *Le Séminaire, Livre XVII, L'envers de la psychanalyse, o.c.*, pp. 124-132 and p. 145.

74. J. Lacan, The Direction of the Treatment and the Principles of its Power, *o.c.*, p. 252.

75. See: S. Cottet, *Freud et le désir du psychanalyste*, *o.c.*, Avant-propos de la seconde édition, pp. i-xii.

76. To distinguish between these two different readings, Dumézil respectively talks about 'le désir de l'analyste' (the desire of the analyst as a subject) and 'le désir d'analyste' (the desire related to the analytic position). Quoted in: Fondation Européenne pour la Psychanalyse (Ed.), *La direction de la cure depuis Lacan*, Paris, Point Hors Ligne, 1994, p. 33.

77. In 1964, Lacan wrote the article *On Freud's 'Trieb' and the Psychoanalyst's Desire* and dedicated his seminar to *The Four Fundamental Concepts of Psychoanalysis*. 1964 was also the year of Lacan's excommunication from the *Société française de psychanalyse*, after which he erected the *Ecole freudienne de Paris*.

78. See: J.P. Muller & W.J. Richardson, *Lacan and Language: A Reader's Guide to Écrits*, *o.c.* p. 264 (comment on *The Direction of the Treatment*).

79. J. Lacan, *Le Séminaire, Livre VIII, Le transfert*, *o.c.*, p. 11.

80. *Ibid.*, p. 66.

81. *Ibid.*, pp. 233-234.

82. *Ibid.*, p. 385 and following.

83. J. Lacan, *The Four Fundamental Concepts of Psychoanalysis*, *o.c.*, p. 270.

84. J.-A. Miller, Commentary on Lacan's text, in R. Feldstein, B. Fink & M. Jaanus (Eds.), *Reading Seminars I and II: Lacan's Return to Freud, o.c.*, p. 422: '[T]he text is nevertheless devoted to the disjunction between the desire and the drive. It emphasizes the fact that they must not be confused as Lacan himself had confused them in "The Signification of the Phallus".'

85. J. Lacan, *The Four Fundamental Concepts of Psychoanalysis*, *o.c.*, p. 273.

86. *Ibid.*, p. 274.

87. J. Lacan, *On Freud's 'Trieb' and the Psychoanalyst's Desire*, *o.c.*, pp. 418-419.

88. Lacan uses the term 'function' in reference to Frege. See, for instance: R. Lévy, La direction de la cure au risque du désir d'analyste, in Fondation Européenne pour la Psychanalyse (Ed.), *La direction de la cure depuis Lacan*, *o.c.*, pp. 31-46, especially pp. 45-46.

89. J. Lacan, *Proposition of 9 October 1967 on the Psychoanalyst of the School*, *o.c.*, p. 7.

90. J. Lacan, *The Four Fundamental Concepts of Psychoanalysis*, *o.c.*, p. 12.

CHAPTER 5

Life and Death in the Glass: A New Look at the Mirror Stage

Dany Nobus

I. Historical Context

Thus it appeared, I say, but was not. It was my antagonist — it was Wilson, who then stood before me in the agonies of his dissolution. His mask and cloak lay, where he had thrown them, upon the floor.[1]

'The discourse one shall find here deserves to be introduced by its circumstances. For it bears their marks.'[2] With these opening sentences of *The Function and Field of Speech and Language in Psychoanalysis*, the written amplification of a keynote address held at a conference in Rome on 26 September 1953, Jacques Lacan drew his readership's attention to a singular tug-of-war within the French psychoanalytic milieu, showing how his sneering Rome discourse had been prompted by specific historical events.[3] Yet, at the same time he unwittingly set an example for all scholars attempting to probe into the fabric of his own, exceedingly abstract theoretical formulations.

Indeed, no matter how much Lacan's Rome discourse may have been sparked off by conflicting personal interests and irreconcilable differences of opinion within the *Société Psychanalytique de Paris* (SPP), Lacan's seminars and writings have always kept track of the *Zeitgeist*. The spirit of the age is for instance clearly detectable in *Seminar XI*, *The Four Fundamental Concepts of Psychoanalysis*, which cannot be disjointed from Lacan's excommunication from the International Psychoanalytic Association (IPA), but it is equally crucial for *Seminar XVII, L'envers de la psychanalyse*, in which Lacan replied to the Paris student revolts of May 1968, as well as for the majority of his other contributions.[4] Furthermore, reconstructing and examining the historical context of Lacan's works is essential in order to understand some of the allusions they contain, and provides an excellent framework to grasp the meaning and the importance of his wording.[5] Such a reading procedure also governed Lacan's own 'return to Freud,' inasmuch as he declared in *Seminar III, The Psychoses*, that 'a text has to be brought to life by what follows and by what precedes.'[6] Lacan refused to read Freud's texts as isolated statements, preferring to revive their original meaning by placing them into their appropriate historical and subjective contexts.[7] In this way, it is possible to understand why Lacan at one point contended that the meaning of his 'return to Freud' was simply a return to the meaning of Freud — a meaning obfuscated by those who failed to see that Freud's works had been written against the backdrop of a particular social-scientific climate and also incorporate a singular subjective desire.[8]

Taking these matters into consideration, it seems only natural to start a discussion of Lacan's seminal paper on *The Mirror Stage* with an analysis of its precipitating historical factors. The first thing that emerges from this vantage point is that the 1949 text on *The Mirror Stage*, first published in *Revue française de Psychanalyse* and subsequently integrated in the *Ecrits*, is the result of a young psychiatrist's failed encounter with the psychoanalytic establishment.[9]

In the Summer of 1936, at the age of thirty-five and still in psychoanalytic training, Lacan attended the fourteenth International Congress of the IPA at Marienbad, presenting a paper entitled *Le stade du miroir* during the second scientific session of 3 August.[10] According to Lacan's own account in *Propos sur la causalité psychique* (1946), his speech was interrupted after ten minutes by Ernest Jones, who apparently felt the need to exhibit his authority as president of the IPA.[11] The following morning, Lacan left the international psychoanalytic arena of Marienbad and travelled to the international Olympic Arena of Berlin in order to capture something of the heroic glory of Goebbels's propaganda machine at the eleventh Olympiad — brushing aside a scornful remark by Ernst Kris that such evasive conduct was unacceptable.[12] This may have been a perfect example of a 'passage à l'acte,' as Lacan himself would define it in the 1960's, insofar as he literally disappeared from the psychoanalytic scene — replacing his mirror stage with another stage whose violent beauty we can still contemplate in the images of Leni Riefenstahl — after having been thwarted in his desire by the highest representative of the institutionalized psychoanalytic law.[13] Lacan did not submit the text of his paper for the conference proceedings, and so it happens that the only remaining trace of his contribution is a title.[14] Indeed, the 1937 Bulletin of the IPA, comprising the proceedings of the Marienbad conference, only mentioned that Dr. J. Lacan from Paris had presented a paper on *The Looking-Glass Phase*.[15] Relying on the title and the context in which it appeared — Lacan was preceded by Lillian Rotter-Kertész who talked about puberty and followed by Edoardo Weiss who spoke on the early diagnosis of psychosis — those who had not attended the congress could have concluded that an unknown Parisian doctor had ostensibly scrutinized the second part of *Alice in Wonderland*.

It was not until thirteen years after the Marienbad débâcle that Lacan devoted a separate new text to his notion of *le stade du miroir*. In an act reminiscent of Prometheus for its bravery in tempting the gods, Lacan rejuvenized his mirror stage and took it to the sixteenth International Congress of the IPA, this time held at Zürich and again presided by the dreaded Ernest Jones.[16] Yet, either Jones was absent when Lacan presented his paper, or Lacan's presentation was simply shorter than the previous one, but he was apparently allowed to say what he had to say and a summary of his report also appeared in the *International Journal of Psycho-Analysis*, under the modified English title of *The Mirror-Stage*.[17]

Between Lacan's first, truncated formulation of the mirror stage — of which nobody has hitherto found a written trace — and his second presentation of it lies a period of thirteen years in which he was not very productive, at least when compared to his output during the 1950's.[18] However, judging by the contents of the 1949 text, the issue of the mirror stage continued to preoccupy Lacan during this thirteen year period. In more than half of the texts Lacan produced between 1936 and 1949, the question as to what is decisive for the installation and maintenance of self-consciousness, which indeed supports the entire conception of the mirror stage, played a prominent part. Therefore, Lacan's 1949 text on the mirror stage should be read as a provisional theoretical terminus rather than a starting point. It was the fruit of a long and difficult gestation period, during which Lacan's reflections on the development of self-consciousness and the psychic agency of the 'me' (*moi*) gradually crystallized into the description of a fundamental (onto)logical experience.[19]

In the course of his ensuing theoretical constructions, Lacan frequently conjured up his mirror stage as a 'generic structure,' a 'paradigm' and a 'first strategic point.'[20] Lacan enjoyed referring to his own works as signposts or beacons for his ongoing elaborations, but there is hardly a personal invention which he cherished so obstinately as the mirror stage. The fact that in 1954, during the seminar on *Freud's Papers on Technique*, Lacan supplemented his original conception with the so-called 'schema of the two mirrors,' further complicating the latter during the 1960's in order to account for what happens during analytic treatment, could instill us with the idea that the mirror stage belongs to Lacanian archaeology, i.e. that it is a construction which was superseded by more adequate, less naive descriptions.[21] Yet, in contrast to a number of his other models — the L schema, the R schema, alienation and separation in the fantasy — the mirror stage has always been viewed by Lacan as a solid piece of theorizing, a paradigm retaining its value to explain human self-consciousness, aggressivity, rivalry, narcissism, jealousy and fascination with images in general.[22] In a sense, this does not come as a surprise when it is appreciated that the 1949 *Mirror Stage* article was not something Lacan had concocted at a moment's notice, but a pearl which he had carefully cultured for some thirteen odd years.

In what follows, I will start with a systematic survey of the main theoretical stakes of Lacan's 1949 paper. Without entering into the details of the 'schema of the two mirrors' in *Seminar I* and in the *Remark on the report by Daniel Lagache* (1960), I will at the same time clarify why Lacan at one stage introduced a more complicated model and to what extent this model added to the ideas contained in the original 1949 paper. Finally, I will discuss some of the practical implications of the mirror stage, opposing Lacan's own use of the concept throughout his works to an interpretation that is more likely to entice educationalists and developmental psychologists.

II. Theoretical Background

> *Not a thread in all his raiment — not a line in all the marked and singular lineaments of his face which was not, even in the most absolute identity,* mine own! *It was Wilson; but he spoke no longer in a whisper, and I could have fancied that I myself was speaking while he said:. . .*[23]

With the risk of hanging Lacan's mirror stage on too inflexible a skeleton, I wish to suggest the following definition of the concept as a general guideline for this section: the mirror stage is the incarnated matheme of the imaginary constitution of the 'me' (*moi*) and its alienating function for the advent of the subject, integrating a Kojèvian interpretation of Hegel's *Phenomenology of Spirit* on the one hand, and a combination of specific neuro-anatomical data and psychological observations on the other hand. This definition of the mirror stage encompasses six different components, which I will address consecutively, starting with the least abstract one.

1. Psychological observations

In 1931, the French psychologist Henri Wallon (1879-1962) published an extensive paper on the development of self-awareness (cenesthesia) in the prestigious *Journal de Psychologie*.[24] Wallon challenged the idea that self-awareness arises as the child becomes conscious of its own physical body-status. In his view, this explanation entails a circular conception of cenesthesia — the idea of a specific form of consciousness arising through consciousness — and, moreover, reduces a complex psychological phenomenon to organic processes. Wallon's alternative theory was that a child only arrives at a relatively integrated notion of itself via a gradual, laborious movement of self-definition, in which positioning oneself in relation to the outside world and the social environment is as important as gaining control over one's bodily functions.[25] In short, Wallon argued that a human being can have no coherent self-image without him or her having distinguished him- or herself from others, i.e. without having acknowledged the difference between inside and outside.

A particularly problematic aspect of this development of self-awareness in relation to the environment is the child's recognition of its mirror image, because this image appears as an external object that is at once intimately connected to oneself. Wallon described the child's assumption of its external self-image as a process requiring two mental operations: 'accepting images which have only an appearance of reality; affirming the reality of images that are withdrawn from perception.'[26] Drawing on the pioneering observations of young children in the works of Charles Darwin, William Preyer and Paul Guillaume, he further charted the child's progressive mastery over mirror images, a process which proceeds from general indifference before the age of three months, to fixating and smiling at the image around four months, and to the rudimentary acknowledgement that the mirror image does not lead a separate existence at the end of the first year.[27]

When Lacan summarized his ideas on the mirror stage in his 1938 encyclopaedia article on the family, he clearly relied on the observational data reported by Wallon, yet blowing up a number of details in Wallon's account.[28] First of all, Lacan underscored that the child's recognition of its mirror image does not occur until the sixth month of infantile development.[29] In his 1931 essay, Wallon had pointed out that at the age of six months the child starts to explore the relationship between mirror images and real objects, but he did not consider this age a 'critical period.' It was Lacan who singled out 'infantile mirror recognition' as a separate developmental stage. Whereas for Wallon, the child's changing attitude towards its reflection in the mirror exemplified how self-awareness does not emerge naturally — in keeping with biological maturation — but follows from an active engagement with the external world, to Lacan, the 'mirror experience' served as a crucial developmental paradigm. Although Wallon regularly employed the notion of stage (*stade*) and even devised his own stage-theory of infantile development, he did not accord a special place or a particular time-span to a '*mirror* stage.' To Lacan, however, the mirror stage coincided with a distinctive phase of infantile development, and he incessantly emphasized the time of its onset.[30]

In Lacan's schema, six months marks the end of a first developmental phase, which he designated as the 'weaning complex' (*le complexe du sevrage*).[31] In his view, the mother induces a vital crisis in the child when she withdraws her breast, because the child is left wanting at a moment when it is still incapable of finding its own food and surviving without the help of somebody else.[32] On a psychic level, this traumatic state is translated as an ongoing mental oscillation between accepting and rejecting the weaning, hence the 'complex'-character of the situation. Accepting the withdrawal of the breast requires that the child develops a 'me' (*moi*), as a coherent agency in its personal conquest for food, whereas rejecting it means that the child endeavours to refind the lost object, which in itself presupposes that it is able to recognize and manipulate objects. As Lacan conceived it at the end of the 1930's, the mirror stage provides a provisional answer to this psychic dilemma of the weaning complex, because it equips the child with a 'me,' as well as a primordial set of object relations.

When considering the mirror stage as a solution to the weaning complex, Lacan had to assume that the child experiences it as an ontological triumph. Therefore, he accentuated the child's affective response when it comes to recognize its mirror image for the first time. Again, Wallon had already noted that a child of eight months is captured by surprise every time it encounters its image in the mirror, but Lacan magnified and centralized this detail, making it a key component of the child's experience.[33] In Lacan's account, the recognition 'is indicated in the illuminative mimicry of the *Aha-Erlebnis*' and ignites in the child 'a flutter of jubilant activity.'[34]

2. Neuro-anatomical data

Although the Lacanian weaning complex hinges on the withdrawal of the breast, it can only acquire the meaning of a traumatic complex due to the fact that the child is at that stage an utterly helpless creature. Lacan qualified this primordial state of helplessness as 'a real specific prematurity of birth,' rephrasing the core idea of the so-called 'foetalization theory.'[35]

This remarkable theory of human evolution was elaborated during the 1920's by the Dutch anatomist Lodewijk (Louis) Bolk (1866-1930) as an alternative to the 'recapitulation theory,' which had achieved immense popularity after its re-discovery and promotion by the German zoologist Ernst Haeckel (1834-1919) during the 1860's.[36] According to Haeckel's 'biogenetic law,' ontogeny (the development of the individual) is but a recapitulation of phylogeny (the development of the species), meaning that, from conception until adulthood, a human being speeds through all the adult forms of his or her animal ancestors, following the appropriate evolutionary sequence, before acquiring a typically human shape and size. For almost half a century, Haeckel's ideas pervaded a panoply of disciplines, including education, anthropology, politics and psychoanalysis, until they eventually perished under the weight of experimental embryology and genetics.[37] In contrast to Haeckel, Bolk argued that humans do not repeat all the adult stages of their ancestors, but that matters are rather the other way round: non-human animals start their development with a human stage, which lasts longer as they become more closely related to human beings.[38] Bolk stated that humans primarily distinguish themselves from other creatures by the fact that they have managed to maintain the juvenile characteristics of their ancestors; compared to other mammals, humans are 'forever young.'

In his reading of Bolk's foetalization theory, Lacan retained its emphasis on somatic retardation, i.e. the fact that the human being develops mature, adult features (teeth, body hair, etc.) at a later stage than his or her evolutionary ancestors, entailing a prolonged period of infantile dependency.[39] As Lacan put it, every child is born prematurely; it is thrown into the world too soon, a condition 'betrayed by the signs of uneasiness and motor unco-ordination of the neo-natal months.'[40] This prematurity of birth explains at the same time why the child is left devastated after the weaning process and why it finds solace in its mirror image. For the mirror image gives the child an impression of relative physical maturity long before it has reached that stage. In the mirror, the child is able to see itself as a unity before it is actually capable of acting in an independent manner. For this reason, the child is eager to adopt its reflection in the mirror as an image of itself.

By relating the mirror stage to the weaning complex and the prematurity of birth, Lacan formulated a psychological answer to a question Wallon had not even asked himself: Why is the child attracted to its mirror image in the first place and why is it willing to adopt this reflection as an image of itself? Looking back at his invention some forty years after its original inception, Lacan divulged that foetalization is the *real* reason for the human being's 'preference for the image.'[41]

However necessary foetalization may be for self recognition in the mirror, as a condition it is not sufficient. Indeed, simply on the basis of prematurity of birth, it is impossible to explain why human beings are capable of recognizing their images, whereas primates are not. As has been described by numerous ethologists, primatologists and physicists, primates also show a keen interest in their own mirror images, but they never manage to regard them as reflections of themselves. They seem to approach their mirror images as if they suddenly found themselves in front of a fellow member of their own species, expressing surprise, anger and disappointment when this 'rival' appears to lack substance and foils every attempt to catch it.[42] This is how the French physicist Henri Bouasse (1866-1953), from whose work on optics Lacan borrowed the so-called 'experiment of the inverted bouquet,' described the peculiar behaviour of apes when confronted with their mirror image:

> One cannot say that they recognize themselves, but they believe that they are in front of an animal of the same species. Their instinctive gesture is to look behind the mirror, or . . . to catch their congener with their hand. As they only grasp emptiness, they think that they have not acted quickly enough, whence the most curious precautions to catch the animal, which *must* exist behind the mirror, by surprise.[43]

In order to account for the differences between the attitudes of monkeys and children vis-à-vis their mirror images, Lacan eventually postulated a triad of necessary and sufficient conditions for self-recognition in humans — a theoretical refinement to which I will return further on.

3. Kojève's interpretation of Hegel's *Phenomenology of Spirit*

As it has been described thus far, the mirror stage is the child's solution to the psychic dilemma of the weaning complex, which derives its traumatic character from the 'prematurity of birth,' inasmuch as it offers the child both a coherent 'me' and a template for subsequent object relations. Instead of conceiving this solution as a relative cognitive equilibrium in a Piagetian sense, Lacan regarded it as a source of new conflicts. Whilst the mirror stage opens new possibilities for the child, its founding relationship between an apparently well-integrated specular other and a totally dependent 'nothing,' drives the child into the world of competition, rivalry and aggressivity. In thus emphasizing conflict over harmony, Lacan followed a philosophical lead, whose starting point was the teachings of Alexandre Kojève (1902-1968) on Hegel's *Phenomenology of Spirit*.

In 1933, Kojève was asked by his mentor Alexandre Koyré to take over his lectures on Hegel at the *Ecole Pratique des Hautes Etudes* in Paris, an invitation which marked the beginning of one of the most reverberating events in the history of French intellectual life. Held on a weekly basis, until his mobilisation for the Second World War in 1939 forced him to stop, Kojève's seminar grew into a meeting place for the most promising young intellectuals in Paris. Through the brilliancy and doggedness of his students rather than through their number, Kojève introduced a whole generation to Hegel's philosophy, leaving indelible traces on the minds of Georges Bataille, Pierre Klossowski, Raymond Queneau, Maurice Merleau-Ponty and Jacques Lacan, to name but a few.[44]

To Kojève, Hegel's *Phenomenology of Spirit* emblematized a sustained effort to explain the historical conditions for the advent of Absolute Knowledge (*das Absolute Wissen*), a mental faculty in which thinking has finally managed to equal being and to coincide with truth, and whose potential Hegel saw realized in himself as a philosopher.[45] Kojève opposed Hegel to Descartes, stating that the latter, in formulating the cornerstone of his philosophy as *cogito ergo sum res cogitans* (I am thinking, therefore I exist as a thinking being), had only addressed the level of thinking, whereas Hegel had examined the very conditions of thinking, asking himself 'what this subject is that is revealed in and by the *I* of "I think".'[46] In Kojève's interpretation of

Phenomenology of Spirit, Hegel had explained the subjective antecedents of thinking, charting the conditions that need to be fulfilled for a human being to be capable of saying 'I think.' Hegel's analysis of the 'I' thus carried him beyond rationality, which is exactly the position Lacan assumed in the opening paragraph of *The Mirror Stage*, asserting that the psychoanalytic experience of the formation of the I 'leads us to oppose any philosophy directly issuing from the *Cogito*.'[47]

The first and foremost condition for the emergence of 'I think' and, by extension, for Absolute Knowledge is, in Kojève's reading of Hegel, self-consciousness (*Selbst-bewußtsein*). This typically human quality differs from consciousness, insofar as the latter merely involves the passive awareness and contemplation of material objects in the outside world. For self-consciousness to arise, a creature must express a desire (*Begierde*) to fill its own emptiness, by actively engaging with non-material objects in the environment. Because it is directed towards these non-material objects, self-consciousness also distinguishes itself from self-sentiment (*Selbst-gefühl*), which is typical of a non-human animal state of mind. Animal desire converges on beings and things, whereas human desire moves beyond these given objects to act upon a non-being, which is nothing else than another desire. This non-biological, 'human desire for another desire' does not prevent a human being from trying to acquire a material object, but he or she will be more interested in gaining recognition (*Anerkennung*) for this act and being given the right to possess the object, than in the possession as such.[48]

The obvious corollary of this human dynamics of desire is a struggle to the death (*Kampf auf Leben und Tod*), since 'each will want to subjugate the other, *all* the others, by a negating, destroying *action*' and since 'Man will risk his biological *life* to satisfy his *nonbiological* Desire.'[49] Yet this struggle to the death poses a limit to the human condition. For if history is to continue and human beings are to maintain their humanity by relying on the recognition of others, the fight for prestige should not be settled in death. The struggling parties must remain alive, the battle reaching a provisional end with the installation of a (subjugating) master (*Herrschaft*) and a (vanquished) slave (*Knechtschaft*).[50] As Kojève's Hegel conceived it, historical progress is predicated upon this ongoing dialectical process between master and slave, the slave attempting to realize freedom by disputing the master's power, which can only end in the complete overcoming (*Aufhebung*) of the opposition.

To this general picture of the first six chapters of *Phenomenology of Spirit*, Kojève added the crucial component of speech (*Logos*), which enables a human being to reveal being and to express desire for desire. Without speech, a creature can never attain self-consciousness; speech constitutes the necessary condition for a human being to transcend consciousness and self-sentiment, and to develop self-consciousness. As Kojève put it: 'Desire is always revealed as *my* desire, and to reveal desire, one must use the word "I".'[51] This implies that 'the Animal attains only Selbst-*gefühl*, *Sentiment* of self, but not Selbst-*bewußtsein*, Self-*Consciousness* — that is, it cannot *speak* of itself, it cannot *say* "I. . . ."'[52] Speech also allows the human being to reveal him or herself as 'self,' but this being revealed through speech is always twofold, since it comprises a revealed being as well as a revealing being. In other words, when presenting him or herself in speech, a human being is both subject and object; he or she is an agency (the revealing being) that reflects upon and objectifies itself (the revealed being).[53]

Lacan attended Kojève's classes between 1934 and 1937, and he embraced Hegel's philosophy of self-consciousness to place the child's recognition of its mirror image within a social context, thereby putting the experience itself under the aegis of a never-ending conflict. As mentioned above, Lacan claimed that the child needs to develop a 'me' in order to supersede the deadlock of the weaning complex. The child needs to become relatively independent from external objects, in a word, it needs to attain self-consciousness. In a Kojèvian fashion, Lacan equalled self-consciousness with the expression of a desire for recognition, yet at once postulating that this can only proceed from a primordial recognition of oneself in the mirror. Whereas this aspect of mirror-recognition was not broached by Kojève, Lacan regarded it as the ontological mould for the social struggle for prestige. Through its identification with the mirror image, the child positions itself as similar to and different from other human beings, from which the aggressive struggle for prestige can follow. In Lacan's own words, the end of the mirror stage — that is to say the child's assumption of its mirror image — entails 'the deflection of the specular *I* into the social *I*' and 'decisively tips the whole of human knowledge into mediatization through the desire of the other.'[54]

With his mirror stage, Lacan clarified how a human being comes to distinguish the desire of the other in the first place, a point which Kojève had hardly addressed. Yet by relating the mirror stage to Hegelian dialectics, he also emphasized the conflictual nature of the experience itself. Indeed, apart from a 'me,' the mirror image also installs a rival other, on whom one can never steal a march and whose good looks are often discordant with one's own feelings of discomfort. Aggressivity is thus as much an intra-psychic, as an 'inter-personal' incident, a phenomenon Lacan linked to 'destructive and, indeed, death instincts,' which explain 'the evident connection between the narcissistic libido and the alienating function of the *I*, [and] the aggressivity it releases in any relation to the other.'[55]

Kojève's presentation of Hegel's philosophy probably also emboldened Lacan to consider 'the function and field of speech and language' within the ontological process of mirror-recognition. In *The Mirror Stage*, the impact of these symbolic dimensions is overshadowed by the power of the imaginary, but from 1953 onwards Lacan progressively conceptualised them as essential preconditions for an adequate structuration of the self-image as opposed to the image of others. Initially, in *Seminar I*, Lacan argued that 'the exchange of symbols' influences decisively the way in which a human being relates to others, but does not affect 'the level of the mirror stage.'[56] From the mid 1950's, he extended this symbolic mediation to every type of imaginary, dyadic relationship, claiming that there can be no distance between two agencies (subject and other) — not even at the level of the mirror stage — without the presence of a third symbolic factor, which he dubbed the discourse of the Other.[57] This gradual reconsideration of the mirror stage as a symbolically mediated event, an experience for which the presence of a symbolic Other is also a necessary condition, coincided with the introduction and elaboration of the 'schema of the two mirrors.'[58]

4. The imaginary constitution of the 'me'. . .

When Bouasse described the behaviour of animals in front of a mirror, he was interested neither in comparative ethology, nor in the development of self-awareness, but in the physical characteristics of various kinds of images. To prove that a monkey's 'hide and seek' game with its specular rival does not only stem from its own mental faculties, but is also ignited by certain features of image formation in plain mirrors, Bouasse underscored that, in contrast to the mirror image, a photographic picture leaves a monkey cold.[59] From these observations, he concluded that images in plain mirrors must have special characteristics and that the animal's recognition of a rival in the mirror must also be induced by physical, image-related factors.

In *The Mirror Stage* Lacan invoked this specific effect of the mirror image owing to its inherent characteristics by referring to biological experiments with female pigeons and migratory locusts.[60] In the case of the former, it had been reported that the visual presence of another (male or female) pigeon, which does not necessarily require the proximity of a real animal, a mirror image being as effective, is sufficient to produce ovulation.[61] In migratory locusts, the gregarious type (with specific morphological features) replaces the solitary type after an individual has been exposed, at a particular point of its existence, to an animal of the same or a related species, whose image must be lively but may be merely visual.[62]

In 1949, Lacan theorized these observations as formative effects of a *Gestalt* or an 'imago,' an isolated, unitary image in the environment (*Umwelt*). This process of subjective transformation due to the occurrence of a certain external 'form' continued to preoccupy him until the mid 1950's.[63] Yet, from the outset Lacan refused to adopt the principle of *Gestalt* psychology (von Ehrenfels), according to which a form is constituted through the organizing perceptive functions of the individual, as a means of explaining what happens during the mirror stage. As Lacan put it, the mirror image does operate for the child as a *Gestalt*, but this form 'is certainly more constituent than constituted' and 'it appears to him above all in a relief of stature [*un relief de stature*] that fixes it.'[64] In other words, it is not the child who constitutes the *Gestalt*, but the *Gestalt* that constitutes the child as a 'me,' and the form itself is fixed (static) rather than mobile (dynamic).

The first aspect follows directly from the fact that Lacan conceived the child as a premature, dependent and uncoordinated creature. Claiming that the *Gestalt* is constituted by the child would presuppose that it functions *ab initio* as a relatively integrated agency, which is exactly what Lacan wanted to counter. To Lacan, relative integration (in the form of a 'me') was an effect rather than a cause of the mirror stage, an opinion for which he found support in a passage from Freud's 1914 paper *On Narcissism*, where Freud had written:

> . . . I may point out that we are bound to suppose that a unity comparable to the ego [*Ich*] cannot exist in the individual from the start; the ego has to be developed. The auto-erotic instincts [*autoerotischen Triebe*], however, are there from the very first; so there must be something added to auto-erotism — a new psychical action — in order to bring about narcissism [*um den Narzißmus zu gestalten*].[65]

Although Lacan rejected the existence of auto-erotic drives, he retained Freud's portrayal of the ego (*Ich*) and the concurrent experience of narcissism as secondary formations, incorporating it into his own paradigm of the mirror stage. In *Seminar I*, Lacan commented upon Freud's remarks on the development of the ego in *On Narcissism*, saying that they 'indicate the imaginary origin of the ego's function.'[66] Obviously, Freud did not really consider the origin — let alone the *imaginary* origin — of the ego; he merely suggested that 'a new psychical action' must be responsible for its emergence. It was Lacan himself who first elaborated upon this action in his reading of the mirror image as a formative *Gestalt*.

Lacan highlighted the aspect of immobility, shared by the *Gestalt* and the mirror image, in order to contrast this to 'the turbulent movements that the subject feels are animating him.'[67] This is yet another way to explain why the mirror image is attractive for the child. When adopting it, the internally felt turbulence can be steered in the right direction. Through its identification with the static mirror image, the child can channel the 'libidinal dynamism' of its 'organic insufficiency.'[68] The fixity of the mirror image can also be inferred from the rigidity of the 'me' to which it gives rise. In *The Mirror Stage*, Lacan contended that the 'me' is represented in dreams via 'a fortress [*un camp retranché*], or a stadium [*un stade*]' surrounded by 'marshes and rubbish-tips,' and that the neurotic formations of the I (me) have a characteristic inertia.[69] In *Seminar I*, he even proffered the thesis that the 'me' 'is structured exactly like a symptom,' even 'the human symptom *par excellence*, the mental illness of man,' which explains why Anna Freud could easily assign a plethora of defence mechanisms to it.[70]

Between 1949 and 1953, Lacan progressively disentangled the physiological effects of the *Gestalt* on animals from the psychic constitution of the 'me' through the mirror image in the human child. Whereas an animal is captivated and influenced by the visual presence of a congener, a child also recognizes, identifies with and distinguishes itself from its mirror image. For this mental operation to occur, the presence of an external imago is necessary, but not sufficient. The imaginary condition needs to be fulfilled, but it will only produce effects if synchronized with foetalization (the real condition) and — as Lacan stressed from the mid 1950's — the discourse of the Other (the symbolic condition).

Moreover, animals and human beings undergo the effects of the *Gestalt* differently due to their differential 'accomodation of the imaginary.'[71] Apart from some exceptional cases, sexual behaviour in animals is only triggered by the presence of one specific imago in the environment, for instance the brightly coloured face of a female. However, in the human species sexual arousal can result from an infinite series of imagos; the effects of the *Gestalt* do not depend on its age, colour, size and shape, and not even on its morphological similarity.[72] To Lacan, this proves that the imaginary is not very well accomodated in human beings. A human being can couple his or her image to basically any object in the environment; no object is perfectly suitable to complement a human being's self-image. Here, Lacan adumbrated the fundamental maladjustment of human sexuality, ascribing this phenomenon to the shaky constitution of the 'me' and seeing the latter in itself as a result of its symbolic mediation.[73]

5. . . . and its alienating function for the advent of the subject

The solution to the weaning complex in the form of a 'mental permanence of the *I*,' which the child finds through its identification with the mirror image, is not only conflictual, it also 'prefigures its alienating destination.'[74] Because the 'me' rests on a mirror image, it epitomizes a form that is completely alien to the one displayed by the child. By identifying with the mirror image, the child assumes a 'me' that is radically exterior, strictly inaccessible and unveraciously complete, and which does not lead a material existence beyond the mirror.

The 'me' is exterior because its matrix does not arise as an internal awareness of bodily status, but as a *Gestalt* within the child's *Umwelt*.[75] Insofar as the imago appears in a mirror, it is moreover inaccessible because it has neither depth, nor contents, and one can neither manage nor wield it. In addition, the imago is complete: unlike the child, it has no insufficiencies and it also seems to enjoy the comfort of having nothing to demand or desire. Yet, the mirror image does not exist outside the virtual space, for in accordance with the laws of image formation in plain mirrors, it is inverted with regard to the object. The image the child sees in the mirror and with which it identifies does not tally with the image of itself as perceived by others. The virtual child is an 'enantiomorph' of the real child; it always behaves 'contrariwise' as Tweedledee to Tweedledum.[76]

When Lacan conveyed that the mirror stage equips the child with 'an alienating identity,' he implied first of all that the nucleus of a human being's self-image is a mirage, no matter how familiar it may seem. In the mirror stage, the human being is alienated from his or her nature, inasmuch as he or she grasps his or her uncoordinated amalgam of sensory and motor processes via an unreal, inverted image with which he or she will never coincide. In 1949, Lacan defined the mirror stage accordingly as 'a drama whose internal thrust is precipitated from insufficiency to anticipation,' designating the self-image in the mirror as 'Ideal-I,' i.e. as an I that can never be realized.[77]

From the idea that the 'me' is a mirage, it is easy to infer that the self-consciousness associated with it cannot point the way to a truthful self-understanding. Rather than considering the 'me' as a mental component through which a human being comes to know and understand him or herself, Lacan regarded the 'me' as a source of *méconnaissance*, that is to say of misunderstanding and failure to recognize. In Lacan's view, the 'me' is not the representative of reality, as Freud conceived it, but a showpiece of illusory mastery, a simulacrum of individual control.[78] The identification with the mirror image permits the child to alleviate its vulnerable condition with an illusion of mastery and to pour its helplessness into a primordial stabilizing form. The 'me' comes to meet the child's fragmentation, covering it with a unitary, recognizable self-image, but completely misrepresents the primordial state of infantile helplessness.

At this point, Lacan criticized Sartre's analysis of consciousness, in which self-consciousness had been defined as a locus of nothingness.[79] Lacan deplored the fact that existentialism had grasped 'negativity only within the limits of a self-sufficiency of consciousness. . .'[80] Contrary to existentialism, he refused to align self-consciousness (and the 'me') with nothingness. To him, the 'me' grants being to nothingness rather than *vice versa*. In other words, whereas Sartre characterized self-consciousness as nothingness and the external objects as being, Lacan ascribed being to self-consciousness and the 'me,' and nothingness to the not-me.[81]

At the end of the 1940's, nothingness was not a crucial concept in Lacan's works. He employed it mainly to designate the psychic component beyond the 'me,' an elusive factor whose unruly character is already signalled physically through the uncoordinated movements of the newborn child. However, in a passage from the 1948 paper *Aggressivity in Psychoanalysis*, the conceptual destiny of this recalcitrant component was clearly announced. Reflecting upon the status of the 'me,' Lacan wrote:

> In short, we call ego [*moi*] that nucleus given to consciousness, but opaque to reflexion, marked by all the ambiguities which, from self-satisfaction to "bad faith" (*mauvaise foi*), structure the experience of the passions in the human subject; this "I" who, in order to admit its facticity to existential criticism, opposes its irreducible inertia of pretences and *méconnaissances* to the concrete problematic of the realization of the subject.[82]

From this sentence, it appears that Lacan opposed the 'me' to 'the realization of the subject,' without really explaining what exactly this subject and its realization entailed. It transpired that this subject is a kind of 'not-me' which is obliged to conform to a 'me' in order to attain self-consciousness, but which at the same time seems to disappear, or at least to be misunderstood (*méconnaissance*) in this very process of objectification.

Until the very end of his career, Lacan devoted himself to the study of this subject and its psychic vicissitudes, at one point formalizing it as a radical split ($). [83] But despite the multifarious meanings Lacan assigned to the subject, he persisted in outlining its dialectical relation with the 'me.' In his theory, the 'me' remained an annoying obstacle for the subject, a symptom requiring dismantlement rather than fortification during psychoanalytic treatment, if the patient were to reorganise the architecture of his or her psychic landscape.[84]

6. An incarnated matheme

At the beginning of *Seminar II*, Lacan pointed out that the word 'form' can be used in two different ways, each corresponding to a distinct scientific paradigm.[85] Firstly, within twentieth century *Gestalt* psychology, 'form' is defined as a complex shape, which can be either static or dynamic, but which always appears to the individual as an organized totality. Secondly, within mathematics, 'form' is related to 'formalisation,' which is meant to capture the relations between phenomena in abstract terms, irrespective of their intrinsic properties. Whereas *Gestalt* psychology investigates the processes governing the *form*ation of images on the basis of their inherent qualities, mathematics heralds the *form*ality of structural laws beyond the concrete characteristics of elements. Asked by Jean Hyppolite which of these two meanings of form he advocated, Lacan unflinchingly expressed his preference for the mathematical one, thus promoting the symbolic instead of the imaginary form.[86]

For the mirror stage, Lacan's privileging of the symbolic over the imaginary had a number of consequences. First of all, he progressively reinterpreted the entire experience as a symbolically mediated event, conforming to his refinement of the 'schema of the two mirrors' during the 1950's. But more importantly, this triggered an insidious theoretical repositioning of the 'stage' as a pivotal axiom, an established principle which requires neither proof nor explanation, but is nevertheless valuable for the development of new hypotheses. Initially conceived as an essential ontological moment for the development of the 'me' and self-consciousness in human beings, Lacan gradually stripped the mirror stage of its psychological dimensions, using it as a formalized theoretical insight, or matheme.[87]

Through this operation of formalisation, the mirror stage not only lost its fixed date, but also its constitutive physical and physiological components. Whereas Lacan's 1949 paper was still largely devoted to what actually happens when animals and human beings are confronted with their mirror images, in his subsequent analyses of the experience the physical presence of a mirror was subordinated to the intervention of the symbolic order (the Other). By 1960, Lacan even identified the mirror with the Other, a construction which had already been foreshadowed in *Seminar I*, where he had claimed 'that the inclination of the plane mirror is governed by the voice of the other.'[88]

In this substitution of the Other for the concrete mirror, one could of course read an additional proof of the priority Lacan assigned to the symbolic. Yet it could also be interpreted as an indication that the presence of a concrete mirror image is of minor importance for the establishment of the 'me.' It is the Other which constructs and controls a human being's external world, and which regulates his or her assumption of a 'self-image.' This does not only imply that a human being's 'self-image' may be distorted despite the presence of mirrors, but also that it can still be formed in the absence of mirror images. Furthermore, the symbolic control of the imaginary implies that the assumption of a 'self-image' can occur outside the field of vision. As such, Lacan's purification of the mirror stage entails a reduction of its basis in the physiology of perception. Insofar as the symbolic governs the imaginary, a blind child can still assume a self-image, as long as the symbolic is there to replace and control its eyes, for it will then see itself through the words of the Other.

As such, Lacan's theoretical move towards the mirror stage as an 'incarnated matheme' during the 1950's and 1960's did not involve a radical modification of the original description — as some authors have suggested — but rather a separation of its substance from the auxiliaries.[89] In retrospect, Lacan stated that he had already taken the symbolic dimension into account in his 1949 text, thus emphasizing rather than inventing its function during the 1950's.[90] In this way, the mirror stage became an epitome of the dynamics between two fundamental registers, which is why Lacan could define the substance of the experience in 1966 as 'the distribution code between the imaginary and the symbolic.'[91]

III. Practical Significance

> *. . . 'You have conquered, and I yield. Yet henceforward art thou also dead — dead to the World, to Heaven, and to Hope! In me didst thou exist — and, in my death, see by this image, which is thine own, how utterly thou hast murdered thyself.'*[92]

Since Lacan took psychological observations as the basis of the mirror stage, it is tempting to view the idea chiefly as a contribution to developmental psychology. One could argue for example that Lacan drew attention to a quintessential moment during the child's development, whose importance in the emergence of self-awareness had remained unexploited in the various accounts of infantile behaviour. One could even venture to say that Lacan was not satisfied with the existing descriptions of this moment, and probed into its conditions and consequences, in order to distinguish a genuinely human experience from what happens within the animal world.

On the basis of such a reading, the mirror stage could be put into a chronological sequence of developmental phases, notably between the (Lacanian) weaning-complex and the (Freudian) Oedipus complex. Educationalists might then try to ensure that a child is indeed being given the opportunity to develop self-awareness during the demarcated critical period, by giving parents, nursery school teachers and child minders concrete guidelines about how and when to assist children in their assumption of self-images, or by advising them about how to recognize and overcome retardation. As it fosters practical recommendations on how to facilitate and control child-rearing processes, and as it finds support in recent research on the emergence of cenesthesia, this reading of the mirror stage appears to be the most valuable one for everyday living conditions, and the most beneficial for widening the acceptance of Lacan's positions.[93]

Yet, this reading is most alien to Lacan's own usage of the mirror stage theory after 1949. In none of his numerous glosses on the mirror stage during the 1950's and 1960's is the concept used within a developmental framework. Lacan's refusal to employ the mirror stage as a developmental concept was instigated partly by his proposal of an alternative, non-chronological time-structure for psychoanalysis, and partly by his rejection of a psychoanalytic ethics geared towards the patient's well-being and the love of one's neighbour.

In contrast to the orthodox psychoanalytic opinion that a patient's symptoms are determined by a salient, yet repressed historical life-event, Lacan demanded that psychoanalysis comply with the time-structure of the future anterior: 'What is realized in my history is not the past definite of what was, since it is no more, or even the present perfect of what has been in what I am, but the future anterior of what I shall have been for what I am in the process of becoming.'[94] The main difference between the classic psychoanalytic present perfect (trying to discover what has been in order to explain what is) and the Lacanian 'future anterior' is that the former sees the truth as coming from the past, whereas the latter implies that it comes from the future. Whereas in the former case, the psychoanalyst urges the patient to discover his or her truth in the past, in the latter case, the psychoanalyst brings the patient to the point where he or she acknowledges that the truth depends on the future, the nature of which is governed by his or her own desire. In other words, a human being is not determined by the past, but determines both the future and the past through the expression of his or her desire. Relying on this particular time-structure, which he also saw at work in the symbolic order, Lacan could no longer regard the mirror stage as a determinative ontological moment within a chronology of life-events, for the determination occurs retrospectively.[95] In other words, the assumption, absence or disintegration of a 'self-image' depends on an event that is posterior to the actual mirror experience. And since it is impossible to predict its meaning, it is useless to secure its occurrence within infantile development.[96]

Lacan's refusal to present his mirror-stage as a key developmental concept also seems to find a rationale in his considerations on the direction of psychoanalytic treatment and the ethics of psychoanalysis.[97] Vehemently opposing the post-Freudian tradition that gained momentum as 'ego-psychology' in the United States during the 1950's, Lacan was at great pains to (re)accentuate the conflictual nature of the mirror stage.[98] As such, he suggested that a stimulation of the patient's 'self-awareness' during psychoanalytic treatment can only result in heightened narcissism, rivalry, aggressivity and jealousy. To Lacan, the ego-psychologists were mistaken in their belief that helping patients to rebuild their egos would contribute to their overall adaptation to reality. In Lacan's view, ego-building could only lead to further alienation and an even more hostile relation with the outside world.[99]

So how did Lacan use the concept of the mirror stage? It seems that he operated in accordance with the 'art of the expert cook,' which he himself put forward as a metaphor for psychoanalytic technique in *Seminar I*.[100] As the expert cook handles knives to dissect birds 'with as little resistance as possible,' Lacan employed his concept of the mirror stage to cut through complex clinical phenomena in the realms of neurosis and psychosis.[101] The 1949 paper on *The Mirror Stage* prefigured this approach, inasmuch as Lacan applied his notion to the surrealistic contents of dreams, the peculiar bodily symptoms in hysteria, the mental fortifications in obsessional neurosis, and the aggressive social relations in paranoia.[102] In *Seminar III*, the mirror stage proved extremely useful to theorize Schreber's remarkable relationship with his environment, a relationship which Lacan initially characterized as an imaginary dissolution, and which he later explained as a topographical regression to the mirror stage.[103] Throughout these clinical 'applications,' the mirror stage often revealed itself as a formula. It enabled Lacan to understand what is going on in neurosis and psychosis, and it regularly induced new hypotheses and additional questions.

In a similar way, a score of literary critics have tried to make sense of fictional characters' relationships with each other by drawing on Lacan's notion. Over the past few decades the mirror stage has been used as a tool to unearth the underlying dynamics in works as diverse as those of Milton, Verlaine and Vargas Llosa.[104] This huge range of literary applications has surely contributed to the progressive hollowing-out of Lacan's concept and its consolidation within the arts and human sciences.

Whereas this could be seen as a favourable movement, from another angle it could also be regarded as a potentially dangerous tendency. When knives can be used to cut everything, they surely prove their value, but they soon become blunt, in which case they need resharpening before somebody decides to throw them away. It is to such a resharpening of Lacan's mirror stage that I have tried to make a contribution.

Notes

1. E.A. Poe, William Wilson (1839), *The Complete Illustrated Stories and Poems of Edgar Allan Poe*, London, Chancellor Press, 1988, p. 48.

2. J. Lacan, The Function and Field of Speech and Language in Psychoanalysis (1953), *Ecrits: A Selection* (trans. A. Sheridan), London, Tavistock, 1977, p. 30. I have modified Sheridan's translation, which is rather a paraphrase of Lacan's first two sentences.

3. Lacan's Rome discourse was not published until three years after the conference, in the first issue of *La Psychanalyse*, the journal created by the *Société Française de Psychanalyse* (SFP) after its secession from the *Société Psychanalytique de Paris* (SPP) in 1953. In this first issue of the journal one can also find the (rarely referenced) transcription of the text which Lacan actually read at the conference, alongside comments on Lacan's discourse by Juliette Favez-Boutonnier, Daniel Lagache, Didier Anzieu and Françoise Dolto, and Lacan's reply to his colleagues. See: J. Lacan, Fonction et champ de la parole et du langage en psychanalyse, *La Psychanalyse*, 1956, no. 1, pp. 81-166; J. Lacan, Discours de Jacques Lacan (26 sept. 1953), *La Psychanalyse*, 1956, no. 1, pp. 202-211. For discussions of the historical circumstances leading to the creation of the SFP, see: J.-A. Miller (Ed.), *La scission de 1953. La communauté psychanalytique en France I*, Paris, Navarin, 1976; E. Roudinesco, *Jacques Lacan & Co.: A History of Psychoanalysis in France 1925-1985* (1986) (trans. J. Mehlman), London, Free Association Books, 1990, pp. 223-276; S. Turkle, *Psychoanalytic Politics: Jacques Lacan and Freud's French Revolution* (2nd Edition, Revised and Updated), London, Free Association Books, 1992, pp. 103-111; D. Macey, *Lacan in Contexts*, London-New York NY, Verso, 1988, pp. 224-229.

4. See: J. Lacan, *The Four Fundamental Concepts of Psychoanalysis* (1964) (trans. A. Sheridan), Edited by J.-A. Miller, Harmondsworth, Penguin Books, 1979; J. Lacan, *Le Séminaire, Livre XVII, L'envers de la psychanalyse* (1969-70), texte établi par J.-A. Miller, Paris, du Seuil, 1994. Sometimes the historical circumstances marking Lacan's itinerary merely encompass the publication of a book, or his invitation to a conference. The former is for instance true for the first chapters of *Seminar IV*, which comprise a vitriolic critique of *La psychanalyse d'aujourd'hui*, a multi-authored, two-volume treatise of mainstream psychoanalysis, published in 1956. See: J. Lacan, *Le Séminaire, Livre IV, La relation d'objet* (1956-57), texte établi par J.-A. Miller, Paris, du Seuil, 1994; S. Nacht (Ed.), *La psychanalyse d'aujourd'hui* (2 vols.), Paris, Presses Universitaires de France, 1956.

5. With all due respect to Anthony Wilden's landmark 1968 translation of Lacan's Rome discourse, it seems unforgiveable that he decided to cut the preface, dismissing it as 'a matter of anecdote.' See: J. Lacan, *Speech and Language in Psychoanalysis* (trans. with notes and commentary A. Wilden) (1968), Baltimore MD-London, The Johns Hopkins University Press, 1981, p. xxiii.

6. J. Lacan, *The Seminar. Book III: The Psychoses* (1955-56) (trans. with notes R. Grigg), Edited by J.-A. Miller, New York NY-London, W.W. Norton & Company, 1993, p. 149.

7. See also: J. Lacan, The Function and Field of Speech and Language in Psychoanalysis, *o.c.*, p. 33, where it is stated: 'In any case, I consider it to be an urgent task to disengage from concepts that are being deadened by routine use the meaning that they regain both from a re-examination of their history and from a reflexion on their subjective foundations.'

8. See: J. Lacan, The Freudian Thing, or the Meaning of the Return to Freud in Psychoanalysis (1956), *Ecrits: A Selection, o.c.*, p. 117. Lacan's editing of this text is contemporaneous with *Seminar III*, in which he defended his reading procedure. On 16 May 1956, Lacan also gave a public address on the occasion of the centenary of Freud's birth, in which he attacked those who had regarded Freud as a man 'without ambition and without needs,' thus reaffirming his own ambition to restore Freud's subjective and cultural-historical dimensions. See: J. Lacan, *The Seminar. Book III: The Psychoses, o.c.*, pp. 231-244.

9. For the first edition of *The Mirror Stage*, see: J. Lacan, Le stade du miroir comme formateur de la fonction du Je, telle qu'elle nous est révélée dans l'expérience psychanalytique, *Revue française de Psychanalyse*, 1949, XIII, no. 4, pp. 449-455. The text reprinted in *Ecrits* (1966), on which the current English translation is based, differs slightly from the original 1949 version, and it would surely be an interesting exercise, however falling beyond the scope of this essay, to interpret the textual variations. The 1970 version of *The Mirror Stage*, which appeared in the first volume of the two-volume, condensed pocket-edition of *Ecrits*, is an exact copy of the 1966 version. See: J. Lacan, Le stade du miroir comme formateur de la fonction du Je, telle qu'elle nous est révélée dans l'expérience psychanalytique (1949), *Ecrits*, Paris, du Seuil, 1966, pp. 93-100; J. Lacan, The Mirror Stage as Formative of the Function of the I as Revealed in Psychoanalytic Experience, *Ecrits: A Selection, o.c.*, pp. 1-7; J. Lacan, Le stade du miroir comme formateur de la fonction du Je, telle qu'elle nous est révélée dans l'expérience psychanalytique (1949), *Ecrits I*, Paris, du Seuil, 1970, pp. 89-97. For the textual variations, see: A. de Frutos Salvador, *Los Escritos de Jacques Lacan. Variantes textuales*, Madrid, Siglo XXI, 1994.

10. Perhaps I ought to tell that Marienbad is now called Máriánské Lázně, and is located a hundred miles to the West of Prague, in the Czech Republic. According to Ernest Jones, this provincial town was chosen 'so that Anna Freud should not be too far away from her father in case she was urgently needed.' Indeed, Freud was recovering from two operations in Vienna and could therefore not be present at the conference. Yet, if Freud's physical condition had to be taken into account when choosing a location for the congress, why did the IPA-board not decide to organize it in Vienna ? Jones's comment that 'Czechoslovakia [was] an island of freedom surrounded by totalitarian states' certainly adds an extra dimension to the geographical proximity of Anna Freud to her father. See: E. Jones, *The Life and Work of Sigmund Freud. Volume III: The Last Phase (1919-1939)*, New York NY, Basic Books, 1957, p. 209.

11. Jones's intervention must have been perceived by the audience as a highly authoritarian gesture, since it not only silenced a Parisian novice, but also put the integrity of Clarence P. Oberndorf, a respected American psychoanalyst who was chairing the session, at stake. See: J. Lacan, Propos sur la causalité psychique (1946), *Ecrits*, *o.c.*, pp. 185-186.

12. See: J. Lacan, The Direction of the Treatment and the Principles of Its Power (1958), *Ecrits: A Selection, o.c.*, p. 239.

13. For 'passage à l'acte,' see: J. Lacan, *Le Séminaire X, L'angoisse* (1962-63), unpublished, especially the seminar of 23 January 1963. It should be noted that whatever the meaning Lacan may have attributed to Jones's act, it does not represent an unambiguous sign of disapproval. Every speaker at the conference had been allocated ten minutes to present a paper, so that Jones's decision to interrupt Lacan could have been merely instigated by a rigid, if not to say obsessional time-management. Neither in his Freud-biography, nor in his (unfinished) autobiography, did Jones comment upon his encounter with Lacan at the Marienbad conference. In any case, Jones's intervention did not prevent Lacan from visiting him at his Sussex cottage, from inviting him back to his own Summer house (an offer Jones declined), and from writing a laudable commemorative essay after his death in 1958. See: E. Jones, *Free Associations: Memories of a Psychoanalyst*, New York NY, Basic Books, 1959; J. Lacan, A la mémoire d'Ernest Jones: Sur sa théorie du symbolisme (1959), *Ecrits, o.c.*, pp. 697-717 and p. 697 in particular.

14. We know that Lacan's paper was not published because he had refrained from submitting it (and for instance not because the editors had refused to publish it), since this is what Lacan himself has indicated on at least two occasions. See: J. Lacan, Propos sur la causalité psychique, *o.c.*, p. 185; J. Lacan, De nos antécédents (1966), *Ecrits, o.c.*, p. 67. Due to the incomplete English translation of Lacan's *Ecrits* and Alan Sheridan's assertion, in his bibliographical note to this translation, that the 1936 text had been published in the *International Journal of Psycho-Analysis*, the 1936 'text' on the mirror stage has puzzled a number of Lacan-scholars in the Anglo-American world. If Sheridan had translated Lacan's 1946 article *Propos sur la causalité psychique*, or if he had checked the 1937 volume of the *International Journal of Psychoanalysis*, he (and those reading his translation) would have known that there is no published 1936 text. Of course, the fact that the bibliographical note at the back of the French *Ecrits* is highly ambiguous about Lacan's paper — it mentions two different papers, whereas the volume includes only one, and it suggests that the 1936 paper had indeed been published — does not excuse Sheridan's mistake. Detailed accounts of the vicissitudes of Lacan's *Mirror Stage* text can be found in: J. Gallop, *Reading Lacan*, Ithaca NY-London, Cornell University Press, 1985, pp. 74-92; B. Ogilvie, *Lacan: La formation du concept de sujet (1932-1949)*, Paris, Presses Universitaires de France, 1987, pp. 96-118.

15. See: Bulletin of the International Psycho-Analytical Association, *International Journal of Psycho-Analysis*, 1937, XVIII, no. 1, p. 78. The gap in the proceedings of the Marienbad conference reminds us of this other remarkable non-event in the history of psychoanalysis: the absence of a protocol of Freud's lecture on *The Aetiology of Hysteria*, held before the Viennese *Verein für Psychiatrie und Neurologie* on 21 April 1896, in the *Wiener Klinische Wochenschrift* of 14 May 1896. See: S.

Freud, The Aetiology of Hysteria (1896*c*), *Standard Edition*, III, pp. 187-221; Verhandlungen ärztlicher Gesellschaften und Congressberichte, *Wiener Klinische Wochenschrift*, 1896, IX, no. 20, p. 420.

16. It is remarkable that Lacan waited until the first post-war IPA congress to present his mirror stage again, for he could have made another attempt at the fifteenth IPA congress of 1938, which was notably held in Paris and by which time he had written an encyclopaedia article on the family in which he had reduced the original paper to its essentials (let us say, to something he could have explained in ten minutes). See: J. Lacan, Propos sur la causalité psychique, *o.c.*, p. 185; J. Lacan, La famille, in H. Wallon (Ed.), *Encyclopédie Française, Vol. VIII: La vie mentale*, Paris, Larousse, 1938, pp. 8.40.3-8.40.16 and 8.42.1-8.42.8. Lacan's text on the family was republished under the editorship of J.-A. Miller in 1984, with a different title and without the original subdivisions and bibliography: J. Lacan, *Les complexes familiaux dans la formation de l'individu* (1938), Paris, Navarin, 1984.

17. See: Bulletin of the International Psycho-Analytical Association, *International Journal of Psycho-Analysis*, 1949, XXX, no. 1, p. 203.

18. The best alternative to the missing 1936 text are probably the (as yet unpublished) notes taken by Françoise Dolto during Lacan's lecture on the mirror stage at the SPP on 16 June 1936, which have been quoted by Elisabeth Roudinesco in her Lacan biography. As regards Lacan's output between 1936 and 1949, the authoritative Lacan bibliography by Joël Dor mentions only nine papers, irrespective of letters and spoken interventions at conferences and meetings. See: E. Roudinesco, *Jacques Lacan* (1993) (trans. B. Bray), New York NY, Columbia University Press, 1997; J. Dor, *Nouvelle bibliographie des travaux de Jacques Lacan*, Paris, E.P.E.L., 1993, pp. 50-54.

19. Since Jean Roussel's first translation of *The Mirror Stage* in 1968, Lacan's notion of *le moi* has been consistently rendered in English as 'ego.' In my opinion, at least four arguments can be given in favour of another option, for example 'me,' which I shall use throughout my text: i/In *The Mirror Stage*, Lacan does not use *moi* as equivalent to Freud's *Ich*; ii/Rendering *moi* as 'ego' may lead to its interpretation along the lines of the ego-analytic conception of the ego, whereas Lacan himself repudiates such an interpretation; iii/In his Rome Discourse, Lacan uses the term 'ego' alongside *moi*, which can no longer be ascertained in the English translation; iv/In translating *moi* as 'ego,' a term taken from everyday language enters an uncommon, pseudo-scientific idiom. Of course, the choice made by English translators to render *moi* as 'ego' is tributary to Strachey's translation of Freud's *Ich* in the *Standard Edition* of his complete works, but the term 'ego' persists in non-English translations of Lacan's works as well. This is exemplified by J. Quackelbeen's Dutch translation of *The Mirror Stage*, in which 'ego' is used for *moi*, although the Dutch also has '*mij*.' See: J. Lacan, Het spiegelstadium als vormend voor de funktie van het ik zoals die ons gereveleerd wordt in de psychoanalytische ervaring (trans. J. Quackelbeen), *Psychoanalytische Perspektieven*, 1984, nos. 4/5, pp. 8-15. For Roussel's translation of *The Mirror Stage*, see: J. Roussel, Introduction to Jacques Lacan, *New Left Review*, 1968, no. 51, pp. 63-77, reprinted without comments in S. Žižek (Ed.), *Mapping Ideology*, London-New York NY, Verso, 1994, pp. 93-99.

20. These qualifications are respectively taken from: J. Lacan, *The Seminar. Book III: The Psychoses, o.c.*, p. 87; J. Lacan, De nos antécédents, *o.c.*, p. 70; J. Lacan, The Subversion of the Subject and the Dialectic of Desire in the Freudian Unconscious (1960), *Ecrits: A Selection, o.c.*, p. 306. For a full survey of references to *The Mirror Stage* in Lacan's published papers, see: D. Lécuru, Thésaurus Lacan, Volume I, annexe. Citations de publications de Lacan par lui-même dans l'ensemble de l'œuvre écrite, *Revue du Littoral*, 1994, no. 40, p. 137.

21. For the 'schema of the two mirrors,' see: J. Lacan, *The Seminar. Book I: Freud's Papers on Technique* (1953-54) (trans. with notes J. Forrester), Edited by J.-A. Miller, Cambridge, Cambridge University Press, 1988, p. 124. For Lacan's reconsideration of this schema, see: J. Lacan, Remarque sur le rapport de Daniel Lagache: "Psychanalyse et structure de la personnalité" (1960), *Ecrits, o.c.*, pp. 647-684 and especially pp. 680-681. For detailed discussions of the 'schema of the two mirrors,' see for example: G. Michaud, L'angoisse et/est le désir de l'Autre, *Esquisses psychanalytiques*, 1991, no. 15, pp. 153-170; J. Attié, N. Charraud, R. Lew & G. Trobas, Lacan: Lagache, *Cahiers de lectures freudiennes*, 1989, nos. 15/16, pp. 23-59; C. Léger, Quel est donc cet autre auquel je suis plus attaché qu'à moi?, in G. Miller (Ed.), *Lacan*, Paris, Bordas, 1987, pp. 31-57; Y. Depelsenaire, La place de l'angoisse, *Quarto*, 1986, no. 25, pp. 48-52; P. Malengreau, Le schéma optique, *Quarto*, 1985, no. 19, pp. 43-48.

22. For the L-schema, see for example: J. Lacan, *The Seminar. Book III: The Psychoses, o.c.*, p. 14. For the R-schema, see: J. Lacan, On a Question Preliminary to Any Possible Treatment of Psychosis (1957-58), *Ecrits: A Selection, o.c.*, p. 197 & pp. 223-224 (note 18, added July 1966). For alienation and separation in the fantasy, see: J. Lacan, *The Four Fundamental Concepts of Psychoanalysis, o.c.*, pp. 203-215.

23. E.A. Poe, William Wilson, *o.c.*, p. 48.

24. H. Wallon, Comment se développe, chez l'enfant, la notion du corps propre, *Journal de Psychologie normale et pathologique*, 1931, XXVIII, nos. 9-10, pp. 705-748. Wallon subsequently divided his paper into four chapters and included it in his book *Les origines du caractère chez l'enfant*, which was first published in 1934 and which still counts as a valuable work within developmental psychology. See: H. Wallon, *Les origines du caractère chez l'enfant. Les préludes du sentiment de personnalité*, Paris, Boivin et Cie, 1934. All further references are to Wallon's original paper. For an introduction into the oeuvre of Wallon, see: H. Wallon, *The World of Henri Wallon* (trans. D. Nicholson-Smith), Edited by G. Voyat, New York NY, Jason Aronson, 1984; E. Jalley, *Wallon, lecteur de Freud et de Piaget*, Paris, Editions Sociales, 1981.

25. H. Wallon, Comment se développe, chez l'enfant, la notion du corps propre, *o.c.*, p. 710.

26. *Ibid.*, pp. 742-743. My translation.

27. For Wallon's sources (which he often fails to mention), see: Ch. Darwin, A Biographical Sketch of an Infant (1877), in P.H. Barrett (Ed.), *The Collected Papers of Charles Darwin*, Vol. 2, Chicago IL-London, The University of Chicago Press, 1977, pp. 191-200; W.T. Preyer, *Die Seele des Kindes. Beobachtungen über die geistige Entwicklung des Menschen in den ersten Lebensjahren*, Leipzig, Gräfenhei-

nichen, 1882; P. Guillaume, *L'imitation chez l'enfant*, Paris, Alcan, 1925. For English translations of the latter two works, see: W.T. Preyer, *The Mind of the Child* (1882), New York NY, Appleton, 1889; P. Guillaume, *Imitation in Children* (trans. E.P. Halperin), Chicago IL-London, The University of Chicago Press, 1971.

28. It should be noted that Wallon had commissioned Lacan to write this entry on the family for the volume of the Larousse encyclopaedia that he was editing at the time.

29. Lacan felt the need to mention this factor no less than three times within the space of three paragraphs. See: J. Lacan, *Les complexes familiaux dans la formation de l'individu. Essai d'analyse d'une fonction en psychologie, o.c.*, pp. 42-43.

30. Indeed, every time Lacan alluded to the mirror stage in texts written before the 1950's, he indicated its time of onset. In *Propos sur la causalité psychique*, he even suggested to call the mirror experience a 'phase' instead of a 'stage', probably in order to highlight its transitional character. See: J. Lacan, Propos sur la causalité psychique, *o.c.*, p. 185; J. Lacan, Aggressivity in Psychoanalysis (1948), *Ecrits: A Selection, o.c.*, pp. 18-19; J. Lacan, The Mirror Stage as Formative of the Function of the I as Revealed in Psychoanalytic Experience, *o.c.*, p. 1. In the latter text, Lacan attributed the periodisation of the mirror stage to James Mark Baldwin, a reference which Ogilvie has interpreted as a malicious lapsus, since Lacan credited neither Wallon, nor Darwin, to whom the dating supposedly accrued. Yet such a reading is itself rather malicious — although it is true that Lacan never referred to Wallon's 1931 article — if one takes into account that neither of them were interested in seeing the child's recognition of its mirror image as a developmental stage. See: B. Ogilvie, *Lacan. La formation du concept de sujet (1931-1949), o.c.*, p. 113. Lacan's reference to Baldwin does not mention a particular book or article, but concerns his *Mental Development in the Child and the Race* of 1895, a book which Freud owned and which attracted his attention, as can be inferred from a letter he wrote to Flieβ on 5 November 1897. See: J.M. Baldwin, *Mental Development in the Child and the Race: Methods and Processes*, New York NY-London, The Macmillan Co., 1895; J.M. Masson (Ed.), *The Complete Letters of Sigmund Freud to Wilhelm Flieβ 1887-1904* (trans. J.M. Masson), Cambridge MA-London, The Belknap Press of Harvard University Press, 1985, pp. 277-278. For re-evaluations of Baldwin's work, see for example: J.M. Broughton & D.J. Freeman-Moir (Eds.), *The Cognitive Developmental Psychology of James Mark Baldwin: Current Theory and Research in Genetic Epistemology*, Norwood NJ, Ablex, 1981.

31. See: J. Lacan, *Les complexes familiaux dans la formation de l'individu. Essai d'analyse d'une fonction en psychologie, o.c.*, pp. 25-35.

32. However simple this representation may be, it is top-heavy with theoretical assumptions. For example, in claiming that the child is left wanting after the withdrawal of the breast, Lacan refuted the Freudian postulates of 'auto-erotism' and 'primary narcissism.' According to Lacan, the child cannot retreat into a state of self-satisfaction, because it does not possess a 'self.' The weaning does not destroy a primitive 'me,' nor obliges the child to seek shelter in complacency, since the 'me' is a secondary formation which comes into existence as a reaction against weaning. For 'auto-erotism' and 'primary narcissism,' see: S. Freud, On Narcissism: An Introduction (1914*c*), *Standard Edition*, XIV, pp. 67-102. For Lacan's refutation of

these notions, see: J. Lacan, *Les complexes familiaux dans la formation de l'individu. Essai d'analyse d'une fonction en psychologie, o.c.*, pp. 29-30.

33. See: H. Wallon, Comment se développe, chez l'enfant, la notion du corps propre, *o.c.*, p. 740.

34. J. Lacan, The Mirror Stage as Formative of the Function of the I as Revealed in Psychoanalytic Experience, *o.c.*, p. 1.

35. *Ibid.*, p. 4. See also: J. Lacan, Propos sur la causalité psychique, *o.c.*, pp. 186-187.

36. See: E. Haeckel, *Natürliche Schöpfungsgeschichte*, Berlin, Georg Reiner, 1868; E. Haeckel, *The History of Creation*, 2 vols. (trans. E.R. Lankester), London, Kegan Paul, Trench, Trubner & Co., 1892. For a concise presentation of Haeckel's life and works, see: S.J. Gould, *Ontogeny and Phylogeny*, Cambridge MA-London, The Belknap Press of Harvard University Press, 1977, pp. 76-85.

37. Throughout his career, Freud remained an ardent defender of the recapitulation theory up to and including its 'racist' corollaries, which he for example implicitly supported in his attempts to draw parallels between the mental lives of children, neurotics and 'savages.' See, for example: S. Freud, Totem and Taboo (1912-13*a*), *Standard Edition*, XIII, pp. 1-161. For a meticulous, yet rather irreverent examination of Freud's espousal of the recapitulation theory, see: F.J. Sulloway, *Freud, Biologist of the Mind: Beyond the Psychoanalytic Legend*, Cambridge MA-London, Harvard University Press, 1992 (2nd edition), pp. 199-204 & 258-261.

38. See: L. Bolk, *Das Problem der Menschwerdung*, Jena, Gustav Fischer, 1926. To the best of my knowledge, this cardinal text has hitherto not been translated into English, but it is fairly accessible in two French translations of the 1960's: L. Bolk, La genèse de l'homme (trans. J.-Cl. Keppy), *Arguments*, 1960, IV, no. 18, pp. 1-13; L. Bolk, Le problème de la genèse humaine (trans. F. Gantheret & G. Lapassade), *Revue française de psychanalyse*, 1961, XXV, no. 2, pp. 243-279. It should be noted that the *Arguments* translation is a strongly abridged version of the original text, which does not comprise any of Bolk's schemas and figures. For a full translation one has to rely on the text in the *Revue française de psychanalyse*, whose only disadvantage is that it is not preceded by an editorial introduction. For illuminating, yet partisan general discussions of Bolk's theory, see: S.J. Gould, *Ontogeny and Phylogeny, o.c.*, pp. 356-362; S.J. Gould, The Child as Man's Real Father (1978), *Ever Since Darwin: Reflections in Natural History*, Harmondsworth, Penguin, 1991, pp. 63-69; S.J. Gould, Racism and Recapitulation (1978), *Ever Since Darwin: Reflections in Natural History, o.c.*, pp. 214-221; S.J. Gould, *The Mismeasure of Man*, New York NY-London, W.W. Norton & Company, 1981, pp. 119-122. In the latter two publications, Gould zooms in on the amazing fact that, despite their radical opposition, proponents of both recapitulation and foetalization were convinced that they had proven the supremacy of the white race.

39. Lacan is not the only figure in the history of psychoanalysis who was devoted to Bolk's ideas, although he is doubtlessly the most prominent one. One Lacanian author has argued that the publication of Bolk's 1926 lecture in a French psychoanalytic journal is due to Lacan's insistent references to Bolk, but in my opinion it was rather the upshot of a fairly wide psychoanalytic interest in his work. See: G. Trobas, La préférence pour l'image, *La lettre mensuelle*, 1986, no. 50, pp. 23-29. For non-

Lacanian psychoanalytic espousals of Bolk's theory, see for example: H. Lampl, The Influence of Biological and Psychological Factors upon the Development of the Latency Period, in R.M. Loewenstein (Ed.), *Drives, Affects, Behavior*, New York NY, International Universities Press, 1953, pp. 380-387; S. Weyl, Retardation, Acceleration and Psychoanalysis, *Journal of the American Psychoanalytic Association*, 1959, VII, pp. 329-349.

40. J. Lacan, The Mirror Stage as Formative of the Function of the I as Revealed in Psychoanalytic Experience, *o.c.*, p. 4.

41. J. Lacan, La troisième (1974), *Lettres de l'Ecole freudienne de Paris*, 1975, no. 16, p. 191. As Freud continued to be an incorrigible Haeckelian, Lacan thus remained a life-long Bolkian.

42. This is perfectly illustrated in the National Geographic Special on Jane Goodall's work with the chimpanzees of Gombe. See also: J. Goodall, *The Chimpanzees of Gombe: Patterns of Behavior*, Cambridge MA-London, The Belknap Press of Harvard University Press, 1986.

43. H. Bouasse, *Optique et photométrie dites géométriques*, Paris, Delagrave, 1932, p. 52. My translation. For the 'experiment of the inverted bouquet,' see: J. Lacan, *The Seminar. Book I: Freud's Papers on Technique, o.c.*, p. 78.

44. For discussions of Kojève's life and works, see: D. Hollier, *Le Collège de sociologie*, Paris, Gallimard, 1979; B. Hesbois, *Le livre et la mort. Essai sur Kojève*, Ph.D. thesis, Université Catholique de Louvain, 1985; J. Butler, *Subjects of Desire: Hegelian Reflections in Twentieth Century France*, New York NY, Columbia University Press, 1987; M.S. Roth, *Knowing and History: The Resurgence of French Hegelianism from the 1930's through the Postwar Period*, Princeton NJ, Princeton University Press, 1988; D. Auffret, *Alexandre Kojève, la philosophie, l'Etat, la fin de l'Histoire*, Paris, Grasset, 1990; S.B. Drury, *Alexandre Kojève: The Roots of Postmodern Politics*, Basingstoke, Macmillan, 1994. For a personal impression of Kojève's influence during the 1960's, see: S. Rosen, Kojève's Paris: A Memoir, *Parallax*, 1997, no. 4, pp. 1-12.

45. This equality of thinking and being can also be read as a correspondence between the word and the thing, between universality (*Allgemeinheit*) and particularity (*Einzelheit*), or (in Heideggerian terms) between essence and existence. For an English translation of Hegel's *magnum opus*, one can rely on: G.W.F. Hegel, *Phenomenology of Spirit* (1807) (trans. A.V. Miller), Oxford-New York NY, Oxford University Press, 1977.

46. A. Kojève, *Introduction to the Reading of Hegel* (1947[1933-39]) (trans. J.H. Nichols, Jr.), Edited by A. Bloom, New York NY-London, Basic Books, 1969, p. 36. It should be noted that this English translation of Kojève's lectures, which were assembled and edited by Raymond Queneau after the war, is an abridged version of the original French edition. For the complete text, see: A. Kojève, *Introduction à la lecture de Hegel*, Paris, Gallimard, 1947. For Descartes' formula, see: R. Descartes, Discourse on the Method (1637[1636]), in *The Philosophical Writings of Descartes*, Vol. I (trans. J. Cottingham, R. Stoothoff & J. Murdoch), Cambridge, Cambridge University Press, 1985, p. 127.

47. J. Lacan, The Mirror Stage as Formative of the Function of the I as Revealed in Psychoanalytic Experience, *o.c.*, p. 1.

48. See: A. Kojève, *Introduction to the Reading of Hegel, o.c.,* pp. 39-40. During the 1950's, Lacan theorized desire along similar lines, although he rephrased the Kojèvo-Hegelian 'desire for recognition' as 'desire is a desire of/for the other' (*désir de l'autre*). In Lacan's view, a human being can only feel recognized when he or she is desired by another human being or when the object he or she desires is also desired by somebody else. Desire for an object, desire to know an object, must be mediated by another desire. In short, no human being desires what no human being desires; one only desires something because it is also desired by somebody else. In *The Mirror Stage*, Lacan designated this mechanism as 'paranoiac knowledge.' See: J. Lacan, The Mirror Stage as Formative of the Function of the I as Revealed in Psychoanalytic Experience, *o.c.*, p. 3. For 'paranoiac knowledge,' see also: J. Lacan, Aggressivity in Psychoanalysis, *o.c.*, p. 17; J. Lacan, Propos sur la causalité psychique, *o.c.*, p. 180. For desire as desire of the other, see for example: J. Lacan, *The Seminar. Book I: Freud's Papers on Technique, o.c.*, pp. 146, 173, 176-178 & 221. From the introduction of the Other in *Seminar II,* Lacan pointed out that recognition is dependent upon the (symbolic) Other rather than the (imaginary) other, thereby reinterpreting his initial formula as 'desire is desire for/of the Other.' See: J. Lacan, *The Seminar. Book II: The Ego in Freud's Theory and in the Technique of Psychoanalysis* (1954-55) (trans. S. Tomaselli, notes J. Forrester), Edited by J.-A. Miller, Cambridge, Cambridge University Press, 1988, pp. 235-247 (introduction of the Other).

49. See: A. Kojève, *Introduction to the Reading of Hegel, o.c.,* p. 41.

50. Hegel's notions of *Herrschaft* and *Knechtschaft* have been rendered as 'Lordship' and 'Bondage' in the standard English translation of *Phenomenology of Spirit*. These terms are unquestionably better than 'master' (*maître*) and 'slave' (*esclave*) when it comes to conveying the precise meaning of Hegel's thought, but Kojève probably preferred the latter — instead of *maîtrise* and *servitude*, for example — in order to show how Hegel's philosophy applied to concrete historical realities. In his comments on Hegel, Lacan always used the first French translation of *Phänomenologie des Geistes* by Jean Hyppolite, in which *Herrschaft* and *Knechtschaft* were also rendered as *maître* and *esclave*. See: G.W.F. Hegel, *Phenomenology of Spirit*, *o.c.*, pp. 111-119; G.W.F. Hegel, *Phénoménologie de l'esprit* (trans. J. Hyppolite), 2 vols., Paris, Aubier, 1939-1941.

51. A. Kojève, *Introduction to the Reading of Hegel, o.c.,* p. 37.

52. *Ibid.*, p. 39.

53. This distinction between 'revealed being' and 'revealing being' tallies with Lacan's opposition between 'subject of the statement' (*sujet de l'énoncé*) and 'subject of the speaking' (*sujet de l'énonciation*), as it can be found, for instance, in *Seminar XI*. See: J. Lacan, *The Four Fundamental Concepts of Psychoanalysis, o.c.*, pp. 138-140. The translations of *sujet de l'énoncé* and *sujet de l'énonciation* I am using have been suggested by Bruce Fink in *The Lacanian Subject*. In most English translations of Lacan's works, *sujet de l'énonciation* is rendered as 'subject of enunciation.' See: B. Fink, *The Lacanian Subject: Between Language and Jouissance*, Princeton NJ, Princeton University Press, 1995, p. 40.

54. J. Lacan, The Mirror Stage as Formative of the Function of the I as Revealed in Psychoanalytic Experience, *o.c.*, p. 5. It should be noted that at this stage of Lacan's theoretical development — the end of the 1940's — me (*moi*) and I (*je*) are interchangeable terms, something I will illustrate by means of Lacan's notions of *je-idéal* and *moi-idéal* further in the text.

55. *Ibid.*, p. 6.

56. J. Lacan, *The Seminar. Book I: Freud's Papers on Technique, o.c.*, p. 140.

57. See, for example: J. Lacan, Remarque sur le rapport de Daniel Lagache: "Psychanalyse et structure de la personnalité", *o.c.*, p. 678.

58. For additional glosses on Lacan's indebtedness to Kojève, see: Ph. Van Haute, *Psychoanalyse en filosofie. Het imaginaire en het symbolische in het werk van Jacques Lacan*, Leuven, Peeters, 1989, pp. 32-63; P. Macherey, Lacan avec Kojève, philosophie et psychanalyse, in M. Deguy (Ed.), *Lacan avec les philosophes*, Paris, Albin Michel, 1991, pp. 315-321; M. Borch-Jacobsen, *Lacan: The Absolute Master* (1990) (trans. D. Brick), Stanford CA, Stanford University Press, 1991; D.H. Bowen, Entre la relation d'objet et la relation intersubjective (trans. P. Nguyen), in S.G. Lofts & P. Moyaert (Eds.), *La pensée de Jacques Lacan. Questions historiques — Problèmes théoriques*, Louvain-Paris, Peeters, 1994, pp. 65-82; E. Roudinesco, *Jacques Lacan, o.c.*, pp. 140-150; D. Auffret, *Alexandre Kojève, la philosophie, l'Etat, la fin de l'Histoire, o.c.*, pp. 440-450; C. Williams, Philosophy and Psychoanalysis: Lacan, Kojève and Hyppolite on the Concept of the Subject, *Parallax*, 1997, no. 4, pp. 41-53. In his biography of Kojève, Auffret mentions that around the time of Lacan's first presentation of the mirror stage (Summer 1936) Lacan and Kojève had conceived the plan to co-author an essay entitled *Hegel et Freud: Essai d'une confrontation interprétative*, which was never finished.

59. See: H. Bouasse, *Optique et photométrie dites géométriques, o.c.*, pp. 52-53.

60. See: J. Lacan, The Mirror Stage as Formative of the Function of the I as Revealed in Psychoanalytic Experience, *o.c.*, p. 3.

61. Lacan derived this information from a 1939 paper by Harrison Matthews: L. Harrison Matthews, Visual Stimulation and Ovulation in Pigeons, *Proceedings of the Royal Society of London* (Series B — Biological Sciences), 1939, CXXVI, pp. 557-560. An incomplete reference to this text and an extensive discussion of its contents can be found in: J. Lacan, Propos sur la causalité psychique, *o.c.*, p. 189.

62. Here, the liveliness of the image is crucial — Lacan wrote that the image must be 'animated by movements of a style sufficiently close to that characteristic of the species' — and may explain why Bouasse observed that animals are indifferent towards photographs of themselves. The experiments Lacan referred to were conducted by Rémy Chauvin during the early 1940's. See: R. Chauvin, *La vie de l'insecte: physiologie-biologie*, Paris, Lechevalier, 1943. Again, a detailed discussion of these experiments can be found in: J. Lacan, Propos sur la causalité psychique, *o.c.*, pp. 190-191. For an English edition of Chauvin's researches, see: R. Chauvin, *Animal Societies, from the Bee to the Gorilla* (trans. G. Ordish), London, Gollancz, 1968.

63. In Latin, the term *imago* has myriad meanings, ranging from image and likeness to deception and semblance. The term was regularly used by Freud and in 1912 Otto Rank and Hanns Sachs even chose it as the title for a new journal devoted to applied psychoanalysis. The notion *Gestalt*, which literally means 'form,' rose to prominence within psychology and ethology thanks to the works of Christian von Ehrenfels, Wolfgang Köhler and Kurt Lewin, amongst others. The term *Umwelt* (environment, external world) was coined by Jakob von Uexküll as a counterpart to *Innenwelt* (internal world). See: J. von Uexküll, *Umwelt und Innenwelt der Tiere* (2. verm. und verb. Auflage), Berlin, J. Springer, 1921. It is possible that Lacan became interested in these authors through an encyclopaedic article by Meyerson on images, which was published in 1929 in *Journal de Psychologie*, but he certainly took his bearings from Merleau-Ponty's *Phénoménologie de la perception* of 1945. See: I. Meyerson, Les images, *Journal de psychologie normale et pathologique*, 1929, XXVI, pp. 625-709; M. Merleau-Ponty, *The Phenomenology of Perception* (1945) (trans. C. Smith), London, Routledge and Kegan Paul, 1962. On Lacan and Merleau-Ponty, see: J. Phillips, Lacan and Merleau-Ponty: The Confrontation of Psychoanalysis and Phenomenology, in D. Pettigrew & F. Raffoul (Eds.), *Disseminating Lacan*, Albany NY, State University of New York Press, 1996, pp. 69-106; B. Baas, Notre étoffe (Lacan et Merleau-Ponty), *La cause freudienne*, 1995, no. 29, pp. 47-57; B. Baas, Over een niet toewijsbaar object: het object *a* (trans. G. Van de Vijver), *Psychoanalytische Perspektieven*, 1994, no. 25, pp. 75-113; J. O'Neill, The Specular Body: Merleau-Ponty and Lacan on Infant Self and Other, *Synthese*, 1986, LXVI, pp. 201-217; A. Lingis, The Visible and the Vision: Merleau-Ponty and Lacan, *Journal of the British Society for Phenomenology*, 1984, XV, no. 2, pp. 155-163.

64. J. Lacan, The Mirror Stage as Formative of the Function of the I as Revealed in Psychoanalytic Experience, *o.c.*, p. 2. I have modified Sheridan's translation of *relief de stature* as 'contrasting size,' opting for the more literal 'relief of stature,' because I think that Lacan intended to convey the liveliness and pregnancy of the mirror image rather than its size.

65. S. Freud, Narcissism: An Introduction, *o.c.*, p. 77.

66. J. Lacan, *The Seminar. Book I: Freud's Papers on Technique, o.c.*, p. 115.

67. J. Lacan, The Mirror Stage as Formative of the Function of the I as Revealed in Psychoanalytic Experience, *o.c.*, p. 2.

68. *Ibid.*, pp. 2 (libidinal dynamism) & 4 (organic insufficiency).

69. *Ibid.*, p. 5.

70. J. Lacan, *The Seminar. Book I: Freud's Papers on Technique, o.c.*, p. 16. For Anna Freud's work, see: A. Freud, *The Ego and the Mechanisms of Defence* (1936), London, The Hogarth Press and the Institute of Psycho-Analysis, 1968.

71. J. Lacan, *The Seminar. Book I: Freud's Papers on Technique, o.c.*, p. 140.

72. Obviously, criteria of age, colour, size, etc. are very important for human beings on a subjective level. In other words, whereas in animals, the *Gestalt* is to a large extent species-related, in human beings it is highly individualized.

73. The problematic nature, or rather culture of human sexuality would become of central importance to Lacan's theory during the 1960's and 1970's, reaching a zenith in the formula 'there is no such thing as a sexual relationship.' For this formula, see

for example: J. Lacan, *Le Séminaire, Livre XX, Encore* (1972-73), texte établi par J.-A. Miller, Paris, du Seuil, 1975.

74. J. Lacan, The Mirror Stage as Formative of the Function of the I as Revealed in Psychoanalytic Experience, *o.c.*, p. 2.

75. In *The Ego and the Id*, Freud had defined the *Ich* as 'a mental projection of the surface of the body' that is 'ultimately derived from bodily sensations.' It is clear that Lacan retained the first qualification, whilst replacing the second by the identification with the mirror image. See: S. Freud, The Ego and the Id (1923*b*) *Standard Edition*, XIX, pp. 25-26.

76. See: L. Carroll, Through the Looking-Glass and What Alice Found There (1896), in M. Gardner (Ed.), *The Annotated Alice*, Harmondsworth, Penguin Books, 1970, pp. 229-244.

77. J. Lacan, The Mirror Stage as Formative of the Function of the I as Revealed in Psychoanalytic Experience, *o.c.*, pp. 4 (drama) & 2 (Ideal-I). From *Seminar I* onwards Lacan replaced 'Ideal-I' (*je-idéal*) by 'ideal-me' (*moi-idéal*), which again indicates that I (*je*) and me (*moi*) were, at that stage of Lacan's itinerary, interchangeable terms. From *Seminar I*, Lacan further distinguished between 'ideal-me' and 'Me-ideal' (*Idéal du moi*), in conformity with Freud's distinction between *Idealich* and *Ichideal* in *On Narcissism*. See: J. Lacan, *The Seminar. Book I: Freud's Papers on Technique, o.c.*, pp. 129-142 (where *moi-idéal* (*Idealich*) has been translated as ideal ego); S. Freud, On Narcissism: An Introduction, *o.c.*, p. 94.

78. For Freud's depiction of the *Ich* as a representative of reality, see: S. Freud, The Ego and the Id, *o.c.*, p. 36.

79. See: J.-P. Sartre, *Being and Nothingness: An Essay on Phenomenological Ontology* (1943) (trans. H.E. Barnes), London, Methuen, 1957.

80. J. Lacan, The Mirror Stage as Formative of the Function of the I as Revealed in Psychoanalytic Experience, *o.c.*, p. 6.

81. In 1966, Sartre proclaimed that all structuralists (including Lacan) had ignored history and the subject, to which Lacan retorted that the influences of existentialism on his work are negligible and that the only thing he had really appreciated in *Being and Nothingness* was its analysis of sado-masochistic relations. The latter point is at least confirmed by a passage in *Seminar I*, where Lacan said that Sartre 'has described this play [of sadism and masochism] in the most magisterial manner.' See: J.-P. Sartre, Jean-Paul Sartre répond, *L'arc*, 1966, no. 30, pp. 87-96; J. Lacan, Entretien avec Jacques Lacan, *Les lettres françaises*, 7 décembre 1966, pp. 16-17; J. Lacan, *The Seminar. Book I: Freud's Papers on Technique, o.c.*, p. 215. On Lacan and Sartre, see for example: S.A. Grolnick, Sartre and Psychoanalysis: A Current View, *Literature and Psychology*, 1977, XXVII, pp. 122-128; C. Howells, Sartre and Freud, *French Studies*, 1979, XXXIII, no. 2, pp. 157-176; P. Vauday, Sartre et la psychanalyse sans inconscient, *Ornicar ?*, 1985, no. 32, pp. 114-131; D. Macey, *Lacan in Contexts*, *o.c.*, pp. 103-107.

82. J. Lacan, Aggressivity in Psychoanalysis, *o.c.*, p. 15. In the first part of the sentence, Lacan talks about *la conscience*, which can mean 'consciousness' as well as 'conscience.' In the second part, *méconnaissance* is singular in the original, but plural in the translation. This fragment proves again that Lacan was using 'me' (*moi*) and I (*je*) as equivalents.

83. See: J. Lacan, *Le Séminaire V, Les formations de l'inconscient* (1957-58), unpublished, in particular the seminars of April, May and June 1958. Summaries of this seminar, drafted by Jean-Bertrand Pontalis and authorized by Lacan, were published in three issues of *Bulletin de Psychologie*. See: J.-B. Pontalis (agréé par Lacan), J. Lacan. Les formations de l'inconscient, *Bulletin de Psychologie*, 1957-58, XI, nos. 4/5, pp. 293-296; 1958-59, XII, nos. 2/3, pp. 182-192; 1958-59, XII, no. 4, pp. 250-256.

84. A detailed discussion of the relations between subject and 'me' exceeds the scope of this essay. Apart from Paul Verhaeghe's chapter in this collection, the following texts provide excellent introductory reading: B. Fink, *The Lacanian Subject: Between Language and Jouissance, o.c.*, pp. 33-79; C. Soler, The Subject and the Other (I) & (II), in R. Feldstein, B. Fink & M. Jaanus (Eds.), *Reading Seminar XI: Lacan's Four Fundamental Concepts of Psychoanalysis*, Albany NY, State University of New York Press, 1995, pp. 39-53.

85. See: J. Lacan, *The Seminar. Book II: The Ego in Freud's Theory and in the Technique of Psychoanalysis*, *o.c.*, p. 34.

86. *Ibid.*, p. 34.

87. See, for example: J. Lacan, De nos antécédents, *o.c.*, p. 69. The term 'matheme' (*mathème*), which Lacan coined by analogy with Levi-Strauss's *mythème*, does not appear in his works until the early 1970's, when he started to examine the possibility of the integral transmission of knowledge via formalized systems. See, for example: J. Lacan, *Le Seminaire XIX, Le savoir du psychanalyste* (1971-72), unpublished, seminar of 2 December 1971. For *mythème*, see: C. Lévi-Strauss, The Structural Study of Myth, *Structural Anthropology* (1958) (trans. C. Jacobson & B. Grundfest Schoepf), New York NY-London, Basic Books, 1963, pp. 206-231.

88. See: J. Lacan, Remarque sur le rapport de Daniel Lagache: "Psychanalyse et structure de la personnalité", *o.c.*, pp. 674-681; J. Lacan, *The Seminar. Book I: Freud's Papers on Technique, o.c.*, p. 140.

89. I have adopted the expression 'incarnated matheme' from J.-A. Miller, who suggested it in: S. Cottet et al., Un mathème incarné, *La lettre mensuelle*, 1986, no. 50, pp. 2-16. The idea that Lacan radically modified his conception of the mirror stage after 1949 has been defended by E. Ragland, who even goes so far as to say that there are three different theories (imaginary, symbolic and real) of the mirror stage in Lacan's works. See: E. Ragland, *Essays on the Pleasures of Death: From Freud to Lacan*, New York NY-London, Routledge, pp. 35-41; E. Ragland-Sullivan, The Imaginary, in E. Wright (Ed.), *Feminism and Psychoanalysis: A Critical Dictionary*, Oxford, Blackwell, 1992, pp. 173-176. From the latter work, the reader will be able to infer that according to Ragland-Sullivan, Lacan has three theories of everything: not only three theories of the mirror stage, but also three theories of the symbolic, three theories of the real, three theories of the death drive, *ad infinitum*.

90. See: J. Lacan, *Le Séminaire X, L'angoisse* (1962-63), unpublished, seminar of 28 November 1962.

91. J. Lacan, De nos antécédents, *o.c.*, p. 69. My translation.

92. E.A. Poe, William Wilson, *o.c.*, p. 48.

93. For an example of how the mirror stage has been integrated into developmental psychology, see: J. Gruber, Das Spiegelstadium ('Stade du Miroir' nach Jacques Lacan) als richtungsweisende Entwicklungsstufe für die Identitätsfindung — 'Normale,' 'Neurotische,' 'Psychotische' Entwicklung, *Zeitschrift für Psychosomatische Medizin und Psychoanalyse*, 1979, XXV, pp. 342-353. The most widely acclaimed empirical research on the development of self-awareness in children, which largely confirms Lacan's dating of the mirror stage between six and eighteen months, has been conducted by Lewis and Brooks-Gunn during the 1970's. See: M. Lewis & J. Brooks-Gunn, *Social Cognition and the Acquisition of Self*, New York NY-London, Plenum, 1979. For a concise discussion of these and related studies, see: J.P. Muller, The Ego and Mirroring in the Dyad, *Beyond the Psychoanalytic Dyad: Developmental Semiotics in Freud, Peirce and Lacan*, New York NY-London, Routledge, 1996, pp. 119-133. In a sense, Winnicott's espousal of the mirror stage in his own theory of maturation as an integrative process is also tantamount to a developmental interpretion of Lacan's ideas. See: D.W. Winnicott, Mirror-role of Mother and Family in Child Development (1967), *Playing and Reality*, London, Tavistock, 1971, pp. 111-118.

94. J. Lacan, The Function and Field of Speech and Language in Psychoanalysis, *o.c.*, p. 86.

95. For the future anterior in the symbolic order, see for example: J. Lacan, The Subversion of the Subject and the Dialectic of Desire in the Freudian Unconscious, *o.c.*, pp. 306-307. It should be noted that in this text Alan Sheridan has translated *futur antérieur* as 'future perfect tense.'

96. For the same reason, it is for example useless to guarantee the 'imprinting' of the Name-of-the-Father in the child by regularly referring to a father-agency during its Oedipal-period, in order to prevent the installation of psychosis.

97. See: J. Lacan, *The Seminar. Book VII: The Ethics of Psychoanalysis* (1959-60) (trans. with notes D. Porter), Edited by J.-A. Miller, New York NY-London, W.W. Norton & Company, 1992.

98. See, for example: J. Lacan, The Subversion of the Subject and the Dialectic of Desire in the Freudian Unconscious, *o.c.*, p. 307. For the principles of ego-psychology, see: H. Hartmann & E. Kris, The Genetic Approach in Psychoanalysis, *The Psychoanalytic Study of the Child*, 1945, I, pp. 11-30; H. Hartmann, E. Kris & R. Loewenstein, Comments on the Formation of Psychic Structure, *The Psychoanalytic Study of the Child*, 1946, II, pp. 11-38; H. Hartmann, E. Kris & R. Loewenstein, Notes on the Theory of Aggression, *The Psychoanalytic Study of the Child*, 1949, III/IV, pp. 9-36; E. Kris, Ego Psychology and Interpretation in Psychoanalytic Therapy, *The Psychoanalytic Quarterly*, 1951, XX, no. 1, pp. 15-30; H. Hartmann, Technical Implications of Ego Psychology, *The Psychoanalytic Quarterly*, 1951, XX, no. 1, pp. 31-43.

99. For a more extensive discussion of this point, see: R. Boothby, *Death and Desire: Psychoanalytic Theory in Lacan's Return to Freud*, New York NY-London, Routledge, 1991, pp. 21-45.

100. J. Lacan, *The Seminar. Book I: Freud's Papers on Technique*, *o.c.*, p. 2.

101. *Ibid.*, p. 2.

102. See: J. Lacan, The Mirror Stage as Formative of the Function of the I as Revealed in Psychoanalytic Experience, *o.c.*, pp. 4-5.

103. See: J. Lacan, *The Seminar. Book III: The Psychoses, o.c.*, pp. 87-88 & pp. 89-101. For 'topographical regression to the mirror stage,' see: J. Lacan, On a Question Preliminary to Any Possible Treatment of Psychosis (1957-58), *Ecrits, o.c.*, p. 209.

104. The following is but a rough selection of papers in which the mirror stage is used to analyze works of literature: J.H. Stewart, Colette: The Mirror Image, *French Forum*, 1978, III, no. 3, pp. 195-205; J. Bem, Verlaine, poète luminaire: mythe et langage poétique, *Stanford French Review*, 1980, IV, pp. 379-393; S.A. Zimmerman, Milton's 'Paradise Lost': Eve's Struggle for Identity, *American Imago*, 1981, XXXVIII, no. 3, pp. 247-267; J.-P. Mourey, Le texte et sa fiction chez Jorge Luis Borges: mirages et miroirs, *Poétique*, 1981, XLV, pp. 67-78; J.-Ph. Lecourt, L'énonciation et la quête de l'identité: personne, espace et temps dans 'One Flew over the Cuckoo's Nest', *Etudes anglaises*, 1982, XXXV, no. 2, pp. 152-164; V. Brady, 'Down at the Dump' and Lacan's Mirror Stage, *Australian Literary Studies*, 1983, XI, pp. 233-237; G. Finney, Self-reflexive Siblings: Incest as Narcissism in Tieck, Wagner and Thomas Mann, *The German Quarterly*, 1983, LVI, pp. 243-256; A. Liu, Toward a Theory of Common Sense: Beckford's 'Vathek' and Johnson's 'Rasselas', *Texas Studies in Literature and Language*, 1984, XXVI, no. 2, pp. 183-217.

CHAPTER 6

Ineluctable Nodalities: On the Borromean Knot

Luke Thurston

I. Introduction

The first step towards an understanding of the Borromean knot — the key figure in the topological elaborations which were the central preoccupation of the last ten years of Lacan's life — is to separate it from its legendary penumbra. A predominant image of the knot as the emblem of a *terra incognita* of dark, abstruse speculation, the incomprehensible grand finale of Lacanian theory, has led to two opposing forms of misunderstanding: on one side, a sort of transferential supposition of knowledge, elevating the knot to the status of a hieratic mystery, a master signifier available only to the initiated; on the other, the idea of the knot as an irrelevant scholastic whim, which has allowed hostile critics to dismiss any talk of psychoanalytic topology as mere *étourderie* (absent-mindedness), echoing the title of a famously difficult Lacanian text from 1973.[1]

If Lacan was himself at times during the 1970's complicit with a certain imaginary notion of the knot (he occasionally allowed his stylistic elegance to slip into self-dramatization, causing one of his followers to refer ironically to 'the epic of the Borromean knot'), we should not allow its legendary aura to hinder our efforts to analyze its emergence and development in Lacan's thought, and to try to grasp some of the problems and questions it raises.[2]

We should begin by noting Lacan's declaration in 1973 that his use of topology does not constitute a theory, and thus not expect the

Borromean knot to supply us with some coherent, finished revision of Lacanian psychoanalysis.[3] Rather, the knot constitutes first of all an *essai de formalisation*, an attempt to consolidate or verify certain aspects of the earlier theories. However, its principle effect was, in the event, the de-stabilization of those theories and the introduction of unsettling new perspectives. One should not, of course, underestimate the interpretive difficulty of the last decade of Lacanian theory. Yet I hope to show that this difficulty does not imply an accident of character or stylistic quirk, but is bound up with a reflexive investigation of the limits of theory, and of what can be taught.

The Borromean knot is developed at different moments of Lacan's teaching, and invested with quite different theoretical stakes. Nevertheless, a certain structure is seen to repeat itself: in the knot, three terms are bound together by a fourth, which is at once a part of the knot and paradoxically beyond it. In the same way, the three central sections of this article are only held together by Lacan's texts on the Borromean knot; a reading of those texts is a necessary supplement to its coherence.

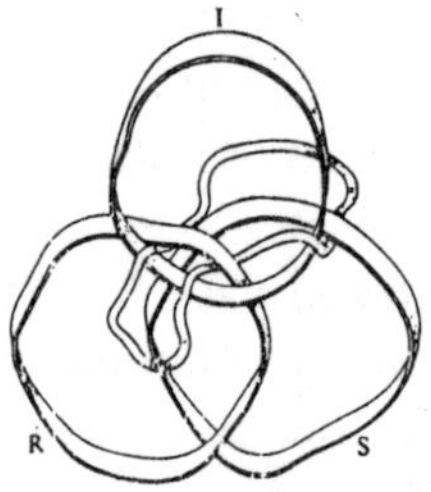

The Borromean knot with four rings[4]

II. Mythemes and Mathemes

> *If what I am saying necessitates not, as is said, a model, but the task of articulating topologically the discourse [of psychoanalysis] itself, this springs from the lack [*défaut*] in the universe, with the condition that what I say does not in turn offer to repair it [*le suppléer*].*
>
> Jacques Lacan[5]

Lacan's interest in a dialogue between psychoanalysis and mathematics had begun in the 1950's. The mathematician Georges Guilbaud, a personal friend of Lacan's whom he would contact for assistance with ideas or problems arising in the seminar, influenced him in particular by sharpening his appetite for and comprehension of topological figures.[6] In a curious way, Guilbaud came to authorize Lacan's introduction of the Borromean knot to the seminar. As Lacan puts it in the seminar *...ou pire* on 9 February 1972:

> A strange thing, while I was puzzling yesterday evening over how I was going to present to you today my tetradic geometry, it chanced that, having dinner with a charming person who attends M. Guilbaud's classes, I was given something like a ring to my finger, which I now wish to show you — as I learned yesterday night, it's nothing less than the coat-of-arms of the Borromei.[7]

The Borromean knot with three rings[8]

The young mathematician had told Lacan about the heraldic crest of the Milanese Borromeo family, which symbolizes a triple alliance by showing three intertwined rings. The three branches of the family are inextricably linked by the coat-of-arms, so that if one ring were broken, the entire knot would disintegrate.[9] Lacan's immediate gusto in embracing the figure perhaps came from his delight in the *coincidentia oppositorum* it embodied: its ostensible representational simplicity, the 'Borromean' quality of mutual interconnection belying its mathematical complexity, and its difficulty as a topological object. Later in Lacan's seminar, as we will see, this antinomy emerged as the troublesome discrepancy between the imaginary dimension of the knot — its *mise à plat*, or two-dimensional inscription — and its real, three-dimensional 'knottedness,' which was only accessible mathematically.

'Mathematical formalisation is our goal, our ideal,' Lacan told his seminar in 1973.[10] If this theoretical ambition was, as Elisabeth Roudinesco writes, 'a final attempt to save psychoanalysis from its origins in the occult and hypnotism,' to translate analytic knowledge from its location in the shifting, aleatory dimension of speech to a place of clearly-defined, reliable formulae, then its principal focus was the teaching of psychoanalysis.[11] The aim of formalisation, concludes Roudinesco, was 'to differentiate [psychoanalysis] from academic knowledge in a society where this, according to Lacan, was beginning to replace religion.'[12]

The term *mathème*, coined by Lacan in 1971 — condensing Lévi-Strauss's *mythème* and the Greek *μάθημα* (knowledge, lesson, science, teaching) — was introduced to articulate this pedagogical ideal: a matheme is that which is capable of integral transmission.[13] The immediate question raised by Lacan's aspiration — to produce, it seemed, a new kind of knowledge along with a new mode of its transmission — concerned the matheme's relation to the contingent discourse of its presentation. An illuminating remark occurs in the 1972-73 seminar, *Encore*:

> [M]athemes . . . are transmitted integrally. One has absolutely no idea what they mean, but they are transmitted. It remains no less true that they are only transmitted with the help of language, and that's what makes the whole business shaky.[14]

The epistemological rigour which the matheme aims to introduce — the quasi-scientific autonomy it seems to entail — is jeopardized, for Lacan, by its linguistic frame, as if the ideal of formalisation somehow necessitated a move beyond discourse. This move, between what Lacan figures with increasing emphasis in the 1970's as the irreconcilably different logics of speech and of writing, is the central stake of the Borromean knot, his last and most ambitious topological endeavour.

If Lacan's references to topology form the concluding chapter of his ambition to formalise, he takes pains to stress that they do not amount to any kind of transcendent knowledge or metalanguage. The Borromean knot is an instance of writing for Lacan, a form of *algèbre littérale* (algebra of letters) which adopts and adapts the signs of mathematics to open new theoretical possibilities and produce new styles of thinking.[15] One should bear in mind Juan-David Nasio's attempt to dispel some of the confusion around the mathematical elements in Lacan's thought by coining the term *topologerie* (modelled on Lacan's term *linguisterie*, used to designate the improper versions of linguistics in his work).[16]

Jacques-Alain Miller warns us to avoid, in our interpretations of the last period of Lacan's teaching, the dangerous tendency to 'extract Lacan's topology from his teaching.'[17] To read the figures sketched on the blackboard during the seminar as neat summaries or blueprints of psychoanalytic theory — rather than as engagements with the theoretical problems of the seminar, and as such strictly continuous with its discourse — is, for Miller, to trivialize Lacanian topology. This is not, on the other hand, to disregard Lacan's privileging of the matheme — his conviction that this new mode of theory offered an access to the real which was unavailable to the discursive field. Rather, it is to prevent the elevation of topology to the impossible position of a metalanguage, a language of being. Topology could never be an ontology, Lacan insisted; unlike the discourse of the master (the *maître* who might take 'my being' (*m'être*) as his subject), psychoanalysis is unable to 'say what is.'[18] The real evoked by topology, emerging in Lacan's final years as a kind of absolute existential negativity, or pure non-being, is never to be confused with any normative reality principle. As Lacan says in *La troisième*: 'The real is not of this world.'[19]

In the 1974-75 seminar *R.S.I.*, Lacan comes to designate the inextricability or intrication of the fundamental registers of his thought — the real, the symbolic and the imaginary — as a knot. If the mathemic status of the knot does not give it the transcendent position of a metalanguage — untouched by the intrication it designates — how are we to situate the knot itself? Lacan's shifting deployment of the knot and the increasing centrality he accords it lead to different formulations of this question (and even to divergent responses to it). There is, we might say, more than one Borromean knot in Lacan's teaching. If on the one hand this is due perhaps to the inherently diverse, elusive properties of the knot, its *nodalité* (quality of being knotted) never realized in any final, definitive form, it is first of all because of its problematic mathematical status.

The invocations of topology in Lacan's teaching fall into two quite distinct periods. Whatever theoretical continuities we can establish between these periods (roughly, the last two decades of Lacan's life), what remains radically different is the kind of mathematical reference at stake. The topological surfaces — the Moebius strip, the Klein bottle and the cross-cap — which take centre stage in the 1960's (from Lacan's *Seminar IX, Identification*) could be termed finished, i.e. fully theorized mathematically, so that the deployment of these objects is, at least on an initial level, mathematically comprehensible.[20] The same is not immediately true when, in the 1970's, Lacan begins to refer to the geometry of knots in support of his theorization.

The theory of knots in mathematics 'forms the core of a wide range of problems dealing with the position of one manifold imbedded within another.'[21] It brings together geometry and algebra to tackle its central problem, the calculation of topological invariants to differentiate knots. It thus presents a series of unresolved questions and mathematical problems, rather than a field of intelligible models or objects to be simply appropriated or manipulated.

The difficulty of establishing mathematical knowledge in knot theory might seem to lend the deployment of Lacan's favourite psychoanalytic *truc*, the Borromean knot, an air of *truquage* (trickery). There was indeed some confusion on *la planète Borromée* (to borrow Roudinesco's mock-epic phrase), some real misunderstandings in the exchanges between Lacan and the group of young philosophers and mathematicians with whom he worked closely in the 1970's to develop the *topologisation* of his teaching.[22] Yet the difficulty of thinking about the knot, which rendered its theoretical deployment at once exciting and precarious, was the greatest appeal it held for Lacan. 'The knot is something to which the mind is the most resistant,' he told an American audience in 1975.[23]. This aligned it as a theoretical object with his lifelong critique of imaginary forms of meaning, of the illusory charms of *sens*.[24]

The topology of the Borromean knot, unlike that of surfaces, is not in the first instance a theorization of the subject in psychoanalysis. It forms part of a wide-ranging reconceptualization of the theoretical terrain within which the Lacanian subject has taken shape, whose key terms are symbolic, signifier and structure. This does not constitute a simple retreat from the linguistic, structuralist moment of theorization, its replacement by models drawn from mathematics, but its re-writing. The *instance de la lettre* (agency of the letter), which for Lacan in 1957 marked the pre-eminence of the signifier for the speaking subject, is re-theorized in a topological *algèbre littérale*, whose object is not mathematical knowledge, but the real of psychoanalytic experience, something 'which has nothing to do with what traditional knowledge has upheld.'[25]

III. Writing the Knot

The aim of the discourse of the master . . . is that things should go in step for everybody. Well, that is in no way the same thing as the real, because the real, precisely, is that which 'won't go', that which gets in the way of the chariot; or better: that which unceasingly repeats itself in order to hinder this advance.

Jacques Lacan[26]

The place of the Borromean knot in Lacan's thought is aptly illustrated by a moment during his 1974 television broadcast, where what could be termed the opening of a gap between speech and writing occurs. Lacan is telling the public about the real, which

> permits the effective unknotting of what makes the symptom hold together, namely a knot of signifiers. Where here knotting and unknotting are not metaphors, but are really to be taken as those knots that in fact are built up through developing chains of the signifying material.[27]

The *mise à plat* of the Borromean knot appears in the text prepared by Jacques-Alain Miller shortly before the broadcast, although it is never named as such. The knot is set apart, positioned in the margin of the discourse proper. Miller explains in a foreword to *Television* that the marginal annotations (couched in the 'mathemic' terms of Lacanian formalisation) were added by him 'in the form of *manuductio*' (brief guide) after his request that Lacan should sift (*cribler*) what he wished to say.[28]

Whatever significance we may assign here to Miller's role (as formalising scribe, introducing 'mathemic' effects into Lacan's discourse), we cannot fail to note the different positions of speech and writing which emerge in this *mise en scène* of Lacanian theory.[29] The place of the Borromean knot is — to borrow a term Lacan coined to designate 'intimate exteriority' — one of 'extimacy' (*extimité*) in the text of *Television*.[30] It appears silently, shown but not given a name, as though it entails something irreducible to the speaking voice, which is always, for Lacan, the *dit-mension* (speech dimension) of the subject's truth.[31] It is not a metaphor, we are told, and thus it is not caught up in the differential weave of the symbolic order, but rather indicates the real construction of signifying chains. 'For these chains,' Lacan continues in *Television*, 'are not of meaning (*sens*) but of enjoy-meant (*jouis-sens*).'[32] The untranslatable pun brings together Lacanian incompatibles: the opaque, 'autistic' substance of jouissance and the virtual domain of meaning. It can be written as one wishes, 'as is implied by the punning [*l'équivoque*, the equivocation] that constitutes the law of the signifier.'[33] Equivocation, which is occluded by the speaking voice, but rendered visible by a written text, encapsulates something of the real signifying material of language, something which is *shown* — silently and literally, beyond speech — by the Borromean knot.

What becomes visible in the text of *Television*, in the dramatic collision of speech and writing, in the gap which opens between Lacan's voice and the marginal sifting (*criblage*), is the spectacle of a thought dominated by the axiomatic of a linguistic subject (the symptom is still a knot of signifiers) striving to exceed itself, to extend its grasp of 'the law of the signifier' beyond (its own) structuralist formulae. The uncanny showing (*monstration*) of the knot is at once a more rigorous expression of this law, and something unspeakable, heterogeneous to it.

For a clearer idea of what this showing constitutes, we need to return to the 'primal scene' of the Borromean knot, namely Lacan's enthusiastic discovery of it in 1972. To what clinical and theoretical problems does the knot first respond? At its introduction in the 1971-72 seminar *...ou pire*, the knot takes part in the formalisation of speech. Lacan takes the spoken phrase '*Je te demande de refuser ce que je t'offre, parce que c'est pas ça*' (I ask you to refuse what I offer you, because that's not it) as an 'enunciation of the impossibility of the sexual relationship.'[34] His first schematization of the phrase is a tetrahedron, a four-faced figure inter-linking its pronouns and verbs. Yet the new discovery of the Borromean knot is brought forward as a more perfect version, fitting Lacan 'like a ring to a finger.'[35] Any two of the circles in the Borromean knot are only held together due to the position of the third, so that all three are simultaneously interconnected. Thus the knot embodies the inextricable verbs of the phrase, the impossibility of any binary *rapport* it figures. '[W]hen I have spoken of the signifying chain,' comments Lacan, 'I have always implied that concatenation.' But more importantly, he adds:

> Demand, Refusal and Offer — it is clear that, in this knot which I have brought forward for you today, each takes on meaning only from the others. But what results from this knot . . . is that it is the foundation, the root, of what belongs to the object *a*.[36]

In later versions of the Borromean knot, the object *a* will be written in its central intersection, wedged 'anamorphically' between real, symbolic and imaginary.[37] But already on its first appearance here, the knot designates something beyond the signifying chain, its signifying concatenation somehow paradoxically evoking the absolute negativity of the object *a* (an object 'for which there is no idea,' as Lacan comments in *La troisième*).[38] The inextricable verbs and pronouns of the phrase — I ask you to refuse what I offer you — are supplemented, crucially, by the final 'that's not it.'

Lacan's next move is to link this impossibility of *rapport*, this objectal stumbling block, to problems in theory. He begins by stating the uncanny proximity of signification and the object *a*, its unspeakable obverse: 'What I am leading you to is this — not how meaning arises, but how it is from a knot of meaning that the object arises, the object itself . . . namely the object *a*.'[39] He goes on to name Wittgenstein as a thinker who concluded that 'we should not speak about that which cannot be spoken of.'[40] 'It is,' Lacan continues, 'precisely that which cannot be spoken of which is in question when I mark as "that's not it" the sole motivation of a demand such as "to refuse what I offer you".'[41]

The object *a*, as negative object knotting together the three verbs, corresponds to the logical limit of language designated as a place of silence, of the non-theorizable, by Wittgenstein. It was Lacan's reading of Wittgenstein, writes Roudinesco, that was a key factor leading him to rethink the status of the discourse of psychoanalysis, seeking its basis no longer in the fluctuations of *la parole* (speech) but instead in *monstration*, a form of 'showing' which aimed beyond the logical limits of speech.[42] François Baudry has gone so far as to argue that, as the purest topological instance of this showing, the Borromean knot is equivalent to — even a *form* of — the object *a*.[43]

From the moment of its introduction to Lacan's teaching — as part of an attempt to theorize the impossible as that which prevents *rapport* — the Borromean knot figures something beyond the logic of a model, of metaphorical representation. It emerges as a paradoxical co-incidence of the inseparable verbs in a phrase and the invisible object embodying the impossible relation it expresses. Lacan's response in 1975 to a sceptical question — 'Despite what you say, in the end isn't this knot a simple model?' — is emphatic: 'It does not constitute a model in so far as it comprises something before which the imagination fails. And the mathematical approach to it in topology is inadequate.'[44]

Unlike the topological surfaces of the 1960's, the Borromean knot — as real *nouage* (knotting), irreducible even to its topological *mise à plat* — offers no representational equivalence to or of the subject. It is strictly identical to structure, not some metaphorical guide to it, to paraphrase a remark in *L'étourdit*.[45]

Lacan addresses the central paradox of the Borromean knot — its non-metaphorical, 'acephalic' essence — in his most concentrated elaboration of it, the 1974-75 seminar *R.S.I.* Announcing the year's project — to try to think the real by first writing the real, the symbolic and the imaginary as a Borromean knot — Lacan states the initial theoretical problem: that of finding the common measure of three terms hitherto understood as being radically heterogeneous.[46]

Real, symbolic and imaginary in the Borromean knot[47]

If the knot's definition as Borromean — its intrication completely undone if any one of its strands is severed — implies, as it were, the homogenization of Lacan's categories, their reconception as components of something larger, a whole series of questions arises vis-à-vis earlier formulations. What becomes, for instance, of the ethical differences between the three registers, such as the oft-stated antinomy between the imaginary as realm of infantile delusion and the symbolic as site of the subject's truth? And, again, in which category — real, symbolic or imaginary — would the knot itself, and the theoretical discourse in which it is embedded, be situated?

In 1974 Lacan gave a paper in Rome entitled *La troisième*, in which he discussed the 'third' of his categories (the real, whose theoretical elaboration came after that of the imaginary and the symbolic) in a self-mocking reprise of his 1953 'Rome discourse,' the *fonction et champ* of the earlier title now becoming *fiction et chant* (fiction and song).[48] He reminded his audience that although to write the real, the symbolic and the imaginary as a Borromean knot might seem a new turn in his thought, it was not the first time he had inter-linked the three terms. A lecture entitled *Le symbolique, l'imaginaire et le réel* had in fact, twenty years before, served as a preliminary outline of the conceptual field developed in the first Rome discourse.[49]

Beyond the ostensible continuity of their terms (although the changed order of those terms does seem to imply a shift in priority, as Lacan occasionally hints), a comparison of these two texts reveals a series of stark contrasts. In 1953, symbolic, imaginary and real, the 'three essential registers of human reality,' are conceived by Lacan as sharply distinct from one another.[50] The relation between the imaginary and the symbolic — by implication, the essential relation in analysis — is presented as syntactic: the symbolic order intervenes in the disorderly cluster of imaginary formations, introducing mediation and thus allowing 'properly human relations' to be realized.[51] In other words, the theoretical relation operates in favour of the symbolic. As for the real, at this point it is barely distinguished from reality of the symbolically mediated type, present, say, in Freud's works under the form of the reality principle.[52] By ascribing theoretical (as well as 'existential') pre-eminence to the symbolic, Lacan's early paper constructs the relation between the three registers in accordance with what, in *Science and Truth*, he terms the 'architecture arrived at by means of combinatory analysis,' or the 'mathematics of the signifier.'[53] The relation between the orders is one of separation and difference, with the real and the imaginary governed by the organisational force of the symbolic.

This privileging of the symbolic — and the concomitant 'ethical' privilege accorded to the subject as site of lawful or truthful mediation — is, to say the least, rendered problematic by the architecture Lacan is working with by 1974. If the definition of the Borromean knot is that no one of its elements is detachable from, or has any priority over the others, then its structuring principle cannot belong to any single register. The intrication of the knot amounts to the abandonment of the neatly organized grid of boundaries and divisions installed by the *évidement* (voidance, clearing) of the symbolic, and its replacement by strange, paradoxical forms of continuity and coalescence.

In the opening session of the seminar *R.S.I.*, Lacan poses the inevitable question about the status of the knot: 'Does it belong to the symbolic, the imaginary or the real?'[54] Lacan's response is characteristically defiant of expectations: 'In so far as it is supported by the number three, the Borromean knot is of the register of the imaginary.'[55] 'The imaginary,' he continues later in the session, 'always tends to reduce itself to a two-dimensional figure (*mise à plat*).'[56] So that the topological diagram, given consistence by its three rings, remains caught in a realm of *méconnaissance* which the knot in itself, its mathematical *nodalité*, eludes.

Elsewhere in the same seminar, Lacan reserves a special place in the knot for the symbolic, in terms which recall the privilege formerly associated with the subject as site of desire, *manque à être* (lack of being): '[T]he symbolic turns around an inviolate hole, without which the knot of three would not be Borromean. That is the meaning of the Borromean knot: the hole of the symbolic is inviolate.'[57]

If the preservation of a symbolic void at its heart is not, it seems, in conflict with the imaginary *mise à plat* of the knot, both these aspects (the attributes, in former times, of the lacking subject and the deluded ego) seem to be radically challenged by Lacan's remarks on 17 December 1974:

> The Borromean knot is a writing. This writing supports a real. So can the real be supported by a writing? Yes indeed, and I shall even say more: there is no other sensible idea of the real than the one offered by writing, by the trait of writing.[58]

This is the notion of the Borromean knot to which Lacan most often returns: its representation of the real does not conform to the logic of the signifier. The signification it entails is ultimately identical with the thing signified. Yet, we might immediately ask, if the knot embodies the non-metaphorical idea of the real, how can one of its constituents be the symbolic, which is defined by the paternal metaphor as precisely the evacuation of the real? And how can the presentation of the knot be termed imaginary, if it supports the absolutely unimaginable real?

Lacan offers another triple schema in *R.S.I.* to untangle some of the complexities of the knot's definition. The series *consistence* (consistency), *ex-sistence* (ex-sistence) and *trou* (hole) is mapped onto that of imaginary, real and symbolic respectively.[59] The classical image of three rings, as shown in the Milanese coat-of-arms, offers a consistent version of the Borromean knot, which is ostensibly at odds with the real of its knottedness. Borrowing the trope *ek-stasis* from Heidegger, Lacan now terms the knot as such *ex-sistent*, i.e. situated beyond meaning, outside of any imaginary or symbolic forms.[60] It is never 'that,' *c'est pas ça*, to recall the negative definition of object *a* in *...ou pire*. The third term, *trou* (hole), is perhaps the hardest to grasp as an aspect or feature of the knot. How is this return of the subject — its symbolic 'nihilation' somehow immanent to the structure of the knot — to be reconciled with the 'demotion' of the symbolic to one of three elements?[61] How can pure *évidement* cohere in the same knot as the brute substance of jouissance? As Jean Allouch writes:

> [T]o present a certain Borromean knotting of R, S and I as the support of the subject as such is to resituate the subject in relation to three types of consistence, and no longer only the symbolic — even if the symbolic was not alone. Henceforth the three consistences would be equivalent in the event of a subjectification.[62]

One way of understanding the shift in Lacan's notion of the subject has been to articulate the changes introduced by topology with the increasing importance, in Lacan's thought, of the psychoanalytic symptom. Pierre Skriabine begins by distinguishing between different topological periods:

> Let us note that Lacan's topology in the 1960's takes the Other as its point of departure, to end . . . by bringing into effect the incompleteness of the Other, the structural position of lack in the Other; beginning with O, it ends with Ø, while the topology of the 1970's, that of knots, is explicitly founded on Ø.[63]

Jacques-Alain Miller argues that the earlier topology — that of surfaces — was especially germane to the Lacanian conception of the unconscious, because 'the place of the Other in a Lacanian sense (which is the unconscious and discourse), has no depth.'[64] This superficial unconscious, lacking any intuitive essence or interiority, was the site of the subject, described by Miller (in an adaptation of the 'triple s' of *sujet supposé savoir*, Lacan's formula for transference) as *sujet sans substance*: a surface-subject, a subject without substance.[65] Now, the shift from a topology of surfaces to one of knots corresponds to a profound change in the conception of the symbolic order. The symbolic is split into signifier and symptom, the latter now defined as substantial, embodying the inert jouissance left behind by signification. As we have seen, another way Lacan figured this — the move from an axiomatic of the Other to an axiomatic of the real — was by contrasting speech and writing, drawing a firm distinction between the *dit-mension* (speech dimension) of the subject and the objectal 'stuff' of the letter (*la lettre*): 'The written is not in any way of the same register . . . as the signifier.'[66]

In the topology of the Borromean knot, Lacanian theory no longer offered an account centred on an insubstantial subject, whose coherence derived from its position as speaking being (*parlêtre*). It constituted in itself — as writing embodying a certain real — a 'subversion of the subject,' a quasi-ontological (or 'onto-graphic') substance, which seemed incommensurable with a notion of the subject as a linguistic instance of pure negativity. 'From the mid-1970's,' writes Miller,

> it was a question, for Lacan — has it ever been grasped? — of an interrogation more radical than had ever been formulated, of the very foundations of psychoanalysis, whose starting-point was the symptom as extra-discursive.[67]

IV. *Dénouements*

> *I consider that my having put forward, in the form of a writing, the real in question amounts to what is usually called a traumatisation.*
>
> Jacques Lacan[68]

> *[I]f the unconscious is structured like a language, it is not immediately discourse of the Other: it only becomes so through the artifice of the analytic experience. Where there was an always autistic jouissance, analysis causes effects of the signified to come about; it operates on the symptom by introducing into it a special effect of signification, known as the 'subject-supposed-to-know'; but in itself, the symptom means nothing to anyone: it is ciphering, it is jouissance, the pure jouissance of a writing-process.*
>
> Jacques-Alain Miller[69]

The changed conception of the symbolic and the consequent questioning of the subject led inevitably to a major re-alignment of Lacanian psychoanalysis. The significance of the father (for Lacan always the key Freudian trope) was radically re-cast by the writing of the Borromean knot. Serge André remarks:

> [I]t is through a progressive purification of the concept of the Name-of-the-Father and the relating of it to Lacan's other great invention, the object *a*, that there opens up the necessity of the last period of his teaching, which he devoted to the Borromean knot.[70]

In Lacan's earlier (pre-topological) period, the Name-of-the-Father functioned as the guarantee of the consistency of the Other, allowing us to write it as S(O), the signifier of an unbarred, coherent Other. Thus, in *Seminar III, The Psychoses* (1955-56), the foreclosure of the Name-of-the-Father indicated the absence of the primordial *Bejahung*, the affirmation which formed the basis of the subject's symbolic coming-to-be.[71] Foreclosure designated a failure of the subject, its absent place in an organized symbolic space swallowed up by the pathological presence of drives.

With the introduction of the object *a* (around 1960, at the same time as the first references to topology) a certain lack in the Other is given a theoretical place. Object *a* is the mark of an impossibility, something irreducible to symbolic structure. Yet the father still retains his place as protective guarantee. Serge André reads the Lacanian matheme for fantasy, $\$ \diamond a$, as a confirmation of this: '[T]he Name-of-the-Father . . . renders the fantasy livable for the subject, by introducing a lozenge [*poinçon*, $\diamond$] between $\$$ and *a*.'[72] By operating as a liaison between the subject and the traumatic object, the Name-of-the-Father enables the organization of jouissance, allowing the subject to take up a position (of identification) as a refuge, a protection, from the real.

The purification of the Name-of-the-Father corresponds to the gradual dissociation of nomination and paternity, of the symbolic act of naming and the 'pathological' singularity of a father. In 1963, Lacan's title for the seminar which was interrupted (owing to a crisis around IPA membership, leading to Lacan's foundation of the *Ecole freudienne de Paris*) was *Les Noms du Père* (The Names-of-the-Father).[73] Although this seminar, which would have pluralized the Name-of-the-Father, was never finished, Lacan had by then definitively moved away from the wish to conceive metaphor as specifically linked to paternity.

By the 1970's, a more general field emerged: that of *suppléance* (suppletion) as particular, symptomatic forms of what could be termed a 'making up' for the lack in the Other.[74]

Bound up with these changes was a reconceptualization of foreclosure, and thus of the diagnostic separation of neurosis and psychosis. If Lacan's 1956 definition of foreclosure, which had adopted Freud's notion of *Verwerfung* to designate the absence of a fundamental signifier in the symbolic, resulting in a psychotic return of the signifier in the real, connected foreclosure closely with the Name-of-the-Father, by the 1970's the outbreak of psychosis is figured through a generalised notion of 'un-knotting': the coming-undone, in various ways, of real, symbolic and imaginary.[75] In radical foreclosure, Lacan states in 1976, the 'orientation of the real . . . forecloses meaning.'[76] The entire field of signification, from the ego's self-delusions to the most privileged symbol, is simply disabled, over-ridden by a particularity, something utterly outside any economy of signs.

The generalisation of foreclosure is bound up with what can only be described as a crisis in Lacanian theory, whose result was the re-centering of psychoanalysis around a new conception of the symptom. If, in an initial moment, the Borromean knot had seemed to offer the possibility of a coherent formalisation of Lacan's three terms, it became clear in the seminar *R.S.I.* that a triple knot was by no means the final or definitive version. With no privileged position accorded to the symbolic as a metaphor assuring the coherence of the knot, there was no reason why a fourth term should not emerge (...and then a fifth, the 'chain-knot' having no limit to the number of its links). By 1975, Lacan came to figure the fourth term in the knot as symptom (marked as Σ in the diagram):

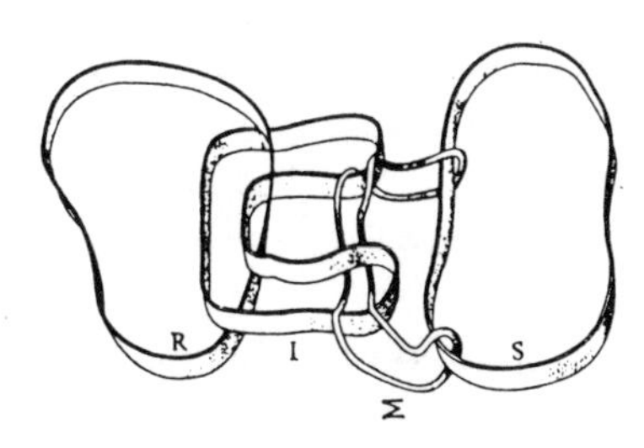

The symptom in the Borromean knot[77]

The abandonment of the triple knot constituted a theoretical crisis: the lack of any normative basis for the knot, centred by a privileged term within it, meant that it could only be constructed — either by a subject in analysis or by a theoretician — in particular, symptomatic ways. The organization of each individual's jouissance — irredeemably 'local' and incompatible with any theoretical code — became the principle of a *clinique du symptôme* (clinic of the symptom), in which no specific term was privileged. Within such a perspective, as Pierre Skriabine writes, 'the paternal metaphor . . . bears a singular resemblance to the delusional metaphor.'[78]

Serge André has explored some of the clinical consequences of this theoretical crisis.[79] Lacan's failure to establish a definitive Borromean structure which could have provided a centre for a newly conceived, consistent psychoanalytic field, raises for André a series of questions. Firstly, the new conception of the symptom as 'on a par with,' able to stand in for, the Name-of-the-Father drastically revises the position of the symptom in analysis. Recasting one of Lacan's titles, André formulates a 'second question preliminary to any possible treatment of psychosis, or even a question preliminary to any psychoanalysis,' namely: 'Is the symptom brought by the subject who comes to ask for an analysis not precisely that which assures him that he is not psychotic?'[80] If the analyst does not comply with the demand to dissolve the symptom, having judged that the analysand might become psychotic, does analysis then seek to nurture or elaborate the symptom? And is it still psychoanalysis then?[81]

André's work further draws upon the Borromean knot to re-think the categories and structures of analytic practice in terms of the relations between real, symbolic and imaginary. He distinguishes between a Freudian knot in which the separate terms R, S, I are bound together by a fourth, the Name-of-the-Father, and a Lacanian variety in which an error in the Borromean structure gives rise to a symptomatic fourth, necessary to prevent un-knotting. The latter situation underlies the 'case' of James Joyce, which Lacan treats in his seminar *Le sinthome*, whereby Joyce's writing of an 'epiphany' is deemed to avert a psychotic collapse.[82] Inspiration for this kind of Borromean clinic is provided by the closing session of *R.S.I.*, where Lacan writes the Freudian trio of inhibition, symptom and anxiety (the title of Freud's 1926 text) as a Borromean knot.[83] Each term is a kind of nomination corresponding, in turn, to the imaginary, the symbolic and the real.[84]

However, some of Lacan's followers have argued that the very possibility of maintaining a distinction between analytic practice and its theory is rendered problematic by the Borromean knot. They claim that as a writing of the real the knot unsettles the entire psychoanalytic field, with its tidy categories of clinical speech, 'secondary' writing, and so on.[85] In this sense, the knot again emerges as a limit of psychoanalytic thought, unassimilable to its established protocols.

Radical foreclosure, where the subject falls away before the meaningless particularity of the real, is also invoked by Lacan as an explanation of a writing process. At the beginning of the 1975-76 seminar *Le sinthome*, he clarifies how the agenda set out the previous year, in *R.S.I.*, has been revised:

> Jacques Aubert . . . has persuaded me to introduce Joyce in a symposium. It is thus that I have allowed myself to be diverted from my project, which I announced to you last year, of entitling this seminar *4, 5, 6*. I am sticking to 4 . . .[86]

This diversion takes Lacan into the domain of the letter, the Joycean text. It is here that the 'fourth' of the knot — the symptom — is reformulated as *sinthome*.[87] Joyce's writing effects a suppletion, makes up for the failure of the knot to cohere, by reconstituting the knot as well as the place it allows the subject. It is no accident that Lacan's teaching remains 'stuck' at the point of this *sinthomatique* writing, that it is unable to progress evenly onto the rest of the series: the move from the knot of three to a symptomatic fourth corresponds to the opening of theory onto the real as non-theorizable. As the real of the symptom, *sinthome* is illegible, asemic — marking, not some logic or structure of signification, but the specific modality of a subject's relation to jouissance.

V. Conclusion

The Borromean knot is a demonstration of the radical continuity between Lacanian theory and its object, formulated by Lacan as the lack of a metalanguage. Access to a real conceived as *ex-sistence*, irreducible to any image or signifier, can only be afforded for Lacan by a writing which is ultimately incommensurable with the symbolic order, beyond metaphor.

Jacques-Alain Miller refers to René Magritte's famous painting *Ceci n'est pas une pipe* as the embodiment of a spatial paradox, similar to Lacan's *mise à plat* of the Borromean knot. To write 'This is not a metaphor' beneath an image of the knot would be to raise a Magrittesque question: 'Are not the image and the words part of the same "picture"?'[88] How can any instance of language escape the semiotic conditions of representation?

The Borromean knot marks the outer limit of Lacanian theory, the point where the formalising ambition of the matheme finally collapses into the non-theorizable, the untranslatable real of the symptom. As Lacan's theoretical legacy, the knot has had an uneven reception. While it has been embraced with enthusiasm by certain followers, others have turned away from it, viewing it as the result of 'a dialogue of confusion' (as Pierre Soury described his exchanges with Lacan).[89] The *dénouement* (un-knotting, dissolution) of Lacan's teaching, which coincided with the dissolution of the *Ecole freudienne de Paris*, has not produced the interpretive consensus amongst his heirs which might have assured its coherence with the body of Lacanian theory. The thought of the real, which Lacan once half-jokingly dubbed his 'symptomatic response' to Freud, embodied a paradoxical *jouis-sens* whose traumatic effects are still being written.[90]

Notes

1. See: J. Lacan, L'étourdit, *Scilicet*, 1973, no. 4, pp. 5-52.
2. For 'the epic of the Borromean knot,' see: J. Dor, The Epistemological Status of Lacan's Mathematical Paradigms (1991) (trans. P. Nagel), in D. Pettigrew & F. Raffoul (Eds.), *Disseminating Lacan*, Albany NY, State University of New York Press, 1996, p. 119.
3. See: J. Lacan, L'étourdit, *o.c.*, p. 34.
4. J. Lacan, Conférences et entretiens dans des universités nord-américaines, *Scilicet*, 1976, nos. 6/7, p. 39.
5. J. Lacan, L'étourdit, *o.c.*, pp. 33-34. My translation.

6. See: E. Roudinesco, *Jacques Lacan & Co.: A History of Psychoanalysis in France 1925-1985* (1986) (trans. J. Mehlman), London, Free Association Books, 1990, pp. 563-564; E. Roudinesco, *Jacques Lacan. Esquisse d'une vie, histoire d'un système de pensée*, Paris, Fayard, 1993, p. 450 & 469.

7. J. Lacan, *Le Séminaire XIX, ...ou pire* (1971-72), unpublished, seminar of 9 February 1972. My translation.

8. *Ibid.*, seminar of 9 February 1972.

9. Although 'Borromean knot' is the term used in this paper, due to its place in the vocabulary of Lacanian psychoanalysis, the figure is not, strictly speaking, a knot in topology (which defines a knot as the homeomorphism in three-dimensional space of a *single* circle). By 1976, Lacan was talking of *une chaînœud borroméenne*, a Borromean 'chain-knot.' Topologists refer to our subject as the 'Borromean rings.' See: J. Lacan, Le Séminaire XXIII, Le sinthome (1975-76), texte établi par J.-A. Miller, *Ornicar ?*, 1976, no. 7, p. 17 (seminar of 13 January 1976); R.H. Crowell & R.H. Fox, *Introduction to Knot Theory*, New York NY, Springer, 1963.

10. J. Lacan, *Le Séminaire, Livre XX, Encore* (1972-73), texte établi par J.-A. Miller, Paris, du Seuil, 1975, p. 108. My translation.

11. E. Roudinesco, *Jacques Lacan. Esquisse d'une vie, histoire d'un système de pensée*, *o.c.*, p. 449. My translation.

12. *Ibid.*, p. 450. My translation.

13. See: J. Lacan, *Le Séminaire XIX, Le savoir du psychanalyste* (1971-72), unpublished, seminar of 2 December 1971. For Levi-Strauss's notion of *mythème*, see for example: C. Lévi-Strauss, The Structural Study of Myth, *Structural Anthropology* (1958) (trans. C. Jacobson & B. Grundfest Schoepf), New York NY-London, Basic Books, 1963, pp. 206-231 and pp. 211-212 in particular.

14. J. Lacan, *Le Séminaire, Livre XX, Encore, o.c.*, p. 100. My translation.

15. See: J. Lacan, L'étourdit, *o.c.*, p. 28.

16. J.-D. Nasio, *Les yeux de Laure. Transfert, objet a et topologie dans la théorie de J. Lacan*, Paris, Aubier, 1987, pp. 151-163.

17. J.-A. Miller, La topologie dans l'ensemble de l'enseignement de Lacan, *Quarto*, 1981, no. 2, p. 13.

18. See: J. Lacan, *Le Séminaire, Livre XX, Encore, o.c.*, p. 33; J. Lacan, L'étourdit, *o.c.*, p. 29.

19. See: J. Lacan, La troisième (1974), *Lettres de l'Ecole freudienne*, 1975, no. 16, p. 184.

20. See: J. Lacan, *Le Séminaire IX, L'identification* (1961-62), unpublished.

21. R.H. Crowell & R.H. Fox, *Introduction to Knot Theory*, *o.c.*, p. vii.

22. See: E. Roudinesco, *Jacques Lacan. Esquisse d'une vie, histoire d'un système de pensée*, *o.c.*, p. 473.

23. J. Lacan, Conférences et entretiens dans des universités nord-américaines, *o.c.*, p. 59. My translation.

24. I follow John Forrester and Sylvana Tomaselli in translating *sens* as 'meaning,' rather than 'sense,' which was suggested by Stuart Schneiderman. See: J. Forrester & S. Tomaselli, Translators' note, in J. Lacan, *The Seminar. Book I: Freud's Papers on Technique* (1953-54) (trans. with notes J. Forrester), Edited by J.-A. Miller,

Cambridge, Cambridge University Press, 1988, p. vii; S. Schneiderman, Translator's Preface, in *How Lacan's Ideas are Used in Clinical Practice* (1980) (Selections edited and translated by S. Schneiderman), Northvale NJ-London, Jason Aronson Inc., 1993, p. vii.

25. J. Lacan, *Le Séminaire, Livre XX, Encore, o.c.*, p. 118. My translation. For 'the agency of the letter,' see: J. Lacan, The Agency of the Letter in the Unconscious or Reason since Freud (1957), *Ecrits: A Selection* (trans. A. Sheridan), London, Tavistock, 1977, pp. 146-178.

26. J. Lacan, La troisième, *o.c.*, p. 183. My translation.

27. J. Lacan, *Television/A Challenge to the Psychoanalytic Establishment* (1973) (trans. D. Hollier, R. Krauss & A. Michelson), Edited by J. Copjec, New York NY-London, W.W. Norton & Company, 1990, p. 10.

28. *Ibid.*, Prefatory Note.

29. Miller has recently commented on this role: 'When I published Lacan's *Television*, which reads like a highly contrived text with a great deal of difficult rhetoric, I included a number of schemas in the margins to indicate that Lacan's rhetoric constitutes a commentary of a very precise nature.' J.-A. Miller, An Introduction to Seminars I and II: Lacan's Orientation Prior to 1953 (III), in R. Feldstein, B. Fink & M. Jaanus (Eds.), *Reading Seminars I and II: Lacan's Return to Freud*, Albany NY, State University of New York Press, 1996, p. 30.

30. For the term 'extimacy,' see: J. Lacan, *The Seminar. Book VII: The Ethics of Psychoanalysis* (1959-60) (trans. with notes D. Porter), Edited by J.-A. Miller, New York NY-London, W.W. Norton & Company, 1992, p. 139; J.-A. Miller, Extimité (trans. F. Massardier-Kenney), in M. Bracher, M. Alcorn Jr., R. Corthell & F. Massardier-Kenney (Eds.), *Lacanian Theory of Discourse: Subject, Structure and Society*, New York NY, New York University Press, 1994, pp. 74-87.

31. J. Lacan, *Le Séminaire, Livre XX, Encore*, *o.c.*, p. 97.

32. J. Lacan, *Television/A Challenge to the Psychoanalytic Establishment, o.c.*, p. 10.

33. *Ibid.*, p. 10.

34. J. Lacan, *Le Séminaire XIX, ...ou pire*, *o.c.*, seminar of 9 February 1972. My translation. The gloss is taken from: S. André, Clinique et nœud borroméen, *Actes de L'Ecole de la Cause freudienne*, 1982, no. 2, pp. 86-94 and p. 90 in particular.

35. See: J. Lacan, *Le Séminaire XIX, ...ou pire*, *o.c.*, seminar of 9 February 1972.

36. *Ibid.*, seminar of 9 February 1972. My translation.

37. For Lacan's discussion of anamorphosis, see J. Lacan, *The Four Fundamental Concepts of Psychoanalysis* (1964) (trans. A. Sheridan), Edited by J.-A. Miller, London, The Hogarth Press and the Institute of Psycho-Analysis, 1977, pp. 79-90. For an account of the 'extimate' place of object *a* in the Borromean knot, see: P. Skriabine, Clinique et topologie (1989), *La Cause freudienne. Revue de psychanalyse*, 1993, no. 23, pp. 117-133 and p. 127 in particular.

38. J. Lacan, La troisième, *o.c.*, p. 183.

39. J. Lacan, *Le Séminaire XIX, ...ou pire, o.c.*, seminar of 9 February 1972. My translation.

40. Of course, the reference is to the concluding statement of Wittgenstein's *TractatusLogico-Philosophicus*. See: L. Wittgenstein, *TractatusLogico-Philosophicus* (1919) (trans. D.F. Pears & B.F. McGuinness), London, Routledge, 1961.

41. J. Lacan, *Le Séminaire XIX, ...ou pire, o.c.*, seminar of 9 February 1972. My translation.

42. See: E. Roudinesco, *Jacques Lacan, Esquisse d'une vie, histoire d'un système de pensée, o.c.*, pp. 469-470.

43. See: F. Baudry, Le nœud borroméen et l'objet *a*, in M. Deguy (Ed.), *Lacan avec les philosophes*, Paris, Albin Michel, 1991, pp. 179-187.

44. J. Lacan, Le Séminaire XXIII, Le sinthome, o.c., seminar of 9 December 1975, *Ornicar ?*, 1976, no. 6, p. 19. My translation.

45. J. Lacan, L'étourdit, *o.c.*, p. 40.

46. See: J. Lacan, Le Séminaire XXII, R.S.I. (1974-75), texte établi par J.-A. Miller, *Ornicar ?*, 1975, no. 2, p. 90 (seminar of 10 December 1974).

47. J. Lacan, Conférences et entretiens dans des universités nord-américaines, *o.c.*, p. 49.

48. J. Lacan, La troisième, *o.c.*, pp. 177-203; J. Lacan, L'étourdit, *o.c.*, p. 18; J. Lacan, The Function and Field of Speech and Language in Psychoanalysis (1953), *Ecrits: A Selection, o.c.*, pp. 30-113.

49. J. Lacan, La troisième, *o.c.*, p. 182; J. Lacan, Le symbolique, l'imaginaire et le réel (1953), *Bulletin de l'Association freudienne*, 1982, no. 1, pp. 4-13.

50. J. Lacan, Le symbolique, l'imaginaire et le réel, *o.c.*, p. 5. My translation.

51. *Ibid.*, pp. 13-14. My translation.

52. See: S. Freud, Formulations on the Two Principles of Mental Functioning (1911*b*), *Standard Edition*, XII, pp. 213-226.

53. J. Lacan, Science and Truth (1965) (trans. B. Fink), *Newsletter of the Freudian Field*, 1989, no. 3, p. 10.

54. J. Lacan, Le Séminaire XXII, R.S.I., seminar of 10 December 1974, *o.c.*, p. 94. My translation.

55. *Ibid.*, p. 94. My translation.

56. *Ibid.*, p. 95. My translation.

57. J. Lacan, Le Séminaire XXII, R.S.I., o.c., seminar of 11 March 1975, *Ornicar ?*, 1975-76, no. 5, p. 21. My translation.

58. J. Lacan, Le Séminaire XXII, R.S.I., o.c., seminar of 17 December 1974, *Ornicar ?*, 1975, no. 2, p. 100. My translation.

59. J. Lacan, Le Séminaire XXII, R.S.I., o.c., seminar of 18 February 1975, *Ornicar ?*, 1975, no. 4, pp. 101-106.

60. Heidegger's term *Ekstasis* had been rendered as *ex-sistance* in the French translations of his *Being and Time*.

61. For the assimilation of hole and structure, see: J. Lacan, L'étourdit, *o.c.*, p. 40.

62. J. Allouch, Tel 36 53 75, *Esquissespsychanalytiques*, 1991, no. 15, p. 29. My translation.

63. P. Skriabine, Clinique et topologie, *o.c.*, p. 119. My translation. The article's notations (A, Ⱥ) are here given an English equivalent (O, Ø).

64. J.-A. Miller, La topologie dans l'ensemble de l'enseignement de Lacan, *o.c.*, p. 16. My translation.

65. *Ibid.*, p. 17.

66. J. Lacan, *Le Séminaire, Livre XX, Encore, o.c.*, p. 31. My translation.

67. J.-A. Miller, Préface, in J. Aubert (Ed.), *Joyce avec Lacan*, Paris, Navarin, 1987, p. 11. My translation.

68. J. Lacan, Le Séminaire XXIII, Le sinthome, o.c., seminar of 13 April 1976, *Ornicar ?*, 1977, no. 10, p. 6. My translation.

69. J.-A. Miller, Préface, *o.c.*, p. 11. My translation.

70. S. André, Clinique et nœud borroméen, *o.c.*, p. 88. My translation.

71. See: J. Lacan, *The Seminar. Book III: The Psychoses* (1955-56) (trans. with notes R. Grigg), Edited by J.-A. Miller, New York NY-London, W.W. Norton & Company, 1993, p. 321.

72. S. André, Clinique et nœud borroméen, *o.c.*, p. 89. My translation. For the matheme of the fantasy, see for example: J. Lacan, *Le Séminaire, Livre VIII, Le transfert* (1960-61), texte établi par J.-A. Miller, Paris, du Seuil, 1991, p. 370.

73. See: J. Lacan, Introduction to the Names-of-the-Father Seminar (1963), *Television/A Challenge to the Psychoanalytic Establishment, o.c.*, pp. 81-95.

74. For discussions of 'suppletion,' see for example: J. Lacan, Le Séminaire XXIII, Le sinthome, o.c., seminar of 18 November 1975, *Ornicar ?*, 1976, no. 6, p. 6; M.-H. Brousse, Question de suppléance, *Ornicar ?*, 1988, no. 47, pp. 65-73; M. Liart, La suppléance comme tentative de guérison, *Actes de l'Ecole de la Cause freudienne*, 1988, no. 15, pp. 17-20.

75. Lacan introduces 'foreclosure' as a translation for *Verwerfung* in the final session of *Seminar III*. See: J. Lacan, *The Seminar. Book III: The Psychoses, o.c.*, p. 321. For Freud's notion of *Verwerfung*, see: S. Freud, From the History of an Infantile Neurosis (1918*b*[1914]), *Standard Edition*, XVII, p. 84.

76. J. Lacan, Le Séminaire XXIII, Le sinthome, o.c., seminar of 16 March 1976, *Ornicar ?*, 1977, no. 9, p. 34. My translation.

77. J. Lacan, Conférences et entretiens dans des universités nord-américaines, *o.c.*, p. 39.

78. P. Skriabine, Clinique et topologie, *o.c.*, p. 133. My translation.

79. See: S. André, Clinique et nœud borroméen, *o.c.*, pp. 91-94.

80. *Ibid.*, p. 92. My translation. Of course, the recasting is of: J. Lacan, On a Question Preliminary to any Possible Treatment of Psychosis (1957-58), *Ecrits: A Selection*, *o.c.*, pp. 179-225.

81. See: S. André, Clinique et nœud borroméen, *o.c.*, p. 92.

82. See: C. Millot, Epiphanies, in J. Aubert (Ed.), *Joyce avec Lacan*, *o.c.*, pp. 87-95.

83. See: S. Freud, Inhibitions, Symptoms and Anxiety (1926*d*[1925]), *Standard Edition*, XX, pp. 87-172.

84. See: J. Lacan, Le Séminaire XXII, R.S.I., o.c., seminar of 13 May 1975, *Ornicar ?*, 1975-76, no. 5, pp. 57-66.

85. See, for example: J.-M. Vappereau, D'un calcul dans les champs d'existence du nœud, *Ornicar ?*, 1984, no. 28, pp. 133-143.

86. J. Lacan, Le Séminaire XXIII, Le sinthome, o.c., seminar of 18 November 1975, *Ornicar ?*, 1976, no. 6, p. 3. My translation.
87. *Ibid.*, p. 3.
88. J.-A. Miller, La topologie dans l'ensemble de l'enseignement de Lacan, *o.c.*, pp. 24-25.
89. *Ibid.*, p. 24.
90. J. Lacan, Le Séminaire XXIII, Le sinthome, o.c., seminar of 13 April 1976, *Ornicar ?*, 1977, no. 10, p. 8. My translation.

CHAPTER 7

Causation and Destitution of a Pre-ontological Non-entity: On the Lacanian Subject

Paul Verhaeghe

'[T]he subject is nothing but the impossibility of its own signifying representation.'

Slavoj Žižek[1]

I. Introduction

The concept of the 'subject' is without any doubt one of the most typical and most important Lacanian concepts, through which the entire evolution of Lacan's thought can be studied. Initially, Lacan wrote about the 'I' (*je*), but very soon this was changed into 'subject' (*sujet*).[2] Both signifiers represent Lacan's attempt to distance himself from the post-Freudian interpretation of the ego and the accompanying conception of the treatment. This attempt resulted in the establishment of a theory of his own.

With the early Lacan, the subject has to be understood in its radical opposition to the ego. The ego belongs to the imaginary order, whilst the subject belongs to the symbolic. The subject is the subject of the unconscious, as described by Freud with his notion of *das Es* (the Id), whilst the ego is a mere concatenation of alienating identifications.[3]

Until the early 1960's, Lacan focused upon this opposition between the imaginary and the symbolic. Yet there is a shift in attention: instead of the opposition and division between ego and subject, the division and splitting within the subject itself comes to the fore. Instead of the term 'subject,' the expression 'divided subject' appears – that is, divided by language.[4]

With the conceptualisation of the category of the real, another major shift occurs. From the 1964 *Seminar XI* onwards, the real becomes a genuine Lacanian concept, within a strictly Lacanian theory, and changes the theory of the subject in a very fundamental way.[5] In this chapter, we will focus mainly on this part of Lacan's development, using three different entrances.

In the first part, we will study the causal background of the subject: how does it come into being? It will be demonstrated that the causation of the subject has everything to do with the drive, and that it has strong links with the status of the unconscious. In addition, the link with Freudian theory will be examined, and reference will also be made to Lacan's theory of causality, thus opening epistemological perspectives.

In the second part, we will discuss the ontological status of the subject, which is radically different from the traditional conceptions. Lacan's ontology is an 'alterology,' alienation being the grounding mechanism and identity always coming from the Other. Moreover, the subject has a mere pre-ontological status, which is again closely linked to the status of the unconscious. The ever divided subject is a fading, a vacillation, without any substantiality.

In the third and final part, we will discuss the link between Lacan's theory of the subject and his theory of the aims and goals of psychoanalysis. Here, the central mechanism is separation, as first formalized by Lacan in *Seminar XI* and further developed during the 1960's.[6]

Several studies and commentaries on the subject of the subject have already been published.[7] Generally speaking, the first topic, concerning the causation of the subject, is the one least commented on, whilst the second has received ample attention. The last topic is the most difficult of all three, as it is very thoroughly marked by Lacan's ulterior evolution.

II. Starting-point of the Process: *La causation du sujet*

Lacan's starting-point, from which he defined the advent of the subject, is significant. In 1964, at the time of *Seminar XI*, Lacan was criticised because of his supposed neglect of the sexual dynamics of the unconscious.[8] He rejected this critique by referring his adversaries to his elaboration of the drive, although he had interpreted it in a totally different way from the object relations theorists.

Following Freud, Lacan considered the drive as essentially partial, without there being any global sexual drive comprising a closed reciprocity between two complementary genders with two complementary instincts. The insistent attempt of the drive to reinstall an original situation stresses the fact that this original state is forever lost. Every drive pulsates around an original loss and thus around an irreversible lack, which puts object relations theory in a totally different light.[9]

At this point a very clear line from Freud can indeed be drawn, especially from his ideas on pleasure and unpleasure, and their importance within ontogeny. In order to acknowledge this line, we have to study some of the lesser known and/or more difficult Freudian works, namely the *Project for a Scientific Psychology* (1895), *Beyond the Pleasure Principle* (1920), the paper on *Negation* (1925) and his metapsychological writings in general.[10]

The gist of these ideas can be found in the *Project*. According to Freud, development starts with the loss of a primary experience of satisfaction and the attempt to regain the original homeostasis. The first reaction consists in hallucinating the lost satisfaction (which will return in the character of wish fulfilment typical of dreamlife), but this is not enough. The primitive organism has to venture in the outside world in order to regain the lost satisfaction. From this point onwards, the relationship between what Freud calls the 'undifferentiated vesicle' (*undifferenziertes Bläschen*) and the 'external world' (*Außenwelt*) is developed.[11] The primary mental apparatus explores the external world by taking samples from it. The two basic mechanisms involved are incorporation and expulsion, through which the external world is divided into a good and a bad part. What yields pleasure is kept inside the ego; what results in unpleasure is spat out. Later, it will become evident that these two mechanisms of incorporation and expulsion are the precursors of the Lacanian ones. For the time being, it is this starting-point which retains our attention.

Freud assumed that there is an original state of primary satisfaction, which he considered to be a state of homeostasis. The inevitable loss of this state sets the development in motion and provides us with the basic characteristic of every drive: the tendency to return to an original state. Thus, the entire development is motivated by a central loss, around which the ego is constituted. With Freud, and especially with the post-Freudians, the emphasis will be upon the installation of substitute satisfactions, ranging from neurotic symptoms and fantasies to sublimation. Yet these substitute satisfactions are never satisfactory enough. The lack is irrevocable.

Freud's key denomination for this lack is castration, which is his attempt at formulating the link between the original, pregenital loss and the oedipal elaboration thereof. For several reasons, the Freudian castration theory itself will never be fully satisfying. Freud's focus on the real, that is to say the biological basis of castration, did not help him any further either, and inevitably brought him to the pessimistic conclusion of 1937, concerning the 'biological bedrock' as the limit of psychoanalysis.[12] Freud's theory is quite unidimensional and Freud himself remained remarkably obstinate in this respect. He refused to take other losses than the loss of a penis into account — with one exception, as becomes clear from his affirmation of Aristophanes' fable about the search for the originally lost counterpart.[13]

This one-sidedness was directed by his conviction regarding the universality of the pleasure principle, i.e. of the desire to restore the original homeostasis. Things became more complicated once he discovered that there is a 'beyond' to the pleasure principle, in which yet another kind of drive is at work, also striving to restore an original condition, albeit a totally different one.[14] The duality of life versus death drives opened up a dimension beyond the one-sidedness of neurosis, castration and desire.

It is this dimension that is taken into account by Lacan. Indeed, Lacan's starting-point is also the very idea of lack and loss, but he will recognize a double loss and a double lack. Moreover, the interaction between those two losses will determine the constitution of the subject. The duality also corresponds to the double level of desire and jouissance and it will find its most elaborate formulation within Lacan's discourse theory, in which it will be expressed by means of the two disjunctions (impossibility and impotence) governing each discourse.[15]

In *Seminar XI*, Lacan began his discussion of the causation of the subject with something that was already well-known to his audience: the drive, being always a partial drive, revolves around a lack. However, at that point, Lacan surprised his audience by stating that there are *two* lacks.[16] The first one is the lack in the chain of signifiers, the interval between two signifiers. This is the typically hysterical — and thus Freudian — level in which desire can never be fully expressed, let alone satisfied. In Lacanian terms, this reads that the subject, confronted with the enigma of the desire of the Other, tries to verbalise this desire and thus constitutes itself by identifying with the signifiers in the field of the Other, without ever succeeding in filling the gap between subject and Other. Hence, the continuous movement from signifier to signifier, in which the subject alternately appears and disappears. The ensuing alienation is a continuous flywheel movement around the lack in the chain of signifiers, resulting in what Lacan called *l'avènement du sujet*, the advent of the subject.[17]

So far, Lacan's theory is not really new. It could also be understood from a Sartrean or an Althusserian point of view. The innovation begins when Lacan surprises his audience by stating that there is yet another lack, which he calls anterior and real in comparison to its counterpart.[18] Furthermore, the lack in the chain of signifiers is only a retake on this primal lack, the originality of which resides in the fact that it has to be understood in the context of *l'avènement du vivant* (the advent of the living being). This entails the emergence of sexual reproduction in phylogeny, which is repeated with every ontogeny.[19] At this point, the level of *Unbegriff* (incomprehension), beyond the psychological comprehensibility of the previous lack, is reached.[20] The anterior lack concerns the price life has to pay for the acquisition of sexual reproduction. From the moment an organism becomes capable of reproducing itself in a sexual way, it loses its individual immortality and death becomes an unavoidable necessity. At birth, the individual loses something and this loss will be represented later on by all other substitute objects.[21]

Lacan tries to depict this primary loss with his myth of the lamella, the object that flies away at birth and that is nothing but pure life instinct. The lamella equals the libido, of which the four forms of the object *a* are the mere representatives. From this moment in Lacan's thought, there is an essential affinity between drive and death.[22] Sexual drive means death drive, as an inevitable consequence of the process of sexualization.[23] Here, Lacan endorses Freud's idea of a *Triebmischung* (a fusion of life and death drives) in *The Ego and the Id*, but he will go much further.[24] Indeed, Lacan will formulate a whole new theory of causality, in which he transcends the level of normal science that is only interested in laws, that is to say in regularity and predictability.

Hence, the constitution of the subject is based on the interaction between life and death, between the two different lacks and their overlap.[25] The Other is 'the field of that living being in which the subject has to appear.'[26] The subject encounters a lack in the discourse of the Other, in which the desire of the Other 'crawls, slips, escapes, like the ferret,' producing an enigma to which the subject has to produce an answer.[27] It is at that point that the subject recurs to the anterior lack which entails its own disappearance. As an answer to the riddle of the desire of the Other, it presents itself and thus its disappearance: does the Other desire me, can s/he afford to lose me? This fantasy, in which one's own death is depicted as a form of testing the limits of the love of the Other, is fairly well-known in adults and children alike: *Veut-il me perdre?*, Does he want to lose me?

The crucial thing concerning these two lacks is that their interaction entails neither reciprocity nor complementarity: 'It is a lack engendered from the previous time that serves to reply to the lack raised by the following time.'[28] The overlap is situated in what Lacan calls 'the intersection between subject and Other,' and it is there that the second operation, which is termed 'separation,' takes place. The ever failing interaction between the two lacks also determines the non-existence of a perfect sexual relationship. This will be further elaborated by Lacan in his theory of the four discourses, in which the two lacks receive their final denomination: the lack on the upper level (the level of desire) concerns an impossibility (*impossibilité*), whereas the lack on the lower level (the level of jouissance) concerns impotence (*impuissance*). The four discourses are four ways of coping with these two lacks.[29]

The elaboration in *Seminar XI* of these two interacting operations, alienation and separation, will bring us to our second point, the ontological status of the subject. As we will see, this status is a very particular one, as the main 'characteristic of the subject of the unconscious is that of being . . . at an indeterminate place.'[30] Yet before going on to examine this, we should situate Lacan's ideas on the causation of the subject into the more general framework of causality and the status of the unconscious as elaborated in the first part of *Seminar XI*.[31]

Indeed, Lacan's theory of the double lack may not be isolated from his ideas on the status of the unconscious and the accompanying conception of causality. From a Lacanian point of view, the 'Gothic' interpretation of the unconscious is totally wrong. In this romantic conception, the unconscious is viewed as the basement of the psyche, in which all ancient dreads and desires lie buried until the unavoidable day of their resuscitation. Freud's theory, including concepts such as 'the return of the repressed,' 'repetition compulsion,' etc., would be nothing more than the scientific elaboration of this unavoidability. Obviously, such a conception implies a complete determinism, insofar as a human being can only become what s/he already was. This tallies with the mechanistic-deterministic conviction of early twentieth century science, but it does not leave much room for therapeutic hope.

Lacan not only distances himself from this substantiated interpretation of the unconscious, he even subverts it: the unconscious is of the order of the μὴ ὄν, the 'non-realised,' the 'unborn,' 'limbo' (*les limbes*).[32] As a process, it is always situated at the border; in itself, it is a void, an abyss: 'For what the unconscious does is to show us the gap through which neurosis recreates a harmony with a real — a real that may well not be determined.'[33] This abyss is pre-ontological: not of the order of to be or not to be, but of the order of the not-realised.[34] And if this unconscious becomes realised, it always happens in a bungled, failed way. The unconscious formations are 'impediments' (*achoppements*), 'failures' (*défaillances*), whose most typical characteristic is their temporal scansion: the unconscious opens and closes at the same time.[35] It is important to understand that this always failing realisation does not take place against a hidden (because unconscious) background of totality or unity. On the contrary, the background is never there. Lacan summarises this subversion with a pun on the 'un' of unconscious: 'Let us say that the limit of the *Unbewußte* is the *Unbegriff* — not the non-concept, but the concept of lack.'[36]

It is evident that this opens completely different perspectives on the subject of determinism. On the whole, Lacan is much more optimistic than Freud in this respect. 'It is always a question of the subject *qua* indeterminate,' and this has effects on the goal and finality of the treatment.[37] But the innovation goes much further, as it also implies a new view on the tricky subject of causality. The novelty resides in the way Lacan puts the lack at the centre of the — indeed — twofold stage. The denominations are provided by Aristotle, but their content is new: *automaton* (αὐτόματον) versus *tuchè* (τύχη).[38]

The automaton is the level that is the easiest to understand. It concerns the network or chain of signifiers, in which the 'pulsatile function of the unconscious' is at work. The barred subject ($) pops up and disappears under these signifiers — 'the signifier represents a subject for another signifier.'[39] In this, the subject is indeed determined, as Lacan had demonstrated time and again with his theory on the unconscious as being structured like a language.[40] The automatic character of this determinism was masterfully demonstrated in his *Seminar on 'The Purloined Letter,'* showing how the chain of signifiers is indeed a chain.[41] This is the level of the law, at which science aims, with its preponderant interest for the *causa efficiens* (efficient cause), and it may convince one of the omnipresence of determinism.[42] It took Freud until 1920, in *Beyond the Pleasure Principle*, to recognize the fallacy in this reasoning, and thus the hole in the mechanistic universe.[43] The hole will prove to be a black one.

This brings us to the second level. The unwinding of the associative chain succeeds only to a certain point, something which Freud experienced time and again during his therapeutic work from the *Studies on Hysteria* onwards.[44] The process of remembering succeeds only to a certain point where the chain stalls and shows an abyss, a gap.[45] This is what Freud termed the 'primal repressed,' and what he also called the *Nabel* (navel) of the dream and the *Kern unseres Wesens* (the core of our being).[46] It is at this point that the real ex-sists, the real in the sense of what cannot be assimilated by the chain of signifiers.[47] Hence, the always missed encounter, due to the lack of a signifier as meeting-point. This radical lack is conceptualised by Lacan with the idea of *tuchè* and it is understood in terms of absence, abyss and cut, where the law and regularity of the chain are failing. This is also the level of pure causality, where law and predictability fail. 'In short, there is cause only in something that doesn't work.'[48]

Hence, we find ourselves again dealing with two levels. On the one hand, there is the chain of signifiers with the lack between them (Freud: the repressed). This is the level of the *automaton*, of the law and predictability, and thus of science. Underlying this chain, we find a more fundamental lack, concerning the real beyond any signifier (Freud: the primal repressed). This is the level of the *tuchè*, of cause and unpredictability.

With this theory, Lacan solves the classical question about the cause of the cause. The first cause lacks any determination whatsoever.[49]

The interaction between the two levels consists in the never ending attempt of the chain of signifiers to produce an answer to the real. This attempt fails and results in the exact opposite: the more signifiers produced, the further one moves away from this real. Therefore, in *Seminar XX*, Lacan defines the real as 'what does not stop not writing itself.'[50]

What is this real all about? Lacan is quite clear on this point. The real beyond the signifier, functioning as cause, is drive-ridden, and that is why Lacan took the drive as his starting-point. With this aspect of the real, the meeting is always a failed one, because it contains no signifier. In the course of his teaching, Lacan enumerated the various manifestations of the real: the Other of the Other, the sexual relationship, Woman (*La femme*), all of them summarized in the notation of the barred Other Ø.[51] In this respect, the subject is fundamentally undetermined, and that is why it has a possibility of choice, beyond the determination of the *automaton*. This aspect of choice was already implicit in Freud's idea of *Neurosenwahl* (choice of neurosis) and it is made explicit with Lacan's idea of *la position du sujet*: the subject has to take a position.[52] Which position? A position vis-à-vis the lack of the Other, of the symbolic order; a position vis-à-vis the desire and the jouissance of the Other. It is this element of choice that provides the subject with a possibility of change, beyond the inescapable determination of the *automaton*. This finds an expression in Lacan's ideas on the future anterior: choices made now will determine the future of the subject, which therefore shows in itself a fundamental indeterminateness.[53] This provides us with the possibility of change, beyond the ever present Freudian determinism. In this respect, Lacan's elaboration of the goal and finality of psychoanalysis will be different, as we will show in the last part of this chapter.

Thus, the 'un' of unconscious has to be taken seriously, just like the bar in the subject ($): it denotes a pre-ontological dimension of non-realisation, of being un-born, within a perpetual process of opening and closing. We must now examine this double process.

III. The Pre-ontological Status: *L'avènement du sujet*

In the first part, we demonstrated how the subject is caused by the primary experience of a lack. The attempt at solving this lack by using signifiers entails a confrontation with another lack, this time within the chain of signifiers. In this second part, we will concentrate on the two constitutive processes within this causation of the subject: alienation and separation. The first one is fully elaborated by Lacan and can easily by traced back to Freud. The second one concerns Lacan's interpretation of the end and the finality of the analytic treatment. His theoretical development in these matters comprises an ever shifting interpretation of this idea of separation.

For Lacan, the advent of the subject takes place in a field of tension between the subject-to-be and the field of the Other: 'The Other is the locus in which is situated the chain of the signifier — it is the field of that living being in which the subject has to appear.'[54] In Freud's works, this field of tension is situated between what must be regarded as a 'primary ego' and the outside world.[55] This primary ego is in a state of tension due to the loss of the original state of satisfaction, which obliges it to try to restore this original state. This is of course the basic characteristic of every drive: the tendency to return to an original situation. Initially, the primary ego tries to satisfy itself by hallucinating the original satisfaction, but this proves to be inadequate. The next step brings the primary ego into interaction with the outside world, in order to find there what was lost.

Freud's understanding of this interaction between the primitive organism and the outside world is very instructive if one wants to understand the Lacanian point of view. We have already referred to Freud's ideas on incorporation and expulsion, the interactions between the primitive ego and the outside world through which the external world is divided into a good and a bad part. These processes are fairly well-known in biology and ethology, and to some extent they can even be recognised in infants. A baby explores the world with its mouth. The first good external world, the mother's milk, is incorporated, and along that path a number of other things will follow. By contrast, the bad parts of the external world are literally spat out. At a further developmental stage, these interactions will make use of perceptual images of the outside world, rather than being carried out literally. Traces of the interactions themselves can be recognised in the language of love and hate: devouring love (the importance of a kiss is to know when to stop — think of Hannibal Lecter), and 'you make me puke.'[56]

This primitive, pre-verbal level suffices to illustrate the fallacy of the idea of two interacting agencies. From a naive point of view, one could consider this process as the interaction of the organism with the world, the 'inside' with the 'outside.' Yet closer examination reveals an unexpected complexity, which destroys the idea of separate entities. The 'inside' is the result of an incorporation of the pleasurable parts of the outside, and the 'outside' is the result of an expulsion of what was considered unpleasurable at the inside. In addition, the real outside is what is unknown in terms of pleasure and unpleasure, and so it simply does not exist for the organism. Thus, the inside is a pleasurable outside, the outside is an unpleasurable inside, and the outside as such is not recognised. This is the reason why Lacan refuses any form of 'two body psychology,' and why he introduces a completely new topology in psychoanalysis, whose basic characteristic is the absence of differences between outside and inside (see, for example, the Moebius strip and the Klein bottle).[57]

Once the pre-verbal perceptual images are superseded by language, we leave biology and enter the truly human realm. Already at the time of the *Project for a Scientific Psychology*, Freud paid full attention to words, because language, that is to say the association between a word and a perceptual image, explains the typically human condition of consciousness, and thus also the fact that something can become or remain unconscious. In this human realm, interactions do not take place between 'organism' and *Umwelt*, but between child and parent. Lacan will stress the language aspect in this interaction by using the denominations of subject and Other. The latter comprises the m(Other)-tongue that will give rise to a second birth, turning the infant into a divided subject. In Freudian terms, the interaction on the verbal level involves different processes from those on the pre-verbal level. Instead of incorporating a piece of the *Umwelt*, the ego now *identifies* with the pleasure-procuring signifiers of the Other; instead of spitting out the bad parts of the outside world, the subject *represses* these parts. Language acquisition divides the human universe into two essentially interwoven parts: 'pleasure — identification —ego— signifier — consciousness' versus 'unpleasure — repression — not-ego — without signifier — unconscious.'

This Freudian metapsychology is usually understood from a developmental point of view. Moreover, the pleasure principle involved is a simple one, for it is based on a singular lack. With Lacan, the accent will be put on a structural point of view, that is to say on a structure beyond development. Hence, the repercussions on the ontological level. Moreover, as we have already pointed out, for Lacan there are two levels, each characterised by a certain lack and a certain pleasure. The implications of this have a particular bearing upon on the goals of psychoanalytic treatment.

The basic Lacanian mechanism is easy to describe: the subject-to-be identifies with the pleasure-procuring signifiers in the field of the (m)Other and represses the unpleasurable ones. Easy as this may seem, it has a number of far-reaching consequences. Firstly, it confronts us with the astonishing fact that the very kernel of our personality is an empty space: peeling off layer after layer of identification in search of the substantial kernel of one's personality, one ends up with a void, with the original lack. In *Seminar I*, Lacan compares the ego to an onion: 'The ego is constructed like an onion, one could peel it, and discover the successive identifications which have constituted it.'[58] Secondly, instead of having an original identity, a human being merely consists of identifications with parts of the other. This is the raw meaning of those classical Lacanian formulae, 'Man's desire is the desire of the other,' 'The unconscious is the discourse of the Other,' echoing T.S. Eliot's 'We are the hollow men/We are the stuffed men/Leaning together/Headpiece filled with straw. Alas!'.[59] No wonder, then, that Lacan coined the basic mechanism in the advent of the subject 'alienation.'[60]

It has already become clear that this process takes place between subject and Other. However, this does not imply a naive two body psychology, as we have seen. This, incidentally, is the reason Lacan stopped using the concept of 'intersubjectivity,' as it reminded him far too much of this two body model.[61] Implicit in Lacan's reasoning, there are two levels in alienation, corresponding to the two lacks mentioned above. The first level concerns the mythical point of origin — mythical because of the very idea of origin — in which *l'être* (being) as such has to make its appearance in the field of the Other, of language. This coincides with what Freud, in his essay on Moses, calls 'hominization' (*Menschwerdung*), the process of becoming a human being.[62]

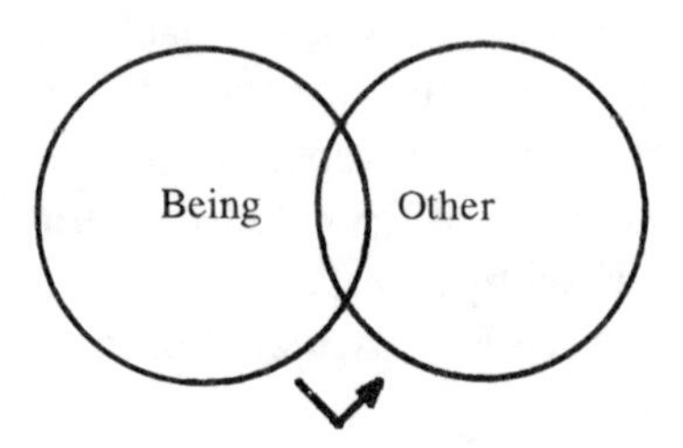

Even at this primary level, the effects are quite dramatic: when being makes its appearance on the level of language, it must disappear under that language, it loses the reality of its being. For Lacan, this is a matter of choice, albeit a very special choice, for whatever decision is made, one element is lost forever. He compares this choice to the classical 'Your money or your life!'. Whatever you choose, you will lose your money anyway. The element lost in the process of becoming a human being is being itself, the pure being, the real, the thing without a name, leaving us with a basic lack as a condition for our becoming, which Lacan calls *manque à être* (want-to-be, or lack of being).[63] Thus, right from the start, the subject is divided between the necessary loss of its being on the one hand and the ever alienating meaning in the Other on the other hand. The subject chooses the (m)Other in order to regain the lost paradise of the primary experience of satisfaction, and the net result will be an ever more clear delineation of this loss.[64]

The second level concerns the chain of signifiers, the *automaton*, in which the subject continuously appears and disappears in an ever repeated division by the signifiers: '[A] signifier is that which represents the subject for another signifier.'[65] Here again, the subject can 'choose' its signifiers in the field of the Other, but this choice reminds one of that mentioned by Ferdinand de Saussure in his *Course in General Linguistics*. There he demonstrated the arbitrary relationship between signifier and signified, and the consequences of this for the freedom of choice. Basically, you can pick your own signifiers, but of course the choice has already been made for you and before you, hence his expression: *la carte forcée de la langue*, meaning that language is a 'set-up.'[66]

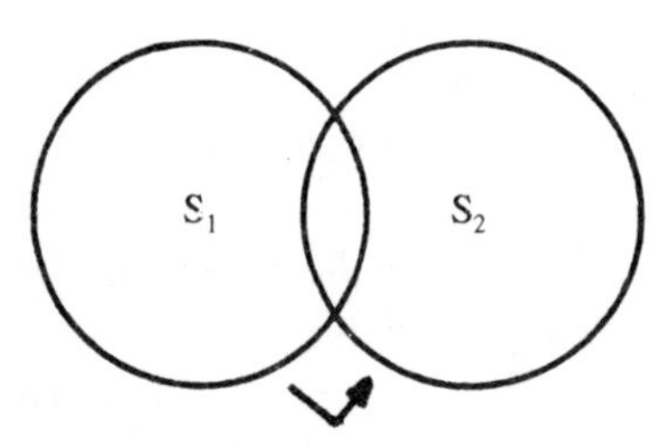

When comparing this Lacanian operation to the Freudian ones, it becomes obvious that alienation comprises both identification and repression. This can be demonstrated with Lacan's definition of metaphor, as 'the substitution of signifier for signifier.'[67] The subject 'chooses' a signifier, which appears on top of another signifier. The latter becomes repressed, whereas the former entails a new identification for the ego and the subject remains divided between the two of them. In Freudian terms, the ego is nothing but a concatenation of identifications, as a result of the successive object losses. In this line of reasoning, the first level of alienation corresponds to the primal repression (*Urverdrängung*) and the primary identification. Indeed, the primal repression constitutes the kernel of the unconscious as something that is forever lost and can never be verbalised, namely the real of the drive.[68] The primary identification is for Freud always the identification with the father, and this identification provides the platform from which development, in the form of the Oedipus complex, takes off.[69] For Lacan, this implies the installation of the S_1, the master signifier.

The second level of alienation corresponds to the Freudian *eigentliche Verdrängung* (repression proper) or *Nachdrängen* (after-pressure), which can be interpreted as a secondary repression and which takes place completely within the chain of signifiers.[70] Unconscious processes or formations, which are made up from signifying material, take place at the border of the unconscious, as is demonstrated by a slip of the tongue, the forgetting of a proper name, etc. The Signorelli example in Freud's *The Psychopathology of Everyday Life* demonstrates both levels in a perfect way. The lost signifiers, due to the secondary repression, can be retrieved by means of free association, but the basic lack cannot be verbalised and is merely hinted at by Freud in his mention of 'death and sexuality' and 'repressed thoughts' at the bottom of his schema.[71]

In Lacan's theory of the four discourses, both levels will be expressed by the master's discourse. The subject is forever barred from the lost object *a* and is thus impotent in matters of and protected against jouissance. It finds its first alienating identity with the S_1, the Oedipal master signifier of the father. From then onwards, the subject will appear and disappear under the never-ending chain of signifiers, S_2, in an attempt to bridge the gap and reach for satisfaction. The result of this impossible attempt is an ever increasing production of the lost object *a*.[72]

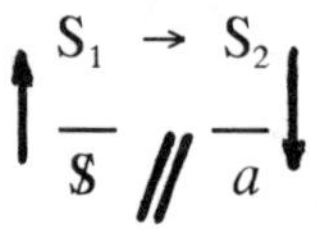

$$\uparrow \frac{S_1}{\$} \to \frac{S_2}{a} \downarrow \quad (\$ \; // \; a)$$

The master discourse

The important thing about the divided subject is that it has no essence, no ontological substance, but, on the contrary, comes down to a pre-ontological, indeterminate non-being which can only give rise to an identity, an ego, in retrospect. Difficult as this may seem, it is rather easy to grasp. Just think of what we will call 'the cocktail experience.' You are invited for a drink with a group of people you do not know. You have to introduce yourself, and so you have to produce signifiers. This production of signifiers will never be satisfactory. Furthermore, the more signifiers produced, the more contradictions, gaps and difficulties will become clear. Therefore, the 'Experienced Cocktail Consumer' will stick to the proverbial 'That's me!' and produce a stock introduction.

From a Lacanian point of view, it would be wrong to assume that the difficulty lies in finding the correct signifiers to present oneself. On the contrary, one is *produced by* the uttered signifiers, which are coming from the field of the Other, albeit in a divided way. It would also be a mistake to assume that the subject is identical to the produced signifier(s). The identification with a number of signifiers, coming from the Other, presents us with the ego. The subject, on the contrary, is never realised as such; it joins the pre-ontological status of the unconscious, the unborn, non-realised etc. In this sense, the Lacanian subject is exactly the opposite of the Cartesian one. In the formula 'I am thinking, therefore I exist' Descartes concludes from his thinking that he has a being, whereas for Lacan, each time (conscious) thinking arises its being disappears under the signifier.[73]

This explains two basic characteristics of the Lacanian subject: it is always at an indeterminate place and it is essentially divided:

> Alienation consists in this *vel*, which — if you do not object to the word *condemned*, I will use it — condemns the subject to appearing only in that division which, it seems to me, I have just articulated sufficiently by saying that, if it appears on one side as meaning, produced by the signifier, it appears on the other as *aphanisis*.[74]

Again, Lacan distances himself from any idea of substantiality. The subject is not an unconscious intention that will interrupt the normal conscious discourse. The interruption or division does not take place between a real or authentic part and a false, external one, but the split defines the subject as such. The subject is split from its real being and forever tossed between eventually contradicting signifiers coming from the Other.

This rather pessimistic view confronts us with the issue of therapeutic and psychoanalytic possibilities. Paradoxical as this may seem, Lacan's point of view is more optimistic than the Freudian one. Freud's theory is by and large deterministic, whereas Lacan leaves an element of choice, albeit a 'forced' choice. It is this element that brings us to the second operation, separation, and to the theme of our final investigation: the goal of psychoanalytic treatment.

IV. The Goal of Psychoanalysis: *La destitution subjective*

The vicissitudes of the subject depend largely on the direction of the treatment and its goal. It is precisely at this point that Lacan will change and revise his theory, with accompanying changes concerning the subject. Generally speaking, the Lacan before *Seminar XI* can be considered as the Lacan of the symbolic and the imaginary, while from

Seminar XI onwards, these categories will be completed and changed by the introduction of the real. The effect thereof is that the whole previous conceptualisation has to be reconsidered, in a typically psychoanalytical process of 'deferred action' (*Nachträglichkeit*).[75]

Before *Seminar XI*, the idea of alienation already occupied a very prominent place in Lacan's thinking. His paper on *The Mirror Stage* demonstrates that alienation is a necessary operation, which cannot be restricted only to the process of socialisation, for it is precisely what determines this process.[76] The further elaboration of the mirror stage introduces the alienation into the structural relation between the imaginary and the symbolic.[77] The primary imaginary alienation is determined by the secondary symbolic one, which relies on the Other. The subject wants to be loved/desired by the Other and models/alienates him or herself on the image of what s/he thinks is desirable for this Other. Here, the goal of psychoanalysis is to recognise this Other and its influence. Separation is understood as a major operation, installed through the paternal metaphor.[78] It is the function of the father/Other to separate the child and the first (m)Other. The real is never mentioned.

In *Seminar XI*, all this is radically changed. Alienation and separation are linked to the twofold lack and they install the subject in a never ending pulsating process of appearing and disappearing. Alienation takes the subject away from its being, in the direction of the Other. Separation is the opposite process, inasmuch as it redirects the subject towards its being, thus opening a possibility of escape from the all-determining alienation, and even a possibility of choice, albeit a precarious one. The two processes are circular and dissymmetrical. The cause of this continuous movement is the twofold lack. The process of alienation conducts the subject towards the signifying chain of the Other. Inevitably, it will stumble upon the lack of the Other: 'He is saying this to me, but what does he want?'.[79] Thus confronted with the nameless desire of the Other, the subject will produce a very typical answer: 'Does the Other desire me?,' 'Am I the one who can fulfil his desire?'. This implies that the subject answers the lack of the Other by presenting his or her own disappearance: 'Can the Other afford to lose me?'. The lack of the Other, within the signifying chain, is answered by a presentation of the lack at the anterior level, i.e. death as a real loss. Hence, the non-reciprocity and dissymmetry, by which the process topples over into the direction of alienation again. This eliminates the possibility of a perfect sexual relationship.

With separation, the effect is the installation of a void between subject and Other, in which the object *a* makes its appearance. This void permits the subject and the Other to fall apart momentarily, to separate. Just think of the well-known metaphor of *le bal masqué*. When the couple finally meets and the partners remove their mask, they discover their mistake: 'They met in Paris, at the Opera ball. When they removed their masks, sheer terror! It wasn't him, her neither by the way.'[80] This negativity implies an escape from the all-embracing determinism of the Other and opens a limited possibility of choice. Within *Seminar XI*, this is hardly elaborated. Lacan plays both on the etymological and the homonymical aspect of separation: *se parere*, to engender oneself and *se parer*, to defend oneself, to dress oneself.[81] He demonstrates the necessity of this process by discussing clinical instances in which it is lacking. This is what Lacan calls the 'holophrase,' exemplified by a peculiar relationship between certain mothers and their children within which there is no gap whatsoever between the signifiers of the (m)Other, thus installing a complete alienation without any possibility of escape.[82] The child is the real obturation of the lack of the (m)Other.[83] But for the 'real' elaboration of this idea of separation, we have to turn to Lacan's later work, focusing on the end of the analytic treatment.

Before doing that, it is necessary to stress the shift that has occurred since Lacan's first theory. In the later stages of his conceptualisation, Lacan states *that the Other of the Other does not exist*; it is lacking, separation being the interaction between the lack of the Other and the lack of the subject. The distance between this idea of separation, and the idea of separation expressed by the paternal metaphor, is immense, and entails a crucial shift in the direction of the treatment.

Lacan abhorred the idea of an analysis ending in an identification with the analyst, which would imply just another alienation. For Lacan, the analyst's desire ought to aim at the exact opposite, namely absolute difference.[84] This brings us back to ontology and ethics. From the point of view of alienation, the subject has no substance whatsoever; it is a mere and, moreover, an ever fading effect of the symbolic order, the Other. At this point, Lacanian theory belongs to constructionism and determinism. Ideas of individuation, self-realisation, and subjective autonomy do not belong to this line of thought. They never will, yet the accent shifts once the real is introduced. Through separation, the subject receives an element of choice. Further elaborations continue to stress the inner difficulty of this idea. The pinnacle of these is to be found in Lacan's elaboration of the 'traversing of fantasy' and the 'subjective destitution,' which replace the original idea of separation.[85] Ultimately, the choice in all this is an impossible one, insofar as the choice has already been made, taking the shape of a peculiar form of identification.[86]

The first developments of this idea can be found in *Seminar XI*. Instead of the abhorred identification with the analyst at the end of analysis, Lacan suggests the existence of another form of identification, inaugurated by the process of separation, *and thus by the object a*: 'Through the function of the *objet a*, the subject separates himself off, ceases to be linked to the vacillation of being, in the sense that it forms the essence of alienation.'[87] This idea is not developed any further in this seminar and can hardly be understood here. Separation does not take place through the intervention of the Other and the symbolic; on the contrary, it takes place through the object *a* and the real. Indeed, the Other of the Other does not exist, the Other is inconsistent. The discovery of its inconsistency is the consequence of analysis and results in a mirror effect. If the Other is inconsistent, then the same goes for the subject, and both of them tumble down from their positions. This is what Lacan calls 'traversing the fantasy.' Applied to Lacan's formula of the fantasy, $\$ \diamond a$, this traversing means that the subject crosses the lozenge and identifies with the lost object, i.e. with the cause of its own advent: $\$ \ominus a$. In this way, the subject comes to subjective destitution: it assumes the non-existence of the Other and the non-existence of itself as a subject. With this, we have reached both the end of Lacan's theory and of his theory of the end of analysis. His final conceptualisations can be understood as an elaboration of the idea of separation, albeit from the point of view of the analytical goal.

What is the goal of analysis? At first sight, the answer is strange: a successful analysis brings the subject to the point where s/he can identify him or herself with the symptom. This identification is a special one, because it concerns an identification with the real of the symptom, and thus concerns an identification on the level of being.[88] This is exactly the counterpart of what the analysand experienced before, namely the identification/alienation with the Other and the accompanying *belief* in this Other, and thus in its existence.[89] The analytic experience makes clear that this Other does not exist, and hence that the subject does not exist either. This is 'subjective destitution' as the most radical form of separation. The analysand not only has to separate him or herself from the Other, s/he even has to discover the non-existence of the Other. The inevitable consequence is that the subject, as a response to the lack of this Other, does not exist either. This paves the way to the real being of the subject, *son être du sujet*. From that point onwards, the subject cannot be considered a mere 'answer to/from the Other' (*réponse de l'Autre*) anymore; on the contrary, the subject is now an 'answer to/from the real' (*réponse du réel*).[90] Thus, the idea of *se parere*, to engender oneself, as it was announced in *Seminar XI*, is realised after all.

This brings us to another important Lacanian dimension, that of creation. Indeed, in our opinion, the 'identification with the real of the symptom' has to be understood via the idea of creation. The gist of it can be recognised in Lacan's earlier ideas on sublimation and *creatio ex nihilo* in his *Seminar VII* on *The Ethics of Psychoanalysis*. The subject can 'choose' to elevate nothing into something and to enjoy this: 'The object is elevated to the dignity of the Thing.'[91] Applied to the end of analysis, this means that the subject has created its own symptom in the real and proceeds by identifying with it. In this way, the symptom takes the place of what is forever lacking. Finally, it takes the place of the lacking sexual rapport and furnishes a self-made answer to it, instead of the previous, Other-made ones. Lacan accentuates this shift by introducing a neologism. The subject has to become a *sinthome*, a combination of *symptôme* (symptom) and *saint homme* (holy man): 'On the level of the *sinthome* . . . there is relationship. There is only relationship where there is *sinthome*.'[92] This delineates a before and an afterwards. Previously, there was a belief in the symptom, which yielded a symbolic suppletion for the lack of the Other and which at once located the jouissance within the Other. At the end of analysis, the identification with the *sinthome* is a real suppletion, providing the subject not only with consistency, but also with jouissance.

The paradox is that the entailing 'rapport' inaugurates absolute difference.

Notes

1. S. Žižek, *The Sublime Object of Ideology*, London-New York NY, Verso, 1989, p. 208.

2. See: J. Lacan, The Mirror Stage as Formative of the Function of the I as Revealed in Psychoanalytic Experience (1949), *Ecrits: A Selection* (trans. A. Sheridan), London, Tavistock, 1977, pp. 1-7; J. Lacan, The Function and Field of Speech and Language in Psychoanalysis (1953), *Ecrits: A Selection*, *o.c.*, pp. 30-113.

3. See: S. Freud, The Ego and the Id (1923*b*), *Standard Edition*, XIX, pp. 1-66; J. Lacan, The Freudian Thing, or the Meaning of the Return to Freud in Psychoanalysis (1955), *Ecrits: A Selection*, *o.c.*, pp. 114-145 and p. 128 in particular.

4. See: J. Lacan, *Le Séminaire V, Les formations de l'inconscient* (1957-58), unpublished.

5. See: J. Lacan, *The Four Fundamental Concepts of Psychoanalysis* (1964) (trans. A. Sheridan), Edited by J.-A. Miller, London, The Hogarth Press and the Institute of Psycho-Analysis, 1977.

6. *Ibid.*, pp. 203-215.

7. Due to the recent boom in Lacanian publications, it is impossible to include a complete bibliography of secondary sources on this subject. These are the two most interesting studies, in my opinion: B. Fink, *The Lacanian Subject: Between Language and Jouissance*, Princeton NJ, Princeton University Press, 1995; D. Nobus, *Choosing Sexuality: A Lacanian Inquiry into the Laws of Sexual Diversity*, Albany NY, State University of New York Press (forthcoming).

8. See: J. Lacan, *The Four Fundamental Concepts of Psychoanalysis*, *o.c.*, p. 203.

9. This had already become clear from Lacan's fourth seminar, *La relation d'objet* (Object-relation), in which he had developed a theory of the *lack* of object. See: J. Lacan, *Le Séminaire, Livre IV, La relation d'objet* (1956-57), texte établi par J.-A. Miller, Paris, du Seuil, 1994, pp. 9-92.

10. See: S. Freud, Project for a Scientific Psychology (1950*c*[1895]), *Standard Edition*, I, pp. 295-343 & pp. 347-387; S. Freud, Beyond the Pleasure Principle (1920*g*), *Standard Edition*, XVIII, pp. 7-64; S. Freud, Negation (1925*h*), *Standard Edition*, XIX, pp. 235-239.

11. S. Freud, Beyond the Pleasure Principle, *o.c.*, pp. 26-28.

12. S. Freud, Analysis Terminable and Interminable (1937*c*), *Standard Edition*, XXIII, pp. 209-253 and p. 252 in particular.

13. See: S. Freud, Analysis of a Phobia in a Five-Year-Old Boy (1909*b*), *Standard Edition*, X, p. 8, note 2; S. Freud, Beyond the Pleasure Principle, *o.c.*, p. 57; Plato, *The Symposium* (trans. W. Hamilton), Harmondsworth, Penguin, 1990, 189*d*-193*e* (Aristophanes' fable).

14. S. Freud, Beyond the Pleasure Principle, *o.c.*, pp. 7-64.

15. See: J. Lacan, *Le Séminaire, Livre XVII, L'envers de la psychanalyse* (1969-70), texte établi par J.-A. Miller, Paris, du Seuil, 1991.

16. Of course, this idea was not completely new. In *Seminar IV*, Lacan had already described two periods in the relationship between a mother and her child: a first one, characterised by a 'primitive identification' (*l'identification freudienne primitive*) in which the child fills the lack of the mother, and a second one, in which the child offers its own lack, which will form the basis for every later infatuation. See: J. Lacan, *Le Séminaire, Livre IV, La relation d'objet, o.c.*, pp. 174-178; J. Lacan, *The Four Fundamental Concepts of Psychoanalysis*, *o.c.*, pp. 204-205.

17. J. Lacan, *The Four Fundamental Concepts of Psychoanalysis, o.c.*, p. 205.

18. *Ibid.*, p. 205.

19. *Ibid.*, p. 205.

20. *Ibid.*, p. 26.

21. *Ibid.*, p. 198.

22. *Ibid.*, pp. 197-199.

23. Due to the nature of science, this truth cannot be expressed by it. Therefore, one has to turn to art and jokes. In the realm of art, we refer the reader to Bataille's *Erotism: Death and Sensuality*. As far as the jokes are concerned, the following selection might suffice: i/Patient: 'Doctor, if I quit drinking alcohol, restrict myself to vegetarian food and leave women for what they are, will I live longer?'; Doctor: 'I don't know whether you will live longer, but I am pretty sure about one thing: you will have the impression that it takes much longer.' ii/A gerontologist wants to answer the question as to why some people live much longer than others do. He interviews a number of people in a home for the elderly. A seventy-year-old assures him that he owes his health to macrobiotic food, an octogenerian adds physical exercise, and a ninety-year-old declares never having touched a woman. At that point, our gerontologist sees what he considers to be his perfect object of study: a man who must be at least a hundred. He asks the man whether he was also particular about his food. Man: 'Indeed I was, only the best was good enough — no margarine for me, cream and butter, that's the thing!'; Gerontologist: 'And what about your drinking habits? Did you restrict yourself on that point?'; Man: 'Of course, I only consume the truly good wines — at least a *grand cru* — and my daily bottle of whisky has to be a single malted one, I don't like the blended stuff, that's pure poison.'; Gerontologist: 'And women, what about women?'; Man: 'Oh, don't ask me about women, I used to do it at least twice a day, but these days I don't get a hard-on that easily anymore.'; Gerontologist: 'But for God's sake, how did you manage to get that old?'; Man: 'Old, old! Let's not exaggerate, my dear chap, twenty-seven is not *that* old!' See: G. Bataille, *Erotism: Death and Sensuality* (1957) (trans. M. Dalwood), San Francisco CA, City Lights Books, 1986.

24. See: S. Freud, The Ego and the Id (1923*b*), *Standard Edition*, XIX, pp. 1-66 and pp. 40-43 in particular.

25. J. Lacan, *The Four Fundamental Concepts of Psychoanalysis, o.c.*, pp. 204-205.

26. *Ibid.*, p. 203.

27. *Ibid.*, p. 214.

28. *Ibid.*, p. 215.

29. See: J. Lacan, *Le Séminaire, Livre XVII, L'envers de la psychanalyse, o.c.*, pp. 202-208.

30. See: J. Lacan, *The Four Fundamental Concepts of Psychoanalysis, o.c.*, p. 208.

31. *Ibid.*, pp. 16-64.
32. *Ibid.*, pp. 128, 22 & 23.
33. *Ibid.*, p. 22.
34. *Ibid.*, pp. 29-30.
35. *Ibid.*, p. 25.
36. *Ibid.*, p. 26.
37. *Ibid.*, p. 26.
38. *Ibid.*, pp. 53-64. For Aristotle's notions, see: Aristotle, *The Physics* (trans. P.H. Wicksteed & F.M. Cornford), Cambridge MA-London, Harvard University Press, 1929, 196*a* 36.
39. *Ibid.*, p. 157.
40. See, for example: J. Lacan, *The Seminar. Book VII: The Ethics of Psychoanalysis* (1959-60) (trans. with notes D. Porter), Edited by J.-A. Miller, New York NY-London, W.W. Norton & Company, 1992, p. 32 & pp. 44-45.
41. See: J. Lacan, Seminar on 'The Purloined Letter' (1956) (trans. J. Mehlman), *Yale French Studies*, 1972, no. 48, pp. 39-72. This translation does not comprise Lacan's three appendices to his original article ('presentation of the sequel,' 'introduction' and 'parenthesis of parentheses'). For these texts, see: J. Lacan, Le séminaire sur 'La lettre volée' (1956), *Ecrits*, Paris, du Seuil, 1966, pp. 11-61.
42. For 'efficient cause,' see: Aristotle, *The Physics*, *o.c.*, 198a.
43. See: S. Freud, Beyond the Pleasure Principle, *o.c.*, pp. 7-64.
44. See: J. Breuer & S. Freud, Studies on Hysteria (1895*d*), *Standard Edition*, II.
45. See: S. Freud, The Dynamics of Transference (1912*b*), *Standard Edition*, XII, pp. 97-108; S. Freud, Remembering, Repeating and Working-Through (Further Recommendations on the Technique of Psycho-Analysis II) (1914*g*), *Standard Edition*, XII, pp. 145-156.
46. See: S. Freud, The Interpretation of Dreams (1900*a*), *Standard Edition*, IV, p. 111 (navel of the dream); *Standard Edition*, V, p. 603 (core of our being); S. Freud, Repression (1915*d*), *Standard Edition*, XIV, pp. 146-158.
47. Lacan borrowed the notion of *ex-sistance* (ex-sistence) from the French translation of Heidegger's *Sein und Zeit*, in which the German *Ekstase* and the Greek *ekstasis* (standing outside) were translated as *ex-sistance*. See: B. Fink, *The Lacanian Subject: Between Language and Jouissance, o.c.*, p. 122.
48. J. Lacan, *The Four Fundamental Concepts of Psychoanalysis, o.c.*, p. 22.
49. See: P. Verhaeghe, La psychanalyse et la science: une question de causalité, *Quarto*, 1994, no. 56, pp. 73-78.
50. J. Lacan, *Le Séminaire, Livre XX, Encore* (1972-73), texte établi par J.-A. Miller, Paris, du Seuil, 1975, p. 87.
51. See: J. Lacan, The Subversion of the Subject and the Dialectic of Desire in the Freudian Unconscious (1960), *Ecrits: A Selection, o.c.*, p. 311 (Other of the Other); J. Lacan, *Le Séminaire, Livre XX, Encore, o.c.*, p. 35 (sexual relationship) & p. 68 (Woman).
52. For the term *Neurosenwahl*, see: S. Freud, The Disposition to Obsessional Neurosis: A Contribution to the Problem of Choice of Neurosis (1913*i*), *Standard Edition*, XII, pp. 311-326. For Lacan's *position du sujet*, see: J. Lacan, *The Four Fundamental Concepts of Psychoanalysis, o.c.*, pp. 246-247.

53. For the time-structure of the future anterior, see: J. Lacan, The Function and Field of Speech and Language in Psychoanalysis, *o.c.*, p. 86.

54. J. Lacan, *The Four Fundamental Concepts of Psychoanalysis, o.c.*, p. 203.

55. In his metapsychological papers, Freud uses different denominations (vesicle, primitive organism, early ego, primitive mental apparatus) to underscore the primary character of the mental apparatus. See: S. Freud, Instincts and their Vicissitudes (1915*c*), *Standard Edition*, XIV, pp. 117-140; S. Freud, Negation, *o.c.*, pp. 233-239; J. Lacan, *The Four Fundamental Concepts of Psychoanalysis, o.c.*, pp. 240-241.

56. For the character of Hannibal Lecter, see: T. Harris, *Red Dragon* (1981), London, Arrow Books, 1993; T. Harris, *Silence of the Lambs* (1989), London, Arrow Books, 1991.

57. For Lacan's critique on the 'two body psychology,' see: J. Lacan, *The Seminar. Book I: Freud's Papers on Technique* (1953-54) (trans. with notes J. Forrester), Edited by J.-A. Miller, Cambridge, Cambridge University Press, 1988, pp. 11, 205, 220, 227 & 261; J. Lacan, The Function and Field of Speech and Language in Psychoanalysis, *o.c.*, p. 90. Lacan introduces the topological figures of the Moebius strip and the Klein bottle from his ninth seminar onwards: J. Lacan, *Le Séminaire IX, L'identification* (1961-62), unpublished.

58. J. Lacan, *The Seminar. Book I: Freud's Papers on Technique, o.c.*, p. 171.

59. J. Lacan, *The Seminar. Book I: Freud's Papers on Technique, o.c.*, p. 146 ('Man's desire is the desire of the other'); J. Lacan, *The Seminar. Book III: The Psychoses* (1955-56) (trans. with notes R. Grigg), Edited by J.-A. Miller, New York NY, W.W. Norton & Company, 1993, p. 112 ('The unconscious is the discourse of the Other'); J. Lacan, The Function and Field of Speech and Language in Psychoanalysis, *o.c.*, p. 71 (*The Hollow Men*); T.S. Eliot, The Hollow Men (1925), *Collected Poems 1909-1962*, London-Boston MA, Faber and Faber, 1974, pp. 87-92.

60. This is not only the basis of suggestion, but of identity as such: *Je est un autre* (I is an other). In this sense, Lacan extends Freud's ideas to their very limits. What Freud decribes in *Group Psychology and the Analysis of the Ego* concerning the individual members of a group taking their identity from the leader in the position of Other, is generalised by Lacan to identity as such. Hence, the possibility of brainwashing, whereby a particular set of signifiers, belonging to a particular other, is replaced in the subject by another set of signifiers. This is the neurotic counterpart of the 'as if'-personality, described by Helene Deutsch. See: J. Lacan, *The Seminar. Book II: The Ego in Freud's Theory and in the Technique of Psychoanalysis* (1954-55) (trans. S. Tomaselli, notes J. Forrester), Edited by J.-A. Miller, Cambridge, Cambridge University Press, 1988, p. 7 (I is an other); S. Freud, Group Psychology and the Analysis of the Ego (1921*c*), *Standard Edition*, XVIII, pp. 65-143; H. Deutsch, Über einen Typus der Pseudoaffektivität ('als ob'), *Internationale Zeitschrift für Psychoanalyse*, 1934, XX, pp. 323-335; H. Deutsch, Some Forms of Emotional Disturbance and their Relationship to Schizophrenia, in J.D. Sutherland & M. Masud R. Khan (Eds.), *Neuroses and Character Types: Clinical Psychoanalytic Studies*, London, The Hogarth Press and the Institute of Psycho-Analysis, 1963, pp. 262-281.

61. See: J. Lacan, *Le Séminaire, Livre VIII, Le transfert* (1960-61), texte établi par J.-A. Miller, Paris, du Seuil, 1991, pp. 20-22.

62. S. Freud, Moses and Monotheism (1939*a*[1934-38]), *Standard Edition*, XXIII, pp. 75 & 113.

63. J. Lacan, *The Four Fundamental Concepts of Psychoanalysis, o.c.*, p. 29.

64. *Ibid.*, pp. 214-215.

65. J. Lacan, The Subversion of the Subject and the Dialectic of Desire in the Freudian Unconscious, *o.c.*, p. 316.

66. F. de Saussure, *Course in General Linguistics* (1906-1911) (trans. with notes and introduction W. Baskin), Edited by Ch. Bally and A. Séchehaye in collaboration with A. Riedlinger, London, Peter Owen, 1960, p. 71. Baskin has translated *la carte forcée* as 'the stated deck'. In the more recent translation of Saussure's work by Harris, *la carte forcée de la langue* is rendered as 'the linguistic Hobson's choice'. See: F. de Saussure, *Course in General Linguistics* (1906-1911) (trans. with notes R. Harris), Edited by Ch. Bally and A. Séchehaye in collaboration with A. Riedlinger, London, Duckworth, 1983, p. 71.

67. J. Lacan, The Agency of the Letter in the Unconscious or Reason since Freud, *Ecrits: A Selection, o.c.*, p. 164.

68. For the notion of 'primal repression,' see: S. Freud, Repression (1915*d*), *Standard Edition*, XIV, pp. 141-158.

69. See: S. Freud, Group Psychology and the Analysis of the Ego, *o.c.*, pp. 105-110.

70. S. Freud, Repression, *o.c.*, pp. 141-158 and pp. 148-149 in particular.

71. S. Freud, The Psychopathology of Everyday Life (1901*b*), *Standard Edition*, VI, p. 5.

72. See: J. Lacan, *Le Séminaire, Livre XVII, L'envers de la psychanalyse, o.c.*, pp. 11-13.

73. For Descartes' formula, see: R. Descartes, Discourse on the Method (1637[1636]), *The Philosophical Writings of Descartes*, Vol. I (trans. J. Cottingham, R. Stoothoff & J. Murdoch), Cambridge, Cambridge University Press, 1985, pp. 125-127. For Lacan's reading of Descartes, see for example: J. Lacan, Science and Truth (1965) (trans. B. Fink), *Newsletter of the Freudian Field*, 1989, no. 3, pp. 4-29 and p. 13 in particular.

74. J. Lacan, *The Four Fundamental Concepts of Psychoanalysis, o.c.*, p. 210. The *vel* refers to a process of forced choice, whereas *aphanisis* indicates a fading of the subject.

75. On *Nachträglichkeit*, see: S. Freud, From the History of an Infantile Neurosis (1918*b*[1914]), *Standard Edition*, XVII, p. 45.

76. See: J. Lacan, The Mirror Stage as Formative of the Function of the I as Revealed in Psychoanalytic Experience, *o.c.*, pp. 1-7.

77. See: J. Lacan, Remarque sur le rapport de Daniel Lagache: "Psychanalyse et structure de la personnalité" (1960), *Ecrits, o.c.*, pp. 647-684.

78. On the paternal metaphor, see: J. Lacan, On a Question Preliminary to Any Possible Treatment of Psychosis (1957-58), *Ecrits: A Selection, o.c.*, p. 200.

79. J. Lacan, *The Four Fundamental Concepts of Psychoanalysis, o.c.*, p. 214.

80. 'Ils se rencontrèrent à Paris, au Bal de l'Opéra; lorsqu'ils ôtèrent leur masque, horreur! Ce n'était pas elle, lui non plus d'ailleurs.'

81. J. Lacan, *The Four Fundamental Concepts of Psychoanalysis, o.c.*, p. 214.

82. *Ibid.*, p. 237.

83. *Ibid.*, p. 238.

84. *Ibid.*, p. 276.

85. For the 'traversing of the fantasy,' see: J. Lacan, *The Four Fundamental Concepts of Psychoanalysis, o.c.*, p. 273. For 'subjective destitution,' see: J. Lacan, Proposition of 9 October 1967 on the Psychoanalyst of the School (1967) (trans. R. Grigg), *Analysis*, 1995, no. 6, pp. 1-13 and p. 8 in particular.

86. This reminds us of the already mentioned 'forced choice' at the basis of language, as described by de Saussure in *la carte forcée de la langue*.

87. J. Lacan, *The Four Fundamental Concepts of Psychoanalysis, o.c.*, p. 258.

88. J. Lacan, Le Séminaire XXIV, L'insu que sait de l'une-bévue s'aile à mourre (1976-77), texte établi par J.-A. Miller, *Ornicar ?*, 1977, no. 12-13, pp. 6-7.

89. See: J. Lacan, Le Séminaire XXII, R.S.I (1974-75), texte établi par J.-A. Miller, *Ornicar ?*, 1975, no. 3, p. 109.

90. J. Lacan, L'étourdit, *Scilicet*, 1973, no. 4, p. 15.

91. J. Lacan, *The Seminar. Book VII: The Ethics of Psychoanalysis* (1959-60) (trans. with notes D. Porter), Edited by J.-A. Miller, New York NY, W.W. Norton & Company, 1992, p. 112.

92. J. Lacan, Le Séminaire XXIII, Le sinthome (1975-76), texte établi par J.-A. Miller, *Ornicar ?*, 1976, no. 8, p. 20. Our translation.

CHAPTER 8

The Seven Veils of Fantasy

Slavoj Žižek

I. Introduction

The standard notion of the way fantasy works within ideology, is that of a fantasy-scenario which obfuscates the true horror of a situation. For example, instead of a full rendering of the antagonisms that traverse our society, we indulge in the notion of society as an organic Whole, kept together by forces of solidarity and cooperation.

However, it is much more productive to look for this notion of fantasy where one would not expect to find it, in marginal and apparently purely utilitarian situations, like the safety instructions prior to the take-off of an airplane. Aren't they sustained by a fantasmatic scenario of how a possible plane-crash will look? After a gentle landing on water (miraculously, it is always supposed to happen on water!), each of the passengers puts on the life-jacket and, as on a beach toboggan, slides into the water and takes a swim, like a nice collective lagoon holiday-experience under the guidance of an experienced swimming instructor. Is this 'gentrification' of a catastrophe (a nice soft landing, stewardesses in dance-like style graciously pointing with their hands towards the Exit-signs), not also ideology at its purest?

Yet the Lacanian notion of fantasy, formalised as $\$ \diamond a$, cannot be reduced to that of a fantasy-scenario which obfuscates the true horror of a situation. The first, rather obvious thing to add is that the relationship between fantasy and the horror of the real that it conceals, is much more ambiguous than it may seem. Fantasy conceals this horror, yet at the same time it creates what it purports to conceal, namely its 'repressed' point of reference. Aren't the images of the ultimate horrible Thing, from the gigantic deep-sea squid to the ravaging twister, fantasmatic creations par excellence? One should specify the notion of fantasy with a whole series of features.

II. The Seven Veils

1. The fantasy is a transcendental schematism

The first thing to note is that fantasy does not simply realize a desire in a hallucinatory way. Its function is rather that of a Kantian 'transcendental schematism.' A fantasy constitutes our desire, provides its coordinates, i.e. it literally 'teaches us how to desire.'

This role of fantasy hinges on the fact that 'there is no sexual relationship,' no universal formula or matrix guaranteeing a harmonious sexual relationship with one's partner.[1] On account of the lack of this universal formula, every individual has to invent a fantasy of his or her own, a 'private' formula for the sexual relationship. For a man, the relationship with a woman is possible only inasmuch as she fits his formula. The formula of the Wolf Man, Freud's famous patient, consisted of 'a woman, viewed from behind, on her hands and knees, and washing or cleaning something on the ground in front of her.' The view of a woman in this position automatically gave rise to love.[2] In the case of John Ruskin, the formula which followed the model of old Greek and Roman statues led to a tragicomic disappointment when, in the course of his wedding night, Ruskin caught sight of his wife's pubic hair, which he had not found on the statues. This discovery made him totally impotent, since he was convinced that his wife was a monster. In Jennifer Lynch's *Boxing Helena*, the fantasy ideal is none other than Venus of Milo herself. The film's hero kidnaps the beloved girl and performs an operation on her in order to make her fit the ideal, and thus to render the sexual relationship possible. He cuts off her hands, makes a scar to match the place where the statue is truncated, etc. The point is, of course, that we are all doing in fantasy what the hero of *Boxing Helena* is doing in reality.

2. The fantasy has two dimensions

The second thing to note is the tension which runs through the very heart of fantasy. On the one hand, fantasy has a beatific side, a *stabilizing* dimension, which is governed by the dream of a state without disturbances, out of reach of human depravity. On the other hand, fantasy has a *destabilizing* dimension, whose elementary form is envy. It encompasses all that 'irritates' me about the Other, images that haunt me about what he or she is doing when out of my sight, about how he or she deceives me and plots against me, about how he or she ignores me and indulges in an enjoyment that is intensive beyond my capacity of representation, etc. Doesn't the fundamental lesson of so-called totalitarianism concern the co-dependence of these two aspects of the notion of fantasy? Those who alleged to have fully realized the (stabilizing) $fantasy_1$, had to have recourse to the (destabilizing) $fantasy_2$, in order to explain their failure. The foreclosed obverse of the Nazi harmonious *Volksgemeinschaft* returned in the guise of their paranoiac obsession with the Jewish plot. Similarly, the Stalinists' compulsive discovery of ever new enemies of Socialism was the inescapable obverse of their pretending to realize the ideal of the 'new Socialist man.' Perhaps freedom from the infernal hold of $fantasy_2$ provides the most succinct definition of a saint.

$Fantasy_1$ and $fantasy_2$ are thus like the front and back of the same coin. Insofar as a community experiences its reality as regulated and structured by $fantasy_1$, it has to disavow its inherent impossibility, the antagonism in its very heart, whereby $fantasy_2$, for example the anti-Semitic figure of the 'conceptual Jew,' gives body to this disavowal. In short, the effectiveness of $fantasy_2$ is the condition for $fantasy_1$ to maintain its hold.

Lacan rewrote Descartes' 'I am thinking, therefore I am' as 'I am thinking: "therefore I am"' — the point being, of course, the non-coincidence of the two verbs 'am,' i.e. the fantasmatic nature of the second 'am.'[3] One should submit the pathetic assertion of ethnic identity to the same reformulation. The moment 'I am French (German, Jew, American, etc.)' is rephrased as 'I am the one who thinks: "therefore I am French",' the gap in the midst of my self-identity becomes visible. The function of the 'conceptual Jew' is precisely to render this gap invisible.

3. The fantasy creates a multitude of subject-positions

The third point is that the question 'Who, where, how is the (fantasizing) subject inscribed into the fantasmatic narrative?' is far from obvious. Even when the subject appears in person within this narrative, this is not automatically his or her point of identification, i.e. he or she by no means necessarily 'identifies with him or herself.' Far more common is the identification with the ego ideal, with the gaze for which, or the point of view from which I, in my activity depicted in the fantasmatic narrative, appear in a likeable way.[4]

Suffice it to recall the standard pornographic scene whereby a man is doing 'it' to a woman. The spectator of the film does *not* identify with the man who is fucking the woman. The woman is as a rule asserted as the exhibitionist subject who fully enjoys doing it, and who is being viewed by the spectator while doing it, in clear contrast to the man who is reduced to the pure, faceless instrument of the woman's enjoyment.[5] The spectator, far from identifying with the male actor, rather identifies with the 'third,' implicit position, which is that of a pure gaze observing the woman who fully enjoys herself. The spectator's satisfaction is of a purely reflective nature; it derives from the awareness that a woman can find full satisfaction in phallic enjoyment.

As a rule, the fantasizing subject does not identify with his or her own appearance in the fantasmatic space (with his or her 'oppositional determination,' as Hegel would have put it). More radically, fantasy creates a multitude of 'subject-positions,' among which the (observing, fantasizing) subject can freely float. The subject is free to shift his or her identification from one to another. Here, the talk about 'multiple, dispersed subject-positions' is justified, with the proviso that these subject-positions are to be strictly distinguished from the void of the subject, which Lacan designated as $\$$.[6] In this sense, the voyeurist sado-masochistic play between Isabella Rossellini and Dennis Hopper in David Lynch's *Blue Velvet* implies three 'subject-positions.' It can be conceived as staged for the voyeur (Kyle MacLachlan) in the closet, who is secretly observing the scene. Or it can be seen as staged for the obscene-impotent father who, obviously aware of being observed, endeavours to project the image of his potency. And finally, it can also be staged for the depressed woman herself, in order to draw her back into the life-circuit by means of a kind of shock-therapy.[7]

4. The fantasy is radically intersubjective

The fourth feature of the fantasy concerns its radically intersubjective character. The critical depreciation and abandonment of the term 'intersubjectivity' by Lacan, in clear contrast to his earlier insistence that the proper domain of psychoanalytic experience is neither subjective nor objective, but intersubjective, in no way also involves an abandonment of the idea that the relation between the subject and the Other, as well as the latter's desire, are crucial for the subject's identity.[8] Paradoxically, one should claim that Lacan's abandonment of 'intersubjectivity' is strictly correlative to the focusing of attention on the enigma of the impenetrable desire of the Other, epitomized in the phrase *Che vuoi?* (What do you want?).[9] What the late Lacan does with intersubjectivity is to be opposed to the early Lacan's Hegelo-Kojèvian motifs of the struggle for recognition, of the dialectical connection between recognition of desire and desire for recognition, as well as to the middle Lacan's 'structuralist' motif of the big Other as the anonymous symbolic structure.[10]

Perhaps the easiest way to discern these shifts is by way of focusing on the changed status of the object. In the early Lacan, the object is depreciated as to its inherent qualities; it counts only as a stake in the intersubjective struggles for recognition and love. In this way, the milk demanded by a child from the mother is reduced to a 'sign of love,' i.e. the demand for milk effectively aims at soliciting the mother to display her love for the child. Likewise, a jealous subject demands from his parents a certain toy, this toy becoming the object of his demand because he is aware that it is also coveted by his brother. In the late Lacan, on the contrary, the focus shifts to the object that the subject itself 'is.' This concerns the *agalma*, the secret treasure that guarantees the minimum of fantasmatic consistency of the subject's being, that is to say the object *a* (*objet petit a*), as the object of fantasy, that 'something in me more than myself' on account of which I perceive myself as 'worthy of the Other's desire.'[11]

One should always bear in mind that the desire which is 'realized' (staged) in fantasy is not the subject's own, but the *Other's* desire. Fantasy, fantasmatic formation, is an answer to the enigma of *Che vuoi?*: 'You are saying this, but *what is it that you effectively want by saying it*?' This renders the subject's primordial, constitutive position. The original questioning of desire is not directly 'What do *I* want?,' but 'What do *others* want from me?, What do they see in me?, What am I for the others?' A small child is embedded in a complex network of relations; it serves as a kind of catalyst and battle-field for the desires of those around it. Its father, mother, brothers and sisters fight their battles around it, the mother sending a message to the father through her care for the son, etc. While being well aware of this role, the child cannot fathom what kind of an object it is for the others, what the exact nature of the games they are playing is. Fantasy provides an answer to this enigma; at its most fundamental level, fantasy tells me what I am for my others.

It is again anti-Semitism, the anti-Semitic paranoia, which renders visible in an exemplary way this radically *intersubjective* character of fantasy. Fantasy (the social fantasy of the Jewish plot, for instance) is an attempt to provide an answer to the question 'What does society want from me?' It contributes to unearthing the meaning of the murky events in which I am forced to participate. For that reason, the standard theory of 'projection,' according to which the anti-Semite 'projects' onto the figure of the Jew the disavowed part of himself, is not sufficient. The figure of the 'conceptual Jew' cannot be reduced to the externalization of the anti-Semite's 'inner conflict.' On the contrary, it bears witness to (and tries to cope with) the fact that the anti-Semite is originally decentered, part of an opaque network whose meaning and logic elude his control.

This radical intersubjectivity of fantasy is discernible even in the most elementary cases, like the one reported by Freud of his little daughter fantasizing about strawberries.[12] What we have here is by no means a simple case of direct hallucinatory satisfaction of a desire (she wanted strawberries, did not get any, and so she fantasized about it...). What we ought to introduce here is precisely the dimension of intersubjectivity. The crucial fact is that when the little girl was voraciously eating strawberries, she noted how her parents were deeply satisfied by this spectacle, i.e. by seeing her fully enjoying it. So, what the fantasy of eating strawberries is really about, is her attempt to form such an identity (of the one who fully enjoys eating strawberries given by the parents) that would satisfy her parents, that would make her the object of their desire.

One can clearly perceive the difference here from the early Lacan, for whom the object is reduced to a token which is totally insignificant in itself, since it matters only as the point in which my own and the

Other's desires intersect. For the late Lacan, the object is precisely that which is 'in the subject more than the subject itself.' It is what I fantasize that the Other (fascinated by me) sees in me. Hence, it is no longer the object which serves as the mediator between my desire and the Other's desire; it is rather the Other's desire itself which serves as the mediator between the barred subject ($) and the lost object that the subject 'is.' The Other's desire provides the minimum of fantasmatic identity to the subject. At this point one can also see in what *la traversée du fantasme* (traversing the fantasy) consists, namely in an acceptance of the fact that *there is no secret treasure in me* at all, that the support of me (the subject) is purely fantasmatic.[13]

We can also see the difference between Lacan and Habermas now. Habermas insists on the difference between the subject-object relation and intersubjectivity proper. In the latter, the other subject is precisely *not* one of the objects in my field of experience, but the partner in a dialogue, the interaction with whom, within a concrete life-world, forms the irreducible background of my experience of reality. However, what Habermas represses, is simply and precisely the *intersection* of these two relations, i.e. the level at which another subject is not yet the partner in an intersubjective symbolic communication and/or interaction, but *remains an object*, a Thing, that which makes a 'neighbour' into a sleazy repulsive presence. This other *qua object* that gives body to an unbearable excess of jouissance is the proper 'object of psychoanalysis.' Lacan's point is thus that symbolic intersubjectivity is *not* the ultimate horizon behind which one cannot reach. There is no 'monadic' subjectivity prior to it, but a pre-symbolic, 'impossible' relation to an Other which is the *real* Other, the Other as *Thing*, and not yet the symbolic Other (the field of intersubjectivity).

5. The fantasy is a narrative

The fifth point is that the fantasy constitutes the primordial form of narrative, which serves to occult some original deadlock. The socio-political fantasy par excellence is the myth of 'primordial accumulation': the narrative of the two workers, the one lazy and free-spending, the other diligent and enterprising, accumulating and investing, provides the myth of the 'origins of capitalism,' obfuscating the violence of its actual genealogy.

Notwithstanding his emphasis on symbolization and/or historicization in the 1950's, Lacan is radically *anti-narrativist*. The ultimate aim of psychoanalytic treatment is *not* for the analysand to organize his or her confused life-experience into (another) coherent narrative, with all the traumas properly integrated. It is not only that some narratives are 'false,' based upon the exclusion of traumatic events and patching up the gaps left over by these exclusions. Lacan's thesis is much stronger: the answer to the question 'Why do we tell stories?' is that *narrative as such* emerges in order to resolve some fundamental antagonism by way of rearranging its terms into a temporal succession. It is thus the very form of narrative which bears witness to some repressed antagonism. The price one pays for the narrative resolution is the *petitio principii* of the temporal loop, i.e. the narrative silently presupposes as already given what it purports to reproduce.[14]

Let us elaborate on this gesture of the narrative resolution of antagonism apropos of the splitting of the domain of the law into the neutral public Law and its obscene superego supplement. The problem with the definition of 'totalitarianism' as the eclipse of the neutral symbolic Law, so that the entire domain of law is 'stained' by the obscene superego, is: how are we to conceive the *prior* epoch, i.e. where was the superego obscenity *before* the advent of totalitarianism?[15] There are two opposed narratives which offer themselves here. Firstly, the narrative according to which, with the advent of modernity, the law rooted in concrete traditional communities and as such still permeated by the jouissance of a specific 'way of life,' gets split into the neutral symbolic Law and its superego supplement of obscene unwritten rules. According to this narrative, it is only with the advent of modernity that the neutral judicial order of Law delivered of substantial jouissance emerges. Secondly, there is the (Foucaultian) counter-narrative, according to which in the epoch of modernity, the rule of the traditional judicial Law is replaced by the web of disciplinary practices. Modernity involves the 'crisis of investiture,' the inability of the subjects to assume symbolic mandates. What hinders them to fulfil the act of symbolic identification is the perception of a 'stain of enjoyment' in the big Other of the Law, the perception of the domain of the Law as permeated with obscene enjoyment. Consequently, the disciplinary exercise of power which supplants the pure symbolic Law is by definition stained with superego enjoyment.[16]

The problem with these two narratives is that they are mutually exclusive as to their crucial aspects. According to the first one, the neutral Law, delivered of the stain of enjoyment, emerged with modernity, while according to the second one, modernity signals the 'crisis of investiture,' the fact that the Law is perceived as stained with superego enjoyment. The only solution to this deadlock is to conceive of these two narratives as the two complementary ideological gestures of resolving/obfuscating the underlying deadlock, which resides in the fact that the Law was smeared, stigmatized by enjoyment *in the very moment of its emergence as the neutral-universal formal Law.* The very emergence of a pure neutral Law, free of its concrete 'organic' life-world support, gives birth to the obscene superego underside, since this very life-world support, once opposed to the pure Law, is all of a sudden perceived as obscene.

It is easy to discern the same paradox in the standard New Age critique of Descartes, whereby Descartes is reproached with 'anthropocentrism.' However, does the Cartesian subjectivity (as correlative to the universe of modern science) not involve the Copernican turn? Does it not decenter man and reduce him to an insignificant creature on a small planet? In other words, what one should always bear in mind is how the Cartesian de-substantialization of the subject, its reduction of the subject to $", to the pure void of self-relating negativity, is strictly correlative to the opposite reduction of man to a grain of dust in the infinity of the universe, to one among the endless objects in it. These are the two sides of the same process. In this precise sense, Descartes is radically anti-humanist, i.e. he dissolves the Renaissance humanist unity of man as the highest Creature, the top of creation, into pure *cogito* and its bodily remainder. The elevation of the subject to the transcendental agent of the synthesis constitutive of reality is correlative to the abasement of its material bearer to one among the worldly objects. Of course, Descartes is also reproached with patriarchal bias (the unmistakable male features of *cogito*). Yet does his formulation of *cogito* as pure thought which, as such, 'has no sex,' not mark the first break out from the pre-modern, sexualized ontology? Descartes is furthermore reproached with conceiving the subject as the owner of natural objects, so that animals and the environment in general are reduced to mere exploitable objects, with no protection. However, is it not that only by way of conferring upon them the status of property, natural objects became for the first time legally *protected* (as only a property can be)?

In all these (and other) cases, Descartes set up the very standard by means of which one measures and rejects his positive doctrine on behalf of a post-Cartesian 'holistic' approach. Narrativization is thus misrepresentational in both of its versions. Firstly, it is a misrepresentation in its guise of the story of the progress from the primitive to the higher, more cultivated form, i.e. from the primitive fetishist superstition to the spiritual monotheist religion or, in the case of Descartes, from the primitive sexualized ontology to the neutral modern thought. Secondly, it is a misrepresentation in its guise of the story of historical evolution as regression or Fall, which, in the case of Descartes, runs from the organic unity with nature to the exploitative attitude towards it, or from the pre-modern spiritual complementarity of woman and man to the Cartesian identification of the woman with the 'natural.' Both versions obfuscate the absolute synchronicity of the antagonism in question.

Consequently, the paradox needs to be fully accepted that, when a certain historical moment is (mis)perceived as the moment of a loss of some quality, upon close inspection it becomes clear that the lost quality only emerged at this very moment of its alleged loss. This coincidence of emergence and loss designates the fundamental paradox of the Lacanian object *a*, which emerges as being-lost. Narrativization occludes this paradox by describing the process in which the object is first given and then gets lost.[17] The conclusion to be drawn from this absolute synchronicity is not that there is no history, since everything is already here from the very outset, but that the historical process does not follow the logic of narration. The actual historical breaks are, if anything, *more* radical than mere narrative deployments, since what changes in them is the entire constellation of emergence and loss. In other words, a true historical break does not simply designate the 'regressive' loss (or the 'progressive' gain) of something, but the shift in the very grid which enables us to measure losses and gains.

The supreme example of this paradoxical coincidence of emergence and loss is provided by the notion of history itself. Where exactly is its place, i.e. which societies can be characterized as properly historical? On the one hand, precapitalist societies allegedly do not yet know history proper, they are 'circular,' 'closed,' caught in a repetitive movement predetermined by tradition. So, history must emerge afterwards, with the decay of 'closed' organic societies. On the other hand, the opposite commonplace tells us that capitalism itself is no longer historical, that it is rootless, with no tradition of its own, and therefore parasitical upon previous traditions, a universal order which (like modern science) can thrive anywhere, from Japan to Argentina, uprooting and slowly corroding all particular life-worlds based on specific traditions. So, history is that which gets lost with the growth of capitalism, with its ultimate world-wide triumph, signalling the moment of the 'end of history.' The solution, again, is that emergence and loss coincide. Properly 'historical' is only a moment, even if this moment is properly unending and goes on for centuries, like the moment of passage from precapitalist societies to a capitalist universal order.

6. The fantasy involves an impossible gaze

The sixth feature is that on account of its temporal loop, the narrative fantasy always involves an impossible gaze, by means of which the subject is already present at the act of his or her own conception. An exemplary case of this vicious circle in the service of ideology, is an anti-abortion fairy-tale written in the 1980's by Joze Snoj, a Slovene right-wing nationalist poet. The tale takes place on an idyllic south-sea island where the aborted children live together without their parents. Although their life is nice and calm, they miss parental love and spend their time in sad reflections on how their parents preferred a career or a luxurious holiday to them. The trick, of course, resides in the fact that the aborted children are presented as having been born, only into an alternative universe (the lone Pacific island), retaining the memory of parents who 'betrayed' them. In this way, they can direct at their parents a reproachful gaze which makes them guilty.

Apropos of a fantasmatic scene, the questions to be asked are thus always: 'For which gaze is it staged? Which narrative is it destined to support?' According to some recently published documents, the British General Michael Rose, head of the UNPROFOR forces in Bosnia, and his special team of SAS operatives, definitely had another 'hidden agenda' in Bosnia. Under the pretence of maintaining a truce between the so-called 'warring factions,' their secret task was to put the blame on Croats, and especially Muslims.[18] These diversions were intended to create the perception of the Bosnian conflict as a kind of 'tribal warfare,' a civil war of everybody against everybody else in which 'all sides are equally to blame.' Instead of the clear condemnation of the Serb aggression, this perception was destined to prepare the terrain for an international effort of 'pacification,' which would 'reconcile the warring factions.' From a sovereign state, victim of aggression, Bosnia was suddenly transformed into a chaotic place in which 'power-mad warlords' acted out their historical traumas at the expense of innocent women and children.

What lurks in the background, of course, is the pro-Serbian 'insight,' according to which peace in Bosnia is possible only if we do not 'demonize' one side in the conflict. Responsibility is to be equally distributed, with the West assuming the role of the neutral judge elevated above the local tribal conflicts. For our analysis, the key point is that General Rose's pro-Serb 'secret war' on the terrain itself was trying not to change the relation of military forces, but rather to prepare the ground for a different narrative perception of the situation. 'Real' military activity itself was here in the service of ideological narrativization. Incidentally, the key event which functioned as a kind of *point de capiton* (quilting point) in turning the previous perspective on the Bosnian war upside-down, and which brought about its depoliticized (re)narrativization as a 'humanitarian catastrophe,' was François Mitterand's visit to Sarajevo in the Summer of 1992.[19] One is tempted even to postulate that General Rose was sent to Bosnia in order to realize, on the terrain, Mitterand's vision of the conflict. That is to say, until Mitterand's visit, the predominant perception of the Bosnian conflict was still a political one. Dealing with the Serb aggression, the key problem was the aggression of ex-Yugoslavia against an independent state. After Mitterand left, the accent shifted towards a humanitarian aspect: down there, a savage tribal war is going on, and the only thing the civilized West can do is to exert its influence to assuage the inflamed passions and help the innocent victims with food and medicine. Precisely through his display of compassion towards the suffering people of Sarajevo, Mitterand's visit gave a crucial blow to Bosnian interests, i.e. it functioned as the key factor of political neutralization in the international perception of the conflict. Or, as the vice-president of Bosnia and Herzegovina Ejup Ganic put it in an interview: 'First we were glad to receive Mitterand, hoping that his visit signals a true concern of the West. All of a sudden, however, we grasped that we are lost.'

The key point is that this gaze of the external innocent observer for whom the spectacle of 'tribal warfare in the Balkans' was staged, has the same 'impossible' status as the gaze of the aborted children who were born into a different reality in the Slovene anti-abortion fairy-tale. The gaze of the innocent observer is also in a way non-existent, since this gaze is the impossible neutral gaze of someone who falsely exempts himself from his concrete historical existence, i.e. from his actual involvement in the Bosnian conflict.

The same operation is easily discernible in the abundant media reports on the 'saintly' activities of Mother Theresa in Calcutta, which clearly rely on the fantasmatic screen of the Third World. Calcutta is regularly presented as Hell on Earth, the exemplary case of the moribund Third World megalopolis, full of social decay, poverty, violence and corruption, with its residents caught in terminal apathy.[20] In this picture of utter gloom, Mother Theresa brings a ray of hope to the dejected with the message that poverty is to be accepted as a way to redemption, since in enduring their sad fate with silent dignity and faith the poor repeat Christ's way of the cross. The ideological profit of this operation is double. Insofar as one proposes to the poor and terminally ill to look for salvation in their very suffering, Mother Theresa deters them from probing into the causes of their predicament, i.e. from politicizing their situation. At the same time, she offers the rich from the West the possibility of a kind of substitute-redemption by making financial contributions to Mother Theresa's charitable activity. And, again, all this works against the background of the fantasmatic image of the Third World as Hell on Earth, as a place so utterly desolate that no political activity, only charity and compassion, can alleviate the suffering.[21]

7. The fantasy stages castration

The seventh and last point is that, contrary to the commonsense notion of fantasizing as indulging in the hallucinatory realization of desires prohibited by the Law, the fantasmatic narrative does not stage the suspension-transgression of the Law, but is rather the very act of its installation, of the intervention of the cut of symbolic castration. What the fantasy endeavours to stage is ultimately the 'impossible' scene of castration. For that reason, fantasy as such is, in its very notion, close to perversion. The perverse ritual stages the act of castration, of the primordial loss which allows the subject to enter the symbolic order. Or, to put it in a more precise way: in contrast to the 'normal,' neurotic subject, for whom the Law functions as the agency of prohibition which regulates (the access to the object of) his or her desire, the pervert's object of desire is Law itself. The Law is the Ideal the pervert is longing for; the pervert wants to be fully acknowledged by the Law, integrated into its functioning. The irony of this fact should not escape us: the pervert, this 'transgressor' par excellence who purports to violate all the rules of 'normal' and decent behaviour, in effect longs for the very rule of the Law.[22]

At the political level, suffice it to recall the interminable search for the fantasmatic point at which German history 'took the wrong turn,' which ended up in Nazism: the delayed national unification, due to the dismemberment of the German Empire after the Thirty Years War; the aestheticization of politics in the Romantic reaction to Kant; the 'crisis of investiture' and the Bismarck state socialism in the second half of the nineteenth century; all the way back to the report of the German tribes' resistance to Romans which allegedly already displayed the features of *Volksgemeinschaft*. Similar examples abound. When exactly did patriarchal repression coincide with the repression and exploitation of nature? Eco-feminism provides a multitude of 'regressive' determinations of this unique fantasmatic moment of the Fall: the predominance of nineteenth century Western capitalism; the modern Cartesian science with its objectifying attitude towards nature; the Greek rationalist Socratic Enlightenment; the emergence of great barbarian Empires; all the way back to the passage from nomadic to agricultural civilization. Is Foucault himself not caught in the same fantasmatic loop in his search for the moment when the Western order of sexuality emerged? He regressed further and further back from modernity, until he finally set the limit at the disintegration of the Antique ethic of the 'care of the Self' into the Christian ethics of confession.[23] The fact that the tone of Foucault's last two books on pre-Christian ethics differs thoroughly from his earlier probing into the complex of power, knowledge, and sexuality — instead of his usual analyses of the material micro-practices of ideology, we get a rather standard version of the 'history of ideas' — bears witness to the fact that Foucault's Greece and Rome 'before the Fall' (into sexuality-guilt-confession) are purely fantasmatic entities.

III. The Common Thread

The common thread of all these seven features consists in the basic paradox of a fantasy formation: in order for a fantasy to be operative, it has to remain 'implicit' i.e., a distance must be maintained between it and the explicit symbolic texture sustained by it.

This constitutive gap between the explicit symbolic texture and its fantasmatic background is obvious in any work of art. Due to the priority of the place over the element which fills it up, even the most harmonious work of art is *a priori* fragmentary. It is lacking with regard to its place, the 'trick' of an artistic success residing in the artist's capacity to turn this lack into an advantage by manipulating skilfully the central void and its resonance in the elements that encircle it. This is how one can account for the 'paradox of the Venus of Milo.' Today, the statue's mutilation is no longer experienced as a deficiency but, on the contrary, as a positive constituent of its aesthetic impact. A simple mental experiment confirms this conjecture. Let us imagine the undamaged, complete statue: the effect is unmistakably that of *kitsch*, the proper aesthetic impact is lost.[24]

Art is thus fragmentary even when it is an organic Whole, since it always relies on the *distance towards fantasy*. In the 'unpublishable fragment' of her unfinished story *Beatrice Palmato*, Edith Wharton provides the detailed X-rated description of a father-daughter incest, with mutual masturbation, cunnilingus, fellatio, as well as, of course, the act itself.[25] It is easy to indulge in quick psychoanalytic explanation, according to which this fragment would offer the 'key' to Wharton's entire literary oeuvre, which is best condensed in the syntagm 'The "No" of the Mother.'[26] In Wharton's parental family, it was the mother who acted as the agent of prohibition, while her father rather embodied a kind of prohibited knowledge permeated with enjoyment. Furthermore, it is easy to play the game of child sexual abuse and to suggest that sufficient 'circumstantial evidence' points to Wharton's child sexual abuse by her father as the traumatic event which marked the course of her life and literary career. It is also easy to emphasize the ambiguity between fantasy and 'reality,' the fact that it is practically impossible to discern neatly their respective parts. Was paternal incest just her fantasy, or was this fantasizing triggered by 'real' sexual molestation? In any case, this vicious circle bears witness to the fact that Edith is not 'innocent': she participated in incest at the level of fantasy.

However, such an approach fails to perceive that there is more truth in the artist's removal from fantasy than in its direct rendering: popular melodrama and *kitsch* are much closer to fantasy than 'true art.' In other words, in order to account for the distortion of 'original fantasy,' it is not sufficient to refer to social prohibitions. What intervenes in the guise of these prohibitions is the fact that fantasy itself is a 'primordial lie,' a screen masking the fundamental *impossibility*.[27] The artifice of 'true art' is thus to manipulate the censorship of the underlying fantasy in such a way as to render visible the radical falsity of this fantasy.

One of the most painful and troubling scenes in David Lynch's *Wild at Heart* deftly manipulates this gap between (social) reality and its fantasmatic support. In a lonely motel room, Willem Dafoe exerts a rude pressure on Laura Dern: he touches and squeezes her, invading the space of her intimacy and repeating in a threatening way 'Say fuck me!,' i.e. extorting from her a word that would signal her consent to a sexual act. The ugly, unpleasant scene drags itself on, and when, finally, the exhausted Laura Dern utters a barely audible 'Fuck me!,' Dafoe abruptly steps away, assumes a nice, friendly smile and cheerfully retorts: 'No, thanks, I don't have time today; but on another occasion I would do it gladly.' The uneasiness of this scene resides in the fact that the shock of Dafoe's final rejection of Dern's forcefully extorted offer gives the final pitch to him. His very unexpected rejection is his ultimate triumph and in a way humiliates her more than her direct rape. He has attained what he really wanted: not the act itself, just her consent to it, her symbolic humiliation. What we have here is rape in fantasy which refuses its realization in reality and thus further humiliates the victim. The fantasy is forced out, aroused, and then abandoned, thrown upon the victim. It is clear that Laura Dern is not simply disgusted by Dafoe's (Bobby Perou's) brutal intrusion into her intimacy: just prior to her 'Fuck me!,' the camera focuses on her right hand, which she slowly spreads out, the sign of her acquiescence, the proof that he has stirred up her fantasy. The point is thus to read this scene in a Lévi-Straussian way, as an inversion of the standard scene of seduction, in which the gentle approach is followed by the brutal sexual act, after the woman, the target of the seducer's efforts, finally says 'Yes!'.

How can such an ugly, properly repulsive figure like Bobby Perou stir up Laura Dern's fantasy? Here we are back at the motif of the ugly. Bobby Perou is ugly and repulsive insofar as he embodies the dream of the non-castrated phallic vitality in all its power: his whole body evokes a gigantic phallus, with his head as the head of a penis.[28] Even his final moments bear witness to a kind of raw energy which ignores the threat of death. After the bank robbery goes wrong, he blows off his own head, not in despair, but with a merry laughter. Bobby Perou is thus to be inserted in the series of larger-than-life figures of self-enjoying Evil whose best-known (although less intriguing and more formulaic than Bobby Perou) representative in Lynch's work is Frank (Dennis Hopper) in *Blue Velvet*. One is tempted to go even a step further here and to conceive the figure of Bobby Perou as the last embodiment of the larger-than-life figure on which all films of Orson Welles are focused:

> [Bobby Perou] is physically monstrous, but is he morally monstrous as well? The answer is yes and no. Yes, because he is guilty of committing a crime to defend himself; no, because from a higher moral standpoint, he is, at least in certain respects, above the honest and just [Sailor], who will always lack that sense of life which I shall call Shakespearean. These exceptional beings should not be judged by ordinary laws. They are both weaker and stronger than others . . . so much stronger because they are directly in touch with the true nature of things, or perhaps one should say, with God.[29]

In this famous description by Andre Bazin of Quinlan in Welles's *Touch of Evil*, we merely replaced the names, and the description seems to fit perfectly.

How, then, are we to grasp the 'No, thanks!' of Bobby Perou, one of the great ethical gestures in contemporary cinema? Perhaps the proper way to do it is to contrast the setting of this scene from *Wild at Heart* to another well-known scene from real life. One of the most humiliating racist rituals in the American Old South was to force the

African-American cornered by a white gang to commit the first gesture of insult. While the African-American was held tightly by his captors, a white racist thug shouted at him 'Spit on me! Tell me I'm scum!,' in order to extort from him the 'occasion' for a brutal beating or lynching — as if the white racist wanted to set up retroactively the proper dialogical context for his violent outburst. Here we encounter the perversity of the injurious word at its purest. The proper order of succession and implication is perverted: in a mocking imitation of the 'normal' order, I compel the victim to insult me voluntarily, i.e. to assume the discursive position of the offender and thereby to justify my violent outburst.

It is easy to perceive the homology with the scene from *Wild at Heart*. The point of this repulsive racist ritual is not simply that white thugs compel the well-meaning humble Uncle-Tomish African-American to offend them against his will. Both parties are well aware that the besieged African-American does cultivate aggressive fantasies about his white oppressors, that he *does* consider them scum (in a quite justified way, considering the brutal oppression he and his race have been exposed to), and their pressure serves to awaken these fantasies, so that, when the African-American finally spits on the white thug or tells him 'You're scum!' he in a way lets go his defences, his sense of survival, and displays his true desire, cost him what it may. This is exactly like Laura Dern in *Wild at Heart* who, in saying 'Fuck me!,' yields not only to external pressure but also to her fantasmatic kernel of jouissance. In short, the poor African-American is beaten (and probably killed) for his desire.

There is, however, a crucial difference between the two scenes. After extorting from Laura Dern her consent, Bobby Perou in *Wild at Heart* does not pass to the act. On the contrary, he reads her consent as a truly spontaneous act and gently rejects it. Unlike Bobby Perou, the racists molesting the African-American, after extorting the 'You are scum!' from him, use this as a legitimation to actually beat or even lynch him. In other words, if Bobby Perou were to act like the KKK racists, he would violently rape Laura Dern after obtaining the forced consent from her; vice versa, if the KKK racists were to act as Bobby Perou, they would follow the African-American's 'You're scum!' by simply retorting 'Yes, we probably are!' and leaving him alone. Or, to put it in yet another way, in the scene from *Wild at Heart* one should be attentive to the way Lynch turns around the standard procedure of male seduction, in which the gentle process of verbal seduction is followed by the forceful physical act of sexual penetration once the consent is obtained. In Lynch, the violence is entirely displaced onto the process of verbal seduction itself, which functions as a nightmarish mockery of the 'proper' gentle seduction, while the sexual act itself simply fails to come.

The traumatic impact of these two scenes thus relies on the gap between the subject's everyday symbolic universe and its fantasmatic support. Let us approach this gap through another disturbing phenomenon. When attention is drawn to the fact that women often do fantasize about being handled brutally and raped, the standard answer to it is either that this is a male fantasy about women or that women only have such fantasies insofar as they have 'internalized' the patriarchal libidinal economy and endorsed their victimization. The underlying idea is that the moment we recognize this fact of daydreaming about rape, we open the door to the male-chauvinist platitudes about how, in being raped, women only get what they secretly wanted; their shock and fear only express the fact that they were not honest enough to acknowledge this. To this commonplace, one should answer that (some) women actually may daydream about being raped, but that this fact not only in no way legitimizes the actual rape, it makes it even more violent. Consider two women, the first, liberated and assertive, active; the other, secretly daydreaming about being brutally handled by her partner, even raped. The crucial point is that, if both of them are raped, the rape will be much more traumatic for the second one, on account of the very fact that it will realize in 'external' social reality the 'stuff of her dreams.' Perhaps a better way to put it would be to paraphrase yet again the immortal lines of Stalin: it is impossible to say which of the two rapes would be worse. They are *both worse*. Rape against one's attitude, of course, is in a way worse, since it violates our disposition. But on the other hand, the very fact that rape was done in accordance with our secret disposition makes it even worse.[30]

In this mental experiment we have of course radically simplified the arrangement. The relationship between a certain type of public, intersubjective behaviour and its fantasmatic support is never direct. It is easily imaginable that a woman who is aggressive and assertive in her relations with men secretly fantasizes about being brutally mistreated.[31] Furthermore, it is easily imaginable that a woman daydreams about being submissive in order to conceal a more fundamental fantasy of a much more aggressive nature. The conclusion to be drawn is that, in contacts with another human being, one can never be sure when and in what way one will touch and disturb somebody's fantasy.

There is thus a gap that forever separates the fantasmatic kernel of the subject's being from the more 'superficial' modes of his or her symbolic and/or imaginary identifications. It is never possible for the subject fully to assume (in the sense of symbolic integration) the fantasmatic kernel of his or her being. When one approaches it too often, or when one comes too close to it, what occurs is the *aphanisis* of the subject: the subject loses his or her symbolic consistency, the subject disintegrates.[32] And, perhaps, the forced actualization in social reality itself of the fantasmatic kernel of the subject's being is the worst, most humiliating kind of violence, a violence which undermines the very basis of one's identity (of the 'self-image').[33]

IV. Fantasy, Drive and Desire

Bearing in mind these meanders of the notion of fantasy, we can now formulate the link between fantasy, drive, and desire, i.e. the way 'traversing the fantasy' (*la traversée du fantasme*) equals the passage from desire to drive. Desire is, at its most fundamental, 'a defence against drive.' Its emergence signals that the subject has renounced the excess of drive, that drive has got caught in the cobweb of Law/prohibition, in the vicious circle in which the object can be attained on the ladder of Law, only insofar as it is first lost. This is also Lacan's definition of castration: 'Castration means that *jouissance* must be refused, so that it can be reached on the inverted ladder (*l'échelle renversée*) of the Law of desire.'[34] Fantasy is the very narrative of this primordial loss, since it stages the process of this renunciation, the emergence of Law.

In this precise sense, fantasy is the screen that separates desire from drive. It tells the story that allows the subject to (mis)perceive the void around which drive circulates as the primordial loss constitutive of desire. Or, to put it in yet another way: fantasy provides a *rationale* for the inherent deadlock of desire; it gives a reason to the enigma of why 'there is no sexual relationship.' Fantasy is thus not simply the fantasy of a successful sexual relationship, but rather the fantasy of why it went wrong. It constructs the scene in which the jouissance we are deprived of is concentrated in the Other, who stole it from us. In the anti-Semitic ideological fantasy, social antagonism is explained away via the reference to the Jew as the secret agent who is stealing social jouissance from us (by amassing profits, seducing our women, etc.). For that reason also, the notion of fantasy is ambiguous: beatific fantasy (the vision of the state of things 'before the Fall') is supported by a disturbing paranoiac fantasy which tells us why things went wrong (why we did not get the girl, why society is antagonistic). Traversing, going through the fantasy, means that we accept the vicious circle of revolving around the void of the object and find jouissance in it, renouncing the myth that jouissance is amassed somewhere else.

It is also crucial to bear in mind that the opposition desire/drive coincides with the opposition truth/knowledge. As was emphasized by J.-A. Miller, the psychoanalytic concept of 'construction' does not rely on the (dubious) claim that the analyst is always right.[35] The point is rather the other, symmetrical side of the coin: it is the analysand who is always, by definition, in the wrong. In order to grasp this point, one should focus on the crucial distinction between construction and its counterpart, interpretation. This couple, construction/interpretation, is correlative to the couple knowledge/truth. That is to say, an interpretation is a gesture which is always embedded in the intersubjective dialectic of recognition between the analysand and the interpreter-analyst. It aims at bringing about the effect of truth apropos of a particular formation of the unconscious (a dream, a symptom, a slip of tongue, etc.). The subject is expected to 'recognize' him or herself in the signification proposed by the interpreter, precisely in order to subjectivize this signification, to assume it as his or her 'own': 'Yes, my God, that's me, I really wanted this.' The very success of interpretation is measured by this 'effect of truth,' by the extent to which it *affects the subjective position of the analysand* (stirs up memories of the hitherto deeply repressed traumatic encounters, provokes violent resistance). In clear contrast to interpretation, a construction (exemplarily, that of a fundamental fantasy) has the status of a knowledge which can never be subjectivized, that is, it can never be assumed by the subject as the truth about him or herself, the truth in which he or she recognizes the innermost kernel of his or her being. A construction is a purely explanatory logical presupposition. As such it is similar to the second stage ('I am being beaten by my father') of the child's fantasy 'A child is being beaten,' which, as Freud emphasizes, is so radically unconscious that it can never be remembered:

> This second phase is the most important and the most momentous of all. But we may say of it in a certain sense that it has never had a real existence. It is never remembered, it has never succeeded in becoming conscious. It is a construction of analysis, but it is no less a necessity on that account.[36]

The fact that this phase 'never had a real existence' indexes its status as the Lacanian real. The knowledge about it, a 'knowledge in the real,' is a kind of 'acephalic,' non-subjectivized knowledge. Although it is a kind of 'Thou art that!,' which articulates the very kernel of the subject's being (or, rather, for that very reason), its assumption *desubjectivizes* me, i.e. I can only assume my fundamental fantasy insofar as I undergo what Lacan calls 'subjective destitution' (*destitution subjective*).[37] Put differently, interpretation and construction stand to each other as symptom and fantasy do: symptoms are to be interpreted, fundamental fantasy is to be (re)constructed.

However, this notion of 'acephalic' knowledge emerges rather late in Lacan's teaching, namely during the early 1970's, after the relationship between knowledge and truth has undergone a profound shift.[38] From the 1940's to the 1960's, Lacan moves within the coordinates of the standard philosophical opposition between the 'unauthentic,' objectifying knowledge which disregards the subject's position of enunciation, and the 'authentic' truth in which one is existentially engaged and by which one is affected. In the psychoanalytic treatment, this opposition is perhaps best exemplified by the clear contrast between the obsessional neurotic and the hysteric. The obsessional neurotic *lies in the guise of truth*. While at the level of factual accuracy, his statements are always true, he uses this factual accuracy to dissimulate the truth about his desire. Say, when my enemy has a car accident because of a brake malfunction, I go to great lengths to explain to anyone willing to listen to me that I was never near his car and, consequently, am not responsible for the malfunction. This is true, but this 'truth' is propagated by me to conceal the fact that the accident actually realized my desire. The hysteric on the other hand *tells the truth in the guise of a lie.* The truth of my desire articulates itself in the distortions of the 'factual accuracy' of my speech. When instead of 'I thereby open this session,' I say 'I thereby close this session,' my desire clearly comes forth. The aim of the psychoanalytic treatment is thus to (re)focus attention away from the factual accuracy and onto the hysterical lies that unknowingly articulate the truth, and then to progress to a new knowledge which dwells at the place of truth. Instead of dissimulating truth, this new knowledge gives rise to truth-effects, i.e. to what Lacan in the 1950's called 'full speech,' the speech in which subjective truth reverberates.[39] As we have already emphasized, Lacan reinserts his theory into a long tradition, from Kierkegaard to Heidegger, of despising the mere 'factual truth.'

From the late 1960's, however, Lacan increasingly focuses his theoretical attention on the drive as a kind of 'acephalic' knowledge that brings about satisfaction. This knowledge involves neither an inherent relation to truth, nor a subjective position of enunciation. This is not because it dissimulates the subjective position of enunciation, but because it is in itself non-subjectivized, ontologically prior to the very dimension of truth.[40] Truth and knowledge are thus related as desire and drive, whereby interpretation aims at the truth of the subject's desire (the truth of desire is the desire for truth, as one is tempted to put it in a pseudo-Heideggerian way), while construction renders the knowledge about the drive.

Isn't the paradigmatic case of such an 'acephalic' knowledge that pertains to the drive provided by modern science, which exemplifies the 'blind insistence' of the (death) drive?[41] Modern science follows its path (in microbiology, in manipulating genes, in particle physics), cost what it may. Satisfaction is provided by knowledge itself, not by any moral or communal goals that scientific knowledge supposedly serves. Ethical committees endeavouring to establish rules for the proper conduct of gene-manipulations, medical experiments, etc. abound. Yet, aren't they ultimately only desperate attempts to reinscribe this inexorable drive-progress of science, which knows no inherent limitation (in short: this *inherent* ethics of the scientific attitude), within the confines of human goals, in order to provide them with a 'human face'? The commonplace wisdom today is that 'our extraordinary power to manipulate nature through scientific devices, has run ahead of our faculty to lead a meaningful existence, to make a human use of this immense power.' At this point, the properly modern ethics of 'following the drive' clashes with the traditional ethics of leading a life regulated by proper measure and by the subordination of all its aspects to some notion of the Good. Of course, the problem is that the balance between the two can never be achieved. The notion of reinscribing scientific drive into the constraints of the life-world is fantasy at its purest — perhaps even the fundamental *fascist* fantasy. Any limitation of this kind is utterly foreign to the inherent logic of science. Science belongs to the real and, as a mode of the real of jouissance, it is indifferent to the modalities of its symbolization, to the way it will affect social life.

Now, although the concrete organization of the scientific apparatus, up to its most abstract conceptual schemes, is socially 'mediated,' this game of discerning a patriarchal (Eurocentric, male-chauvinist, mechanistic and nature-exploiting) bias of modern science, in a way, *does not really concern science*, i.e. the drive which effectuates itself in the run of the scientific machine. Heidegger's position here seems utterly ambiguous. Perhaps it is all too easy to dismiss him as the most sophisticated proponent of the thesis that science *a priori* misses the dimension of truth.[42] Heidegger's more crucial point is rather that modern science, at its most fundamental, cannot be reduced to some limited ontical, 'socially conditioned' option (expressing the interests of a certain social group), but is rather the real of our historical moment, that which 'remains the same' in all possible (progressive and reactionary, technocratic and ecological, patriarchal and feminist) symbolic universes. Heidegger is thus well aware that all fashionable 'critiques of science,' according to which science is a tool of Western capitalist domination, patriarchal oppression, etc., fall short and thus leave unquestioned the 'hard kernel' of the scientific drive.

What Lacan imposes us to add is that science is perhaps also 'real' in an even more radical sense. It is the first (and probably unique) case of a discourse which is *stricto sensu non-historical*, even in the most fundamental Heideggerian sense of the historicality of the epochs of Being. Science's functioning is inherently indifferent towards the historically determined horizons of the disclosure of Being. Precisely insofar as science 'does not think,' *it knows*, ignoring the dimension of truth, and as such it is the drive at its purest. Lacan's supplement to Heidegger would thus be: why should this utter 'forgetting of Being,' at work in modern science, be perceived only as the greatest 'danger'? Is there not in it an already perceptible 'liberating' dimension? Is the suspension of ontological Truth in the unfettered functioning of science not already a kind of 'passing through' the metaphysical closure?

Within psychoanalysis, this knowledge of the drive, which can never be subjectivized, assumes the form of the knowledge about the subject's 'fundamental fantasy,' the specific formula which regulates his or her access to jouissance. That is to say, desire and jouissance are inherently antagonistic, exclusive even. Desire's *raison d'être* is not to realize its goal, to find full satisfaction, but to reproduce itself as desire. So, how is it possible to couple desire and jouissance, to guarantee a minimum of jouissance within the space of desire? It is the famous Lacanian object *a* that mediates between the incompatible domains of desire and jouissance. In what precise sense is the object *a* the object-cause of desire?[43] The object *a* is not what we desire, what we are after, but rather that which sets our desire in motion, in the sense of the formal frame which confers consistency on our desire. Desire is of course metonymical, it shifts from one to another object. However, through all these displacements, desire nonetheless retains a minimum of formal consistency, a set of fantasmatic features which, when encountered in a positive object, make us desire this object. Object *a* as the cause of desire is nothing else than this formal frame of consistency. In a slightly different way, the same mechanism regulates the subject's falling in love: the automatism of love is set in motion when some contingent, ultimately indifferent (libidinal) object finds itself occupying a pre-given fantasy place.

Recently, Slovene feminists reacted with a great outcry at the publicity poster of a large cosmetics factory for sun lotion, depicting a series of well-tanned women's behinds in tight bathing suits, accompanied with the logo 'Each has her own factor.' Of course, this publicity is based on a rather vulgar double-entendre. The logo ostensibly refers to the sun lotion, which is offered to customers with different sun factors so as to fit different skin types. However, its entire effect is based on its obvious male-chauvinist reading: 'Each woman can be had, if only the man knows her factor, her specific catalyst, what arouses her!' The Freudian point regarding fundamental fantasy would be that each subject, female or male, possesses such a 'factor' which regulates her or his desire. As we pointed out above, 'A woman, viewed from behind, on her hands and knees' was the Wolf Man's factor, whereas 'A statue-like woman without pubic hair' was Ruskin's factor. There is nothing uplifting about our awareness of this 'factor.' This awareness can never be subjectivized; it is uncanny, horrifying even, since it somehow 'depossesses' the subject, reducing her or him to a puppet-like level 'beyond dignity and freedom.'

Notes

1. For Lacan's formula *Il n'y a pas de rapport sexuel* (There is no sexual relationship), see for example: J. Lacan, *Le Séminaire, Livre XX, Encore* (1972-73), texte établi par J.-A. Miller, Paris, du Seuil, 1975.

2. For the Wolf Man's formula, see: S. Freud, From the History of an Infantile Neurosis (1918*b*[1914]), *Standard Edition*, XVII, pp. 89-103.

3. For Lacan's rewriting of Descartes' formula, see for example: J. Lacan, Science and Truth (1965) (trans. B. Fink), *Newsletter of the Freudian Field*, 1989, no. 3, pp. 4-29 and p. 13 in particular.

4. See: J. Lacan, *The Four Fundamental Concepts of Psychoanalysis* (1964) (trans. A. Sheridan), London, The Hogarth Press and the Institute of Psycho-Analysis, 1977, p. 268.

5. If the man sometimes wears a mask, this mask does not allow every spectator to identify with the man doing it to the woman, but rather hides the fact that there is nothing to hide, i.e. it emphasizes the man's desubjectivized, mechanical status.

6. See for example: J. Lacan, The Subversion of the Subject and the Dialectic of Desire in the Freudian Unconscious (1960), *Ecrits: A Selection* (trans. A. Sheridan), London, Tavistock, 1977, pp. 292-325.

7. For a more detailed analysis of this scene, see Chapter 5 of: S. Žižek, *The Metastases of Enjoyment: Six Essays on Woman and Causality*, London-New York NY, Verso, 1994, pp. 113-136 and pp. 119-121 in particular.

8. For Lacan's insistence on the intersubjectivity of the psychoanalytic experience, see: J. Lacan, *The Seminar. Book I: Freud's Papers on Technique* (1953-54) (trans. with notes J. Forrester), Edited by J.-A. Miller, Cambridge, Cambridge University Press, 1988, pp. 208-219. For Lacan's critical depreciation of intersubjectivity, see: J. Lacan, *Le Séminaire, Livre VIII, Le transfert* (1960-61), texte établi par J.-A. Miller, Paris, du Seuil, 1991, pp. 11-26.

9. For *Che vuoi?*, see: J. Lacan, The Subversion of the Subject and the Dialectic of Desire in the Freudian Unconscious, *o.c.*, p. 312.

10. For the struggle for recognition, see: J. Lacan, Aggressivity in Psychoanalysis (1948), *Ecrits: A Selection, o.c.*, pp. 8-29 and p. 26 in particular. Lacan introduced the Other in: J. Lacan, *The Seminar. Book II: The Ego in Freud's Theory and in the Technique of Psychoanalysis* (1954-55) (trans. S. Tomaselli, notes J. Forrester), Edited by J.-A. Miller, Cambridge, Cambridge University Press, 1988, pp. 235-247.

11. For the *agalma*, see: J. Lacan, *Le Séminaire, Livre VIII, Le transfert, o.c.*, pp. 163-178. For the object *a* as 'something in me more than myself,' see: J. Lacan, *The Four Fundamental Concepts of Psychoanalysis, o.c.*, p. 268.

12. See: S. Freud, The Interpretation of Dreams (1900*a*), *Standard Edition*, IV, p. 130.

13. See: J. Lacan, *The Four Fundamental Concepts of Psychoanalysis, o.c.*, p. 273.

14. The narrative of 'primordial accumulation' effectively explains nothing, since it already presupposes a worker behaving like a full-blown capitalist.

15. For such a notion of 'totalitarianism,' see Chapter 6 of: S. Žižek, *For They Know Not What They Do: Enjoyment as a Political Factor*, London-New York NY, Verso, 1991, pp. 229-277.

16. The fact that Schreber was possessed by the vision of the obscene God who wanted to use him as the feminine partner in the act of copulation is thus strictly correlative to the fact that he was the victim of a proto-Foucaultian, disciplinary father. See: S. Freud, Psycho-Analytic Notes Upon an Autobiographical Account of a Case of Paranoia (1911*c*[1910]), *Standard Edition*, XII, pp. 3-82. As to the political stakes which overdetermine D.P. Schreber's psychosis, see: E. Santner, *My Own Private Germany: D.P. Schreber's Secret History of Modernity*, Princeton NJ, Princeton University Press, 1996.

17. Although it may appear that the Hegelian dialectic, with its matrix of the mediatization of immediacy, is the most elaborate philosophical version of such a narrativization, Hegel was rather the first to provide the explicit formulation of this absolute synchronicity. As he put it, the immediate object lost in reflection 'only comes to be through being left behind.' See: G.W.F. Hegel, *Science of Logic* (1812-16), London, Allen & Unwin, 1969, p. 402.

18. Soon after the fall of Srebrenica, Rose's operatives suddenly 'discovered' in northern Bosnia some Serb bodies allegedly slaughtered by the Muslims. Their attempts to 'mediate' between Muslims and Croats actually inflamed the conflict between them.

19. For the notion of the quilting point, see: J. Lacan, *The Seminar. Book III: The Psychoses* (1955-56) (trans. with notes R. Grigg), Edited by J.-A. Miller, New York NY-London, W.W. Norton & Company, 1993, pp. 258-270. See also: S. Žižek, *For They Know Not What They Do: Enjoyment as a Political Factor, o.c.*, pp. 16-20.

20. The facts are, of course, rather different. Calcutta is a city bursting with activity, culturally much more thriving than Bombay, with a successful local Communist government maintaining a whole network of social services.

21. See: C. Hitchens, *The Missionary Position: Mother Theresa in Theory and Practice*, London-New York NY, Verso, 1995.

22. A further point about the pervert is that, since for him the Law is not fully established (the Law is his lost object of desire), he supplements this lack with an intricate set of regulations (see the masochist ritual). The crucial point is thus to bear in mind the opposition between Law and regulations (or 'rules'): the latter witness to the absence or suspension of the Law.

23. See: M. Foucault, *The History of Sexuality: Introduction* (1976) (trans. R. Hurley), London, Allen Lane, 1978; M. Foucault, *The Use of Pleasure* (1984) (trans.

R. Hurley), New York NY, Random House, 1985; M. Foucault, *The Care of the Self* (1984) (trans. R. Hurley), New York NY, Random House, 1987.

24. During the nineteenth century, art historians were actually busy 'complementing' the statue. In different 'reconstructions,' the missing hand holds a spear, torch, even a mirror. What is significant in these 'reconstructions' is their very multiplicity. The object destined to fill the void is *a priori* secondary, and as such exchangeable. A typically 'post-modern' counterpart to this nineteenth century *kitsch* is provided by recent attempts to fill the void around which some canonic work is structured. Again, the effect is inevitably that of obscene vulgarity. Suffice it to mention *Heathcliff*, a recent novel that deals with the central void of *Wuthering Heights*. What was Heathcliff doing between his disappearance from Wuthering Heights and his return as a rich man a couple of years later? One of the earlier, more successful examples of it is the classic film noir *Killers*, based on Hemingway's short story with the same title. In its first ten minutes, the film faithfully follows the original; what then follows, however, is an attempt to reconstruct the mysterious, past traumatic experience that caused the 'Swede' to vegetate as a living dead and to wait calmly for his death.

25. The plot summary and the surviving fragment of *Beatrice Palmato* were for the first time published in: G. Erlich, *The Sexual Education of Edith Wharton*, Berkeley-Los Angeles CA, University of California Press, 1992.

26. This is actually the title of a sub-chapter in Erlich's book.

27. Of course, in the case of Edith Wharton we are dealing with the fantasmatic notion that doing it with one's father would really be 'it,' the fully realized sexual relationship the woman is looking for in vain in her relation with her husband or her other partners.

28. See: M. Chion, *David Lynch*, London, BFI Publications, 1995.

29. A. Bazin, *Orson Welles: A Critical View*, New York NY, Harper and Row, 1979, p. 74.

30. And the same goes for the male side: a gay man who has fantasies of being sodomized will probably be more hurt when actually raped than a straight man.

31. Suffice it to recall, from the opposite side, the proverbial cliche of the aggressive executive who regularly visits prostitutes and pays them to submit him to a masochistic ritual which enables him to realize his secret submissive daydreams.

32. For the notion of aphanisis, see: J. Lacan, *The Four Fundamental Concepts of Psychoanalysis*, *o.c.*, pp. 216-229.

33. Another way to make the same point is to draw attention to the crucial fact that men who actually perform rapes do not fantasize about raping women. On the contrary, they fantasize about being gentle, about finding a loving partner. Rape is rather a violent *passage à l'acte* emerging from their incapacity to find such a partner in real life. Another point of ambiguity: men who rape women are either totally ignorant of how the victim reacts to being raped, or they force her to fake pleasure, or they find supplementary pleasure in her being horrified.

34. J. Lacan, The Subversion of the Subject and the Dialectic of Desire in the Freudian Unconscious, *o.c.*, p. 324.

35. If the patient accepts the analyst's proposed construction, it is valid; if the patient rejects it, this rejection is a sign of resistance which, consequently, again confirms that the construction has touched some traumatic kernel in the patient. See: S. Freud, Constructions in Analysis (1937*d*), *Standard Edition*, XXIII, pp. 255-269; J.-A. Miller, E = UWK: Towards the 9th International Encounter of the Freudian Field (1994) (trans. V. Palomera), *Analysis*, 1995, no. 6, pp. 14-31.

36. S. Freud, 'A Child is Being Beaten' — A Contribution to the Study of the Origin of Sexual Perversions (1919*e*), *Standard Edition*, XVII, p. 185.

37. For 'subjective destitution,' see for example: J. Lacan, Proposition of 9 October 1967 on the Psychoanalyst of the School (1967) (trans. R. Grigg), *Analysis*, 1995, no. 6, pp. 1-13.

38. See for example: J. Lacan, *Le Séminaire, Livre XVII, L'envers de la psychanalyse* (1969-70), texte établi par J.-A. Miller, Paris, du Seuil, 1991.

39. For the notion of 'full speech,' see for example: J. Lacan, *The Seminar. Book I: Freud's Papers on Technique, o.c.*, pp. 107-108.

40. Of course, the very predicate 'ontological' thereby becomes problematic, since ontology is by definition a discourse on truth.

41. See: J.-A. Miller, Retour de Grenade. Savoir et satisfaction, *La Cause freudienne. Revue de psychanalyse*, 1996, no. 33, pp. 7-15.

42. Didn't he claim that 'science does not think,' i.e. that it is by definition unable to reflect upon its own philosophical foundation, the hermeneutic horizon of its functioning, and, furthermore, that this incapacity, far from playing the role of an impediment, is a positive condition for the very possibility of its smooth functioning ?

43. For the object *a* as cause of desire, see for example: J. Lacan, *Le Séminaire X, L'angoisse* (1962-63), unpublished, seminar of 16 January 1963.

NOTES ON CONTRIBUTORS

DYLAN EVANS trained as a Lacanian psychoanalyst in London, Paris and Buenos Aires, and is now in private practice in London. He is the author of *An Introductory Dictionary of Lacanian Psychoanalysis* (Routledge, 1996) and the co-author, with Dany Nobus, of *Jacques Lacan and the Clinical Practice of Psychoanalysis* (Routledge, forthcoming). E-mail: D.EVANS@lse.ac.uk

BRUCE FINK is Associate Professor of Psychology at Duquesne University and a psychoanalyst in private practice. He is the author of *The Lacanian Subject: Between Language and Jouissance* (Princeton University Press, 1995) and *A Clinical Introduction to Lacanian Psychoanalysis: Theory and Technique* (Harvard University Press, 1997). He is also the translator of Lacan's *Seminar XX: Encore*, *Seminar VIII: Transference* and *Ecrits* (new complete edition), forthcoming from W.W. Norton. E-mail: fink@duq3.cc.duq.edu

RUSSELL GRIGG teaches in philosophy and psychoanalytic studies at Deakin University, Australia. He is a member of the *Ecole de la Cause freudienne* and the Australian Centre for Psychoanalysis. He has translated Lacan's *Seminar III: The Psychoses* (Routledge, 1993) and *Seminar XVII: The Other Side of Psychoanalysis* (Routledge, forthcoming). He is currently writing on Lacan's later seminars and also editing a collection of the early papers on female sexuality for Rebus Press. E-mail: rgrigg@deakin.edu.au

KATRIEN LIBBRECHT is Professor of Psychology at the Free University of Brussels and a consulting psychoanalytic psychotherapist at the Psychiatrische Centra Sleidinge, Belgium. She is the author of *Hysterical Psychosis: A Historical Survey* (Transaction, 1995). E-mail: klibbrec@vub.ac.be

DANY NOBUS is a Lecturer in Psychology and Psychoanalytic Studies in the Department of Human Sciences at Brunel University. He is the author of *Choosing Sexuality: A Lacanian Inquiry into the Laws of Sexual Diversity* (State University of New York Press, forthcoming) and the co-author, with Dylan Evans, of *Jacques Lacan and the Clinical Practice of Psychoanalysis* (Routledge, forthcoming). E-mail: dany.nobus@brunel.ac.uk

LUKE THURSTON studied at Oxford University, Université de Paris VII and the University of Kent, Canterbury. He has recently completed his Ph.D. on Lacan and Joyce at the University of Kent. His papers have appeared in *Parallax* and *Free Associations* and he is the translator of *On Otherness* by Jean Laplanche (Routledge, forthcoming). He teaches critical theory at the University of Warwick.

PAUL VERHAEGHE is Professor of Psychoanalysis at the University of Ghent, Belgium, a member of the European School of Psychoanalysis and a psychoanalyst in private practice. He is the author of *Does the Woman Exist? From Freud's Hysteric to Lacan's Feminine* (Rebus Press, 1996). E-mail: Paul.Verhaeghe@rug.ac.be

SLAVOJ ŽIŽEK is Senior Researcher at the Institute for Social Sciences at the University of Ljubljana, Slovenia. He is the author of numerous articles and books on Lacan, philosophy, politics and film, the most recent ones being *The Indivisible Remainder: An Essay on Schelling and Related Matters* (Verso, 1996), *Gaze and Voice as Love Objects* (Renata Salecl & Slavoj Žižek, editors — Duke University Press, 1996), *The Abyss of Freedom/Ages of the World* (The University of Michigan Press, 1997) and *The Plague of Fantasies* (Verso, 1997).

INDEX

C

D

Q

R

S

T